PUTIN

PUTIN

CHRIS HUTCHINS

with Alexander Korobko

Matador
Troubador Publishing Ltd
9 Priory Business Park
Wistow Road
Kibworth Beauchamp
Leicester LE8 0RX, UK
Tel: 0116 279 2299
Email: books@troubador.co.uk
Web: www.troubador.co.uk/matador

ISBN 9781780881140

A CIP catalogue record for this book is available from the British Library

Matador is an imprint of Troubador Publishing Ltd
Printed in the UK by TJ International, Padstow, Cornwall

Contents

Prologue

A Little Place in the Country

LITTLE DID THE locals know what lay ahead when the bulldozers trundled through their village, cutting huge swathes through the forest, taking care to preserve the centuries-old pine and birch trees. These were the woods where they had played as children, courted as teenagers and gathered fuel for their fires to stave off the bitterly cold Russian winters. In earlier days, you would hardly have noticed their village, Kalchuga, home to a community of just a few dozen souls inhabiting picturesque wooden cottages. Even today, it draws scant attention from those who speed by on the Rublyovo-Uspenskoye highway. What is unmissable, though, are the high walls and security fencing surrounding the nouveau mansions which have sprung up on either side of Lovers Lane, where villagers once lay, shielded by the trees from intrusion.

In modern times, these sylvan glades have long attracted Russia's elite. Now the exclusive fiefdom of some of the country's richest men and women – oligarchs, pop stars and politicians – Novo-Ogaryovo was once the haunt of the Soviet political elite, housing Premier Malenkov, alongside senior members of the CPSU's Central Committee. In 2000, it became home of the country's new leader, Vladimir Putin. Now, bristling with antennae, surrounded by high-tech forts and protected by a small army, this is Putin's 'dacha' which – far removed from the traditional country cottage – serves both as the Russian leader's office and entertainment centre, and is as grand as any European or American country house.

Putin kept the estate when he stepped down as president in 2008 to become prime minister. He needed a place close to his family home, a mansion buried deep in the woods, just as much as his successor Dmitri Medvedev had, in order to receive some of the world's most influential leaders. In earlier times, this is where George W. Bush came to argue with Putin about whether or not Saddam Hussein had nuclear weapons. The former German Chancellor Gerhard Schroeder brought his wife here to thank Putin and his wife for facilitating their adoption of a Russian baby named Viktoria. Like many others, they were transported from the main gate up to the dacha in golf buggies.

Putin is not fond of unexpected guests, but to those who really interest him he is a superb host. The privileged few who have witnessed Putin at home will testify that in a domestic setting they found a very different character from the tough-guy politician we see on the international stage. The world's best-known Russian once allowed Bush to drive him around the estate in his beloved reconditioned Volga – although he grabbed the steering wheel when the American President's driving turned dangerous; he poured tea and buttered toast for the German photographer Konrad Muller, and fed apples to Obereg – the favourite of his five stallions – in front of a young training partner who turned up regularly for a session in unarmed combat. Lord Browne's lasting memory of his visit there to say goodbye after his demise as boss of BP, is of Putin's black Labrador, Koni, walking in circles around his ankles.

It is ironic, perhaps, that Russia's oligarchs are among the elite who live here on Putin's doorstep. For these are the very people he holds in contempt for having taken advantage of Boris Yeltsin's plight by buying up the country's principal assets during the financial crisis of the mid-1990s. Theirs are the enormous blinging palaces Putin's armoured limousine drives past every day on his way to work.

Nowhere is their prosperity more marked than in the luxury village of Barvikha, where Yeltsin and his family once lived; now the spot where dolled-up wives and mistresses buy their essential supplies from Gucci, Prada and Dolce & Gabbana (a private salon in D&G here has mink-covered doors), while their men browse in Armani, or perhaps visit the car dealership which specialises in Lamborghinis and Bentleys. The couples rendezvous at the Avenue restaurant, where a lunchtime snack of seafood risotto costs half as much as the average Russian worker spends to support his family in a week.

Personally disinterested in what he regards as the 'high life', Putin himself rarely eats out in public restaurants and with good reason: on one occasion when he took his wife to Rublyovka's Prichal restaurant he found himself seated at the table next to former Vice-President Alexander Rutskoy, who seized the opportunity to try to engage Putin in small talk. So Putin ignores such places as his motorcade, ablaze with flashing blue lights, reaches speeds of up to 160 kilometres per hour on its journey eastwards into Moscow: 'My home is just twenty or so miles outside the city and I can be in the office in less than half an hour,' he told a visiting ambassador. But this high-speed travel is also a way of avoiding sniper attacks. Some years ago, a vehicle loaded with explosives was found in Moscow, a stone's throw from a major street, Kutuzovskiy Prospekt, on which Putin regularly travelled. The would-be bomber was Alexander Pumané, an active member of the Kingiseppskaya criminal group, headed by Bashkiria senator, Igor Izmestiev. A total of five attempts have been made on Putin's life to date.

The speed of Putin's convoy along the Rublyovo-Uspenskoye Highway poses no danger to the public, since the highway and all surrounding streets are cleared of traffic – and every junction blocked – to ensure an unhindered journey. Any vehicle which does manage to evade the roadblocks risks being rammed by one of the escorting police cars – just such an incident occurred in 2006, killing the hapless driver of a Volvo who had inadvertently pulled out of a parking space.

When the motorcade turns left into Kutuzovskiy Prospekt on Putin's journey into town, the prime minister can recall illustrious passages in his country's history, looking out at the monument commemorating Russia's victory over Nazi Germany in 1945, and the Triumphal Arch built to celebrate victory over Napoleon in 1812. Then his journey takes him, by sharp contrast, along the Novy Arbat, a garish street lined with sushi bars, a lively market and ugly high-rise office blocks.

Heading for Red Square – he still uses his suite of offices in the Kremlin's Old Senate building – Putin can reflect comfortably on his leadership, which started on the first day of the 21st century; perhaps recalling how, just a few years ago, jobless and fast running out of money to feed his family, he contemplated the prospect of becoming one of St Petersburg's army of unlicensed taxi drivers, trawling the streets in the very same Volga saloon in which he and an American president toured the majestic country estate he now calls home.

Indeed, Novo-Ogaryovo is on a similar scale to Sandringham – and just like the British Royal Family's sprawling country retreat, it too boasts stables, vegetable gardens, a helipad, as well as its own recently restored church. Just like Queen Elizabeth, Putin shuns the must-have gadgets that modern technology has thrown up. He doesn't use a Blackberry, contribute to a personal blog or send emails. Indeed he even has staff place most of his telephone calls, admitting, 'They do it very well. It makes me envious of them'.

It is fitting that the incredible story of Vladimir Vladimirovich Putin, a boy who grew up on the wrong side of the tracks in the USSR to become one of the most powerful men on the planet, should begin with a visit to meet Her Majesty, one of the closest living relatives of Russia's last tsar . . .

1

Vlad the Conqueror

AS VLADIMIR PUTIN drove into London on a warm June day in 2003, he was acutely aware that he was making history. Not since Queen Victoria welcomed Tsar Alexander II to Windsor Castle in 1874 had a Russian leader been accorded a state visit, the highest honour Britain can bestow on a foreign power. Mikhail Gorbachev had visited London in his capacity as general secretary of the Communist Party, whereas Putin – 50 years old at the time – had been the democratically elected President of the Russian Federation for less than three years.

Putin and his wife Lyudmila were greeted at Heathrow Airport by the heir to the throne, Prince Charles, who escorted them to Horse Guards Parade for a display of pomp and pageantry to mark the official arrival of the second President of the Russian Federation. From there the newly arrived guests rode with the Queen and Prince Philip in horse-drawn carriages along a brilliantly sunny Mall, festooned with British and Russian flags, to Buckingham Palace, where they would be staying in the Belgian Room.

The Bolsheviks had executed the Queen's cousin, Alexander's son Tsar Nicholas II. Indeed, her first meeting with a visiting Soviet leader had been a frosty encounter with Nikita Khrushchev; but this occasion passed extremely well, with Putin describing Her Majesty in a speech at a state banquet that evening as 'a noble example of faithful and selfless service'.

Now, escorted by police outriders, he was on his way to the Guildhall in the City of London to be honoured by the Lord Mayor of London. The previous Tsar had arrived at Windsor with an entourage of 70 – including four food tasters (or cooks as they were diplomatically named in the official list); and, although only 10 people were listed in Putin's official party, he was accompanied by a force of no fewer than 150, including his security detail (to prevent potential attack by a Chechnyan death squad since many Chechens live in the capital) and a complete medical team (to swing into action should his bodyguards fail in their duty). There were no food tasters on this occasion, but because of fears for the President's safety over Chechnya, the kitchens at the Palace and the Guildhall – and the people working in them – were subjected to a rigorous security check. And whereas the Tsar had demanded – and ploughed his way through – 22 courses, including seven desserts, Putin had been happy to settle for a simpler menu of chilled melon, lobster thermidor, breast of Norfolk duckling and fruit crème brûlée, finishing off with a digestif of iced vodka. No expense had been spared to make Russia's strongman feel welcome – a portrait of Nicholas II with his cousin King George V and a startling colour photograph of Leo Tolstoy, dressed in his favoured peasant's tunic and long boots, had been borrowed for the occasion.

There was just one oversight.

From the very first glance, Putin was aware that the throne he had to ascend was so high that his feet wouldn't touch the floor. 'He was visibly uncomfortable,' says Sergei Kolushev, the head of Russia's London-based Economic Forum. 'I saw the apprehension in his eyes as he approached it. But he adapted very quickly and, as the proceedings kicked off, he displayed no outward signs of anxiety about it, whatever he might have been thinking or feeling. He managed to adjust very smoothly and in the end he charmed many people in the hall. In fact, he even looked quite at home up there on that throne!'

THE LONDON organisers may have gone to great lengths to research their visitor's needs (including, according to one Royal source, his and

Lyudmila's preference for the mattress on their bed in the Belgian Room) but no one had thought to provide him with a footstool, and in this they had missed a vital point – the President's sensitivity about his diminutive stature.

Putin's height – he is 1.65 metres or five feet five inches tall, two inches taller than Mahatma Gandhi – had already been seized on by the merciless British press at Horse Guards. Vladimir Putin, however, measured up to the British Queen just fine, at 1.60 metres she was still five centimetres shorter than him. But after the band had played the Russian national anthem, Major Martin David of the Grenadier Guards invited Putin to inspect the guard of honour. 'Major David plus bearskin towered far above him,' wrote a reporter for *The Times*. 'Like a block of Moscow flats over a dacha.'

Such cracks have been a constant feature of Putin's life ever since he stepped out from the shadows to become a potent force in Russian politics. As a small boy, he was often bullied about his height, and learned to handle the bullies by taking up judo. As an adult, he is said to have solved the problem by wearing built-up heels, just like Tom Cruise, Silvio Berlusconi and Nicolas Sarkozy, with the latter allegedly using secret insoles, adding an extra seven centimetres.

SO WHO IS the man occupying the Royal bed in the Belgian Room at Buckingham Palace? In public life – often parodied as the bare-chested Judoka with a glare of cold steel – Vladimir Putin presents an image of toughness that neither Bush nor Chirac nor Blair nor any of their successors could ever dream of matching, while the apparently spontaneous gesture of kissing a young boy on the stomach suggests a tenderness that is the exact opposite. The contradiction is typical of the man, but is either image true? 'He rarely talks about himself unless it is part of a PR operation,' says one of his closest friends, 'and he is more PR-conscious than most people would believe. Indeed, he once told us that the only difference between a rat and a hamster was: "The hamster has better PR".'

First impressions on the world stage were favourable when Putin,

PRESIDENT Putin and his wife Lyudmila welcomed the Queen and Prince Philip to Spencer House in London, where they hosted a reception for the royal couple during Putin's state visit to Britain in 2003 – the first time a Russian leader had been accorded such an honour since Queen Victoria had welcomed Tsar Alexander to Windsor Castle 129 years earlier.

replaced an ailing Boris Yeltsin, his Kremlin mentor, as Russia's head of state in March 2000. Even before that date Tony Blair had developed a 'special relationship' with the acting president and became his strongest advocate in the international arena. His wife Cherie sounded a note of caution: 'This is not a man you want to cross,' she warned her husband after spending a few days with Putin in St Petersburg.

At the first meeting between the new Russian leader and the American president – in Slovenia in 2001 – George W. Bush peered into Putin's blue-green eyes and thought he could see into his soul. Putin duly infuriated both Bush and Blair by crossing them over the invasion of Iraq. Before his departure, Putin's preferred Western leader was Italy's mercurial Silvio Berlusconi.

Putin's eyes continue to attract attention. Irene Pietsch, a German banker's wife who befriended Lyudmila Putina in the 1990s, joked that his eyes resembled 'two hungry, lurking predators' and claimed that Lyudmila had jokingly described him as 'an energy vampire'. Alastair Campbell too paid note, stating in his diary that 'Vlad' – he was on first-name terms with all the important people during his years as Blair's communications supremo at 10 Downing Street – might look thoroughly modern but would suddenly turn into 'the old KGB man'. 'Vlad's eyes were real killers,' he recounts, 'piercing blue and able to move from sensitive soul to hard nut in one blink.' A leading British businessman drew his own conclusions, confessing that when he looked into them he saw nothing at all.

Indeed, Russian liberals and Western conservatives alike have demonised Putin as an anti-democratic KGB automaton; and he makes no secret of his links to the security services, or of his pride in being the KGB's most famous 'old boy'. Western tycoons eager to do business with Russia have embraced him. 'Regardless of what this man stands for,' declares Lord Browne, ex-chief executive of BP – one of the petroleum super-majors that were prepared to turn a blind eye to such matters if it meant getting a share of the country's immense oil deposits – 'he is exceedingly competent.' Browne's comments could well have been endorsed by Putin's school-teachers, who agreed he had an ability to absorb knowledge at an exceptionally high speed.

Ask any twelve people who have met Vladimir Putin what he is like and you are likely to get a dozen different answers. Although the truth is that very few people really know him at all. To his family he is loving, to his adversaries he is foul-mouthed and dangerous, to his religious friends he is a devout Christian, to the Russian public (or around 73 per cent of them, according to one count) he is their saviour – the man who restored their nation's pride. Although even some of his most loyal citizens have reservations: 'I feel empathy towards him but that is now tinged with a little bitterness,' said one man who voted for Putin in the most recent elections. 'He has not improved the lot of the average Russian in the way he could have. Alaska shares its wealth with the people – they each receive

$1,000 a month from the profits of natural resources. Russians do not enjoy similar benefits.'

Vladimir Putin is first and foremost a Russian patriot. Although he professes to believe in democracy, he could hardly be described as a democrat. Boris Yeltsin publicly vouched for him: 'As Putin's Godfather, I can tell you democracy is safe in his hands,' he said – a dubious testimonial as Yeltsin himself had changed from democratic saviour to autocratic despot during his years in the Kremlin. Putin's political enemies say he has followed a similar path. Putin does not quarrel with them. His view is that after Gandhi died, 'there was nobody left to talk to' – another of Putin's asides which would later be quoted *ad nauseum*.

In fact, Putin believes in 'sovereign democracy' or 'managed democracy' rather than the Western variety; his democracy is one that operates through a rational, hierarchic system that he calls 'the vertical of power'; in other words, power flows naturally downwards from the presidential office in the Kremlin to the various echelons of officials, including the *siloviki* (the security men, soldiers and spies who joined the state bureaucratic apparatus on his coat-tails), and only then down to the masses.

Putin is not a man who bows to international political convention: he became prime minister and then acting president of Russia without ever having to stand for elected office. Certainly his views on democracy do not endear him to others. 'Elections are fine as long as they vote for me,' he reportedly said on one occasion. Putin also claims to support a law-governed state – as distinct from the old party-governed Soviets – which he calls the 'dictatorship of the law'. The degree of democratic freedom here depends, of course, on who is making the laws. Indeed, 'Putinism' has flourished because the usual sources of opposition, such as the Russian intelligentsia, who led dissent against the Communists, have lost their power. Some regard Putin as being too close to this faction to fear any real challenge.

According to the billionaire oil tycoon Gordon Getty, Putin is 'the most dangerous man in the world' and indeed, he does hold a terrifying trump card in terms of world power. 'He could close down China tomorrow,' notes one of the his closest confidants. 'If he cut off Russian oil and gas, there would be no smoke coming from many of China's chimneys. The same goes for India. And what a chill Italy, Germany, France and Britain would feel if he did the same to Western Europe. He could shake America's fragile economy to the core because America could not supply all of those other countries – it doesn't have enough oil and gas for its own needs.

'So of course he's the most dangerous man in the world. The difference between him and his predecessors is he doesn't need nuclear weapons. He could bring the world to its knees without firing a shell or a bullet.'

And what might induce him to use his energy weapon? 'He would only do it if he thought Russia was threatened by an outside power. He is watching the expansion of NATO very carefully, as it pushes ever closer to Russia's borders. He would not have taken kindly to it going into Ukraine – that would have been his Cuba; then you would have seen some serious action.'

Alleged readiness to 'bring the world to its knees', however, should not be mistaken for willingness to do it, Putin's close friend insists. 'He's a realist. He knows the power of his position and for him Russia comes first, second and third; that does make him potentially dangerous. As Putin himself once said in an open letter to all Russians published in the newspaper *Izvestiya* on 25 February 2000: "One insults us at one's own peril".'

'His role model is Catherine the Great and he rules by her principles: there is no compromise,' his friend continued. And, like Catherine with her lovers, Putin is inclined to use businessmen and then discard them. 'It's all in keeping with his aspiration to unravel the mess that Yeltsin left behind and restore Russia's political greatness.'

There was a lot of unravelling to do. One of Putin's main targets had been the oligarchs, the Russian tycoons who became fabulously wealthy when Yeltsin sold them valuable state assets at very low prices in the notorious 'loans for shares' auctions. Putin assessed the oil, gas and metal industries and quickly realised many of the oligarchs were making considerable profits from them, and so the President set out to make their lives intolerable. His public mantra was (and is): 'We have to share! With whom? With the State!'

Roman Abramovich, one of the few oligarchs still in favour, did not collect the $13 billion he was reported to have received when he sold his controlling interest in Sibneft to the state-owned Gazprom in September 2003 – at least not for his own purse. Putin persuaded Abramovich – who owns four yachts and Chelsea Football Club – that $13 billion would be an obscene amount of money with which to walk away from a company which had already made him and his former partner Berezovsky rich beyond all dreams of avarice since taking it over barely a decade earlier. Knowing full well that while he might have the billions, Putin owns the prisons, Abramovich did not resist presidential pressure to hand over a huge chunk of the Gazprom money.

ANOTHER IMPORTANT aspect of Putin's personality is his highly suspicious nature. Putin trusts no one. It may be his KGB training, or perhaps it goes back further. His former teacher Vera Dmitrievna Gurevich warned that even as a child he 'never forgave people who betrayed him'. He is deeply suspicious of everyone, and perhaps with good reason: he is, after all, well aware that plots against him have been made deep within the Kremlin and the State Duma (which replaced the Supreme Soviet as the Russian parliament in 1994). Some of his own ministers have had it in their minds from time to time to overthrow him. He has not relied solely on the FSB – successor to the KGB as Russia's domestic security service – to keep him informed of such manoeuvres. Such a body is not above infiltration and, indeed, is not always capable of penetrating the highest echelons of government.

One of my most surprising discoveries is that a group of businessmen and borderline politicians who call themselves the VVP men regularly send him missives based on their own research and opinions. Whether or not he takes their home-spun advice seriously is debatable, but he is certainly acquainted with several of their number.

ONE OF THE VVP men's more outlandish claims is that it was they who planned and executed Operation Yukos, to capture then oil boss Mikhail Khodorkovsky. Khodorkovsky was one of the few who dared to defy the uncompromising demand made by Putin after he became President: 'You can keep your ill-gotten gains and your freedom providing you stop meddling in politics'. According to Andrey Karaulov (a famously controversial TV host), Khodorkovsky – Russia's wealthiest man when he was first arrested in 2003 on charges of fraud – was allegedly responsible for a number of murders. But at the trial where he received an eight-year sentence, he was never actually accused of such crimes. Environmentalists have suggested that those at the head of a number of companies – including Yukos – that turned part of the Komsomol youth movement into oilmen overnight are guilty of destroying hundreds of thousands of acres of tundra in Russia's far north.

IT WAS smiles all round when Putin visited an American school with President Bush – the man who said he looked into Putin's eyes and saw his soul.

Another interesting aspect of Putin's personality is his way of dealing with any politician he suspects of plotting against him. He does nothing to remove such men and women but subscribes to the much-quoted line in *Godfather II*: 'Keep your friends close… and your enemies even closer.'

Putin has been unfairly blamed for many catastrophes, including the crashing of the Estonian Internet. The Russian affairs expert Orlando Figes suggested, 'They blamed the Kremlin [for that], so you begin to think, "Well perhaps they believe they can put the clock back ideologically to the point where criticism of Putin becomes a hostile act against Russia".' Another well-placed source put it like this: 'The Estonian Internet crashed after the Estonian authorities removed the monument to the memory of Red Army soldiers who had died fighting fascist Germany. Either way, it is incorrect to think that Putin himself is orchestrating this. He is a part of the system which, for lack of a better expression, we call the secret service.'

Putin's powers of persuasion should never be underestimated. At one of his regular meetings in the Kremlin with the president, Rabbi Beryl Lazar, a leading member of the Jewish community, told him about a young Moscow woman who had been badly burned when she triggered a rigged explosive as she moved an anti-Semitic sign from the roadside. She lived in dreadful conditions, Rabbi Lazar explained, with neighbours who made her life unbearable, and yet the authorities refused to provide any help. Lazar was not convinced that Putin was even listening until, as he was leaving the building, a guard told him he was wanted back in the president's office. Putin had already telephoned Mayor Luzhkov, drawn the woman's plight to his attention and been assured that remedial action would be taken. The delighted rabbi said later: 'He gets extremely frustrated with the incompetence of the state'.

It was more than frustration with bureaucracy which spurred the president into action. The 58-year-old – who has announced his intention to seek a third non-consecutive term in the 2012 presidential elections – has never forgotten his humble roots, nor has he tried to hide them. Indeed in his autobiography, *First Person*, he is at pains to point out that he grew up in a loving atmosphere. Vladimir Vladimirovich Putin, known in his family as Vovka or Volodya, was brought up by his mother Maria Ivanovna Putina and his father Vladimir Spiridonovich Putin in the kind of grinding poverty that most Russians endured during the arms race of the 1950s – and many still do today despite the country's new-found prosperity. He was born in St Petersburg's Snegiryov maternity hospital on 7 October 1952, when his mother was 41 years old. He is her only surviving child.

Putin's neighbours during his childhood days in St Petersburg describe him as 'delicate' and 'precious', with one recalling a 'shy but generous boy who always shared his sweets with other kids'. Having lost her first two sons – one died shortly after birth, the other of diphtheria during Hitler's infamous siege of their home city, in which more than one million people perished – Maria Ivanovna took special care of her little Volodya. Fearing for his safety, she refused to send him to kindergarten, as most working mothers did, but instead took jobs close to home to help put food on the table while her young son stayed indoors playing on his own. He did not attend school until he was almost eight years old. The preference he developed for isolation in childhood was to mould his character into one of self-reliance and independence. To this day, he likes his own company and prefers to eat alone. When a *Time* magazine journalist asked him what he did in his spare time, he retorted: 'I do not have any spare time'. The truth is, he doesn't want any – these days, the man lives to work.

IN THE EARLY days, the Putin family occupied a single room with no bathroom, no running hot water and a shared lavatory and kitchen, in a *kommunalka*, or communal flat, at No.12 Baskov Lane – just a short tram-ride from Nevsky Prospect in the historical centre of Russia's imperial capital. In those earlier days, Vladimir Spiridonovich worked as a foreman at the Yegorov engineering works, where they made railway carriages. At night, he entertained his first wife and their young son on a battered accordion. He was an accomplished player; there is certainly no record of neighbours ever complaining about the noise. Maria must have been exhausted most of the time from her several part-time jobs as a concierge,

TONY BLAIR may look as though he has the upper hand, but Putin wrong-footed him when he invited the Prime Minister to Russia even before he was elected President.

taking deliveries at a bakery and as a technical assistant in a laboratory. Against her husband's wishes, she had their son secretly christened at the Russian Orthodox Cathedral of the Transfiguration: to this day, Putin wears his little aluminium baptismal crucifix on a chain around his neck. His father, Vladimir Spiridonovich – a devout atheist – turned a blind eye to the christening, which Maria made sure was performed in secret. Like their neighbours, the Putins owed the little they had to the anti-religious authorities – and it could easily be taken away.

VLADIMIR PUTIN'S grandfather, Spiridon Ivanovich Putin, worked hard for what he'd achieved, training as a chef in his home town of St Petersburg, as Leningrad was then known (before it became Petrograd in 1914). He had a great talent for cooking and before he was 20 years old he was preparing meals for the aristocracy in the Astoria, a five-star hotel on St Isaac's Square in the Tsarist capital. His patrons included the Tsar's Romanov relatives and the notorious monk Grigory Rasputin. The Astoria was said to pay Spiridon the princely sum of 100 roubles a month in gold. He married a country girl, Olga Ivanovna, and between 1907 and 1915 they had three sons – Alexei, Mikhail and Vladimir Spiridonovich (born on 23 February 1911) – and a daughter, Anna.

When the Bolshevik Revolution of 1917 deposed the Provisional Government (which had recently replaced the abdicated Tsar) and the ruling caste either fled or faced execution or imprisonment, the Putins' world came crashing down. There were no more aristocrats demanding caviar and *foie gras*, in fact, there was precious little food of any description to be had in the capital (by this time renamed Petrograd as 'Petersburg' was considered too Germanic during the First World War). As the Russian civil war brought chaos to the length and breadth of the vast empire, Spiridon moved his family to a relative's house in the village of Pominovo in the Tver region (Putin likes to remind anyone who will listen that the house is still standing and relatives travel there to spend their holidays).

The legend goes that many years later, when Vladimir Spiridonovich sat his son on his knee in their grim room on Baskov Lane and told him Spiridon's story, the boy shuddered more at the thought of the humiliation his grandparents had suffered than at their hunger. But like so many stories about Putin's background, this is apocryphal: 'My grandfather kept pretty quiet about his past life,' he says. 'My parents didn't talk much about the past either. People generally didn't back then. My parents never told me anything about themselves, especially my father. He was a taciturn man.'

After World War I, Spiridon was offered a job in the Gorky district on the outskirts of Moscow, where Lenin and his family lived. He was employed at Lenin's country house and, following the revolutionary leader's death in January 1924, continued working for his widow, Nadezhda Krupskaya. Three days after Lenin's death, Petrograd was renamed Leningrad in his honour. Olga wanted to move back there, but Spiridon knew that the Communist administration regarded the city as vulnerable to attack from Finland. Spiridon calculated that the future for skilled people like him lay in the new capital, Moscow. He was right. His culinary skills were soon in demand among the new Communist elite. Stalin took a liking to him and he was transferred to one of his dachas.

Perhaps it was his loyalty to Stalin as much as his cooking that landed him a plum job at 'Ilichovsky', the country guesthouse of the Moscow City Communist Party. As head chef, he was given a two-room flat – almost unheard of for a man of his background – and Olga could pick fruit, vegetables and flowers from their very own allotment, another rare privilege. Few people who spent much time around Stalin came out alive, but Spiridon survived. Putin's memories of his grandfather come from this period when he visited Ilinskoye on school holidays with his parents.

Chain-smoking but teetotal, Spiridon died in 1965 at the age of 86, having retired just six years earlier. He was buried in the cemetery at Ilinskoye. Still mentally alert in his twilight years, he enjoyed fishing trips with his grandson, even if he failed to impart any great wisdom to the boy. Olga lived to be 90. Putin recalls that he learned most things about his family by picking up 'snatches and fragments' from his parents' conversation whenever relatives visited the Putin home on Baskov Lane. This was the only time they would open up and talk about themselves. For good reason: the past was an emotional minefield.

VLADIMIR SPIRIDONOVICH PUTIN met Maria Ivanovna Shelomova in Pominovo, where he had spent his childhood. She had been born in the neighbouring village of Zarechie on 17 October 1911. They became sweethearts at an early age and were both just seventeen when they took their wedding vows in 1928 (asked by a reporter looking for a skeleton in the Putin cupboard if there was a reason why they had married so young, Putin huffed before replying: 'Why should there be a reason? Love is the main reason, but my father was also due to be conscripted. Maybe they were looking for some sort of commitment from each other.')

Four years later, the onset of collectivisation forced them to move to Leningrad. Maria spent some time as a street sweeper and later worked in a factory, while Vladimir Spiridonovich was drafted into the fledgling submarine division of the Soviet navy. Within a year of him completing his term of service, the Putins had two sons. The first, Oleg, died a few months after birth, but Maria became pregnant almost immediately and they were overjoyed when she gave birth to a healthy boy named Viktor. The Putins were living in an apartment at Peterhof – home of the fabled Summer Palace – when Hitler launched Operation Barbarossa against the Soviet Union on 22 June 1941. Leningrad was one of the Wehrmacht's primary objectives. Peter the Great had raised the city from the swampy banks of the Neva River; Hitler ordered his troops to bury it.

Vladimir Spiridonovich joined a demolition battalion of the NKVD – the grandly-named People's Commissariat for Internal Affairs; in fact this unit of the Soviet secret police was a combat squadron engaged in sabotage behind German lines. His team of 28 men was sent to Kingisepp near the Estonian border, where they blew up a munitions depot. While they were withdrawing towards the Russian lines, they ran out of rations and approached some Estonians who brought them food but then tipped off the Germans. The Russians' camp was surrounded. Vladimir Spiridonovich was in a small group who fought their way out and headed east, pursued by German soldiers with a pack of dogs. Apparently he jumped into a swamp and performed the time-honoured trick of breathing through a hollow reed until the search party had passed. Only four out of the 28 men in his unit made it back home.

As the Germans completed the encirclement of Leningrad in early 1942, Vladimir Spiridonovich was sent back into action as one of the defenders of the so-called Neva pocket, a tiny redoubt on the left bank of the river which the Germans were never able to capture, despite saturation bombing and repeated assaults. Maria, meanwhile, had opted to stay in Peterhof, which was being pulverised by German bombing and shellfire. When the Summer Palace was overrun, looted and destroyed, her elder brother Ivan Shelomov came for her and Viktor. Ivan was a naval officer serving at fleet headquarters in Smolny, once a private girls' school on the banks of the Neva, now covered in camouflage netting that was painted by the thespians of the Mariinsky Theatre to change colour with the seasons. He gave his sister some of his rations and then took her and Viktor to one of the shelters in Leningrad, which had been set up in an effort to save children's lives. It was there that the five-year-old boy contracted diphtheria. Maria not only lost her child, her mother had been killed by a stray German bullet and her older brothers, including Ivan, would later disappear without trace at the front.

Then, in the winter of 1942, Vladimir Spiridonovich was seriously wounded in both legs by a German grenade. He would have died from loss of blood if a former neighbour hadn't recognised him at the dressing station and carried him on his back across the frozen Neva to a hospital in Leningrad. Maria visited him every day. Seeing her pitiful condition, her husband secretly saved his hospital rations for her until the nurses realised from his sickly state what he was doing and banned her from the ward. Once she fainted from starvation in the street and was laid out with other corpses. It was only when someone heard her moan that her life was saved.

When Vladimir Spiridonovich had recovered sufficiently to leave hospital, he was demobilised from the army as an invalid. His wounds had left him with a permanent limp, so he drove a horse and cart at a collective farm until he was able to walk again. By 1944 he was well enough to work as a toolmaker in the Yegerov Carriage Building Works, an engineering plant which at that time was making shells for Russian guns. He and Maria were reunited – this remarkable woman had stayed in Leningrad through the entire siege. As the German army was driven back, the Putins picked up the pieces of their lives in one of the rooms at the factory's *kommunalka* in Baskov Lane. They had both turned forty by the time their third son – the president-to-be – was born eight years later.

CONSIDERING HER wartime experiences, Maria's desire to protect her little Volodya from harm was entirely understandable. It wasn't until 1 September 1960 that she enrolled him at School No. 193 across the road from their home, and he still keeps a photograph taken on his first day, of him clutching a flower pot for the teacher. The experience came

A WELCOME VISITOR: While some other oligarchs rebelled, Roman Abramovich
promised Putin he would not interfere in politics.

as something of a shock. He stood out, not only because he looked small
and frail but because, unused to communicating with others of his age,
he arrived at school late and left early. His classmates concluded that he
was avoiding their company and judged him a snob. He was bullied at
every turn, but Volodya struck back in the only way he knew how: 'He
fought as hard as he could,' says a former classmate. 'He scratched, bit,
pulled hair and screeched. It wasn't nice to watch.'

PUTIN'S OWN recollection of himself in those early days is of a boy
who was not eager to go to school: 'I liked to hang out in our courtyard.
There were two courtyards joined like a well and it was there that we
spent most of our time. Mother would look out of the window
occasionally and shout "Are you in the courtyard?" I was in the courtyard
and she was happy that I had not run away – I was not supposed to leave
the courtyard without permission.' On one occasion, however, he
disobeyed and was left fearful by the experience: 'When I was five or six

I walked up to the big street corner for the first time. Without permission, of course. It was on a May Day. I looked around. The people were all swirling around, brouhaha was everywhere, life was boiling over, and yes, I was scared.'

Staring up from his bed at the peeling ceiling of their room, young Volodya ached to give his parents a better life. Each day he saw his mother struggle up five flights of stairs to their room at the top of the dreary, yellow five-storey building. These were momentous times for Russia. Stalin had been replaced as First Secretary of the Communist Party by the complex – though oft-noted humane – political commissar Nikita Khrushchev, who stunned the world with his denunciation of his predecessor in a well-leaked 'secret' speech at the Twentieth Party Congress in February 1956. Khrushchev divided regional committees in two: agriculture and industry – an unfortunate split in Soviet times for what lay ahead. There were hopes that under Khrushchev the Soviet system might be capable of reforming itself into a more democratic form of socialism, although most of Khrushchev's domestic policies aimed at improving the lot of the ordinary Soviet citizen proved ineffective.

Volodya was perceptive enough to learn lessons from the squalid environment around him. The Putins shared the kitchen – nothing more than a sink and gas cooker in a corridor – with an elderly Jewish tailor, his wife and grown-up spinster daughter, Khava. In that confined space, arguments were inevitable. Although Volodya was fond of the Jewish couple, he made the mistake of intervening on his parents' side in one of their disputes. His parents were furious. 'Mind your own business,' they told him. He was nonplussed. It took him some time to realise that his parents considered his rapport with the old couple to be much more important than those petty kitchen squabbles. 'After that incident, I never got involved in the kitchen quarrels again,' he says. 'As soon as they started fighting, I simply went back to our room or to the old folks' room.'

TO COUNTERACT the bullying her son was experiencing at school, Maria, a sensible woman, encouraged him to go out by himself in the hope that he would make new friends. In his new-found freedom, Volodya chose bad company and found himself doing what he now describes as 'wrong things' to impress his peers. He spent a lot of time in the courtyard at the bottom of the building's stairwell. This was the 'turf' of the local gangs. 'Growing up in the yard was like living in the jungle,' he says. 'Very much so. Oh yes!' One of the gangs' favourite pastimes, he explains, was chasing rats up the stone stairs with sticks, a pursuit he enjoyed until he made 'the interesting discovery that if you corner a rat it turns on you and attacks you, attacks you aggressively. A rat will even chase its adversary when it tries to run away' – a tactic he doubtless remembers even today when dealing with his judo opponents. The gang was ruled over by a couple of young tearaways called the Kovshov Brothers. Although he was a lot younger, Volodya tried to keep up with them – with everything that they got up to. He started carrying a hunting knife for self-protection. Despite his puny frame and pale complexion, the little boy with a lick of blonde hair over his right eye got into trouble with the police and was branded a hooligan. 'I really was a bad boy,' he says. When it was discovered that he took a knife to school, his teachers threatened him with being sent to a borstal. Indeed, he was one of a handful of boys in a class of 45 pupils who were not permitted to join the Young Pioneers because of their rowdy behaviour. 'It doesn't matter,' he said, 'I've always got the Kovshovs.'

Vladimir Spiridonovich ordered his son to take up boxing. But after his nose was broken in an early bout his ring career came to an abrupt and undignified end. His life might well have gone into a downward spiral, but around this time Vera Dmitrievna Gurevich, who taught him from grades five to eight – age 11 to 14 – noticed a dramatic change in his attitude. In April 1964, he expressed an interest in learning German, which he took as an extra subject in after-school classes with Ms Gurevich, who realised that he had a fantastic memory. She found him a strong-willed, energetic, kind and even loving pupil, with an aptitude for languages, history and literature.

In the autumn of 1965, Volodya joined the Trud (Labour) Club – an athletic club which was part of the Russian Republic's Voluntary Sports

HE MAY have upset George Bush with his opposition to the invasion of Iraq, but Putin's love of dogs endeared him to the President's father, former President George Bush Snr, when he went to stay at the family home, Walker's Point, near Kennebunkport in the state of Maine in 2007.

Society – for which good marks were a prerequisite. It was here he fell under the influence of Anatoly Semyonovich Rakhlin, a neighbour of the Putins in Baskov Lane and an expert in the art of self-defence known as sambo. The sport, a combination of wrestling and ju-jitsu, appealed enormously to the 13-year-old boy. Rakhlin taught him that while he might not be able to out-punch his foes he could *out-think* them. Under Rakhlin's tutelage, he became fanatical about sambo and then judo. He also made some good friends at the club – particularly Arkady Rotenberg and his brother Boris. 'They were probably the first close friends Volodya ever had,' according to one person who remembers them training together. 'Like most of the others who used the club, the Rotenberg brothers were from as poor a background as Putin himself.' They were, however, to go on to achieve incredible success and to accrue great riches, as we shall see.

Explaining today how martial arts changed him, Putin says that judo is not just a sport, but a philosophy: 'Sport teaches us about relationships between people and to respect your partner. It also teaches us that a seemingly weak partner can not only resist you but also beat you. It's not only strength that can change the result of a match. It's the ability to think and use the right stance. This is very important. What is also very important is to have a strong character and a strong desire for victory.' Enormously grateful to Rakhlin, he still sees him occasionally when he visits the city of his birth.

Indicative of the change in young Volodya, he was permitted to join the Young Pioneers, an essential move in any young person's life in the Soviet Union. Failure to do so would have barred him from the Komsomol (the Communist Youth League) and without Komsomol membership, he would have been denied a university education and access to the professions. His father, a life-long Communist who had been educated along strict Party lines, was delighted when Volodya was elected chair of his Pioneer council. He was also proud of his son's sporting prowess. He and his wife never missed one of his contests if they could help it. Volodya went on to win many trophies in the Leningrad sambo championships and became a master in both sambo and judo.

SKIING PRESIDENTS, past and present: Putin and Dmitri Medvedev both enjoy the delights of Russia's favoured ski resort, Sochi – the venue chosen for the 2014 Winter Olympics.

By now the family were able to afford a small three-room dacha at Tosno, a small town to the south-east of Leningrad. Maria happily observed the growing closeness between father and son as they chopped wood together, went fishing and generally shared whatever work was necessary during the summer holidays.

Although Volodya hadn't inherited his father's musical abilities, he was very keen on learning to play the accordion. Perhaps he did not sing exactly in time, but he also happily joined in with his father singing folk songs. In turn, the father would listen tolerantly to his teenage son's much-loved collection of Beatles records – his favourite song was Paul McCartney's *Yesterday* – and eventually bought him a cheap guitar, which he strummed all day long. He was not much of a dancer either, but in those days that was no handicap: his main interest in the opposite sex was seeing if *they* admired *him*. By all accounts, he had plenty of admirers.

Putin – and many would say most of Russia – has a lot to thank Anatoly Rakhlin for. The martial arts expert still lives close to Baskov Street and, when asked, will take the curious to visit the apartment where the Putins shared that room with a peeling ceiling. Its present occupants, Police Captain Anton Matveev and his wife Nina, are reluctant to show visitors around and are clearly grateful that there is no plaque on the building to draw attention to the fact that one of the most powerful men in the world once lived there. Thanks to Yeltsin's course towards a market economy – a course that Putin inherited – the rent has soared on the modest abode the Matveevs share with their daughter Zhenia.

There is little demand for bus tours of the district offered by a firm called Falkon and conducted by a man known only as Kirill, although business does pick up around the time of Putin's birthday in October. The tour starts at the maternity hospital where he was born and takes in the cathedral where he was baptised and the *banya*, or bathhouse, where the Putins went for their weekly ablutions. Kirill takes pride in pointing out to anyone who is interested that Putin is the first native of the city to head the country since the last Tsar almost a century ago. Then he shows them the restaurants, Russkaya Rybalka and Podvoriye, where Putin entertained two other presidents, George W. Bush and Jacques Chirac.

Putin himself has felt no inclination to return to the room in which he lived for many years or to walk through his old neighbourhood. He would not enjoy the experience: School No. 193 has been converted into a technical college, the gym in which Anatoly Rakhlin trained him lies derelict and the streets he once roamed with his gang are now filled with the debris left by the alcoholics and drug addicts who inhabit the district. It would never occur to him that he might have joined their ranks. He was too smart for that, too disciplined. He still abhors disorder and lack of discipline.

It is almost five decades since Putin was accepted into the Komsomol, in a ceremony before the Party district committee, in the autumn of 1967. To the country's leader it must feel like a lifetime ago. In 1968, without consulting either his parents or his teachers, 16-year-old Putin suddenly changed tack. Forsaking the humanities, he opted to spend the final two years of schooling at Grammar School No. 281, which specialised in chemistry. It was still some time before the strong-minded Russian would make his explosive entrance on the world stage.

2

Agent and Lover

IN THE SUMMER of 1968, while Tony Blair was play-acting with a group called The Pseuds at Fettes College in Edinburgh (where he broke all the rules on drinking and smoking and his main interest lay in playing the guitar) and Bill Clinton was at Oxford University (where he famously "didn't inhale, didn't get drafted and didn't get a degree"), Vladimir Putin took a walk down Leningrad's Liteiny Street to the KGB offices, where he hoped his services would be enlisted.

His physique and confidence had been boosted by his prowess at judo and, like many of his generation, he was looking for a job in what were known as 'the agencies', the various arms of state security, membership of which represented a significant step up the Soviet career ladder. Putin already saw himself as a leader. As a member of the Komsomol, he was expected to give a lead to other pupils at Grammar School No. 281, a task he took to heart, handing out autographed pictures of himself inscribed with messages such as 'A healthy mind in a healthy body', and offering advice to other pupils about how they should conduct themselves.

He was a student who would speak about current affairs in weekly presentations to his class, grasping the lectern with both hands as he expounded his views. There was a lot for the young Soviet mind to take in. Khrushchev had been deposed in 1964 and the lugubrious old Ukrainian Leonid Brezhnev was at the Kremlin helm. He abandoned

'Mr K's' liberal reforms, invested heavily in arms and invaded Afghanistan, ushering in a period known to Russians as *zastoinoe vremya*, the time of stagnation.

If some thought Putin big-headed and self-promoting, such opinions did not deter him. He developed a knack for telling improbable stories with a straight face and enjoyed it when he was believed. More importantly, he lost his desire to become a chemist when, in the flickering light of the October cinema on Moscow's Novy Arbat Street, his life took a completely new direction.

Putin loved the cinema and his boyhood dream (or so he later confided to Hollywood film star, Jack Nicholson) was to become an actor. All that changed when he saw *The Sword and the Shield (Schit i mech)*, a thriller about a Russian spy who infiltrated SS headquarters in Berlin and stole Hitler's secrets. The following day he told his classmate Viktor Borisenko, 'I am going to be a spy – *they* are the people who win wars, not armies. The soldiers are just servants, the brawn not the brains'. He was thrilled to learn that the KGB was known in Lenin's day as 'the sword and shield' of the Revolution.

The most immediate effect of his sudden conversion was that he dropped physics and chemistry in favour of Russian literature and history, and continued with his German. 'He was one of the rare students who had a very clear idea about his future,' says Tamara Stelmashova, his social history teacher. 'He was focused, determined, with a strong character, very serious, responsible and just.' On a visit to his home, she noted that on one of the walls there was a picture of Felix Dzerzhinsky, the founder of the Bolshevik special services, the Cheka – forerunner of the KGB, now the FSB.

Volodya worked hard at his studies and spent weekends cramming for his school leaving exams at his parents' three-room dacha at Tosno. Vera Brileva lived in the same street. She met Volodya in 1968, when she was 14 and he was 16. She became a frequent visitor to the Putins' dacha and also to their home in Leningrad. In an interview with the *Sobesednik* newspaper, she portrayed the future president as a muscular student who feared no one and had a magnetic effect on women. When he arrived in

Tosno, 'girls just threw themselves at him,' Vera said. 'He had some kind of charm about him. To this day, I remember his hands – he had short, strong fingers.'

Vera recalls a New Year's Eve party at the Putins' dacha where somebody suggested playing Spin the Bottle. Volodya gave the bottle a spin and it pointed at Vera. He kissed her on the lips. 'It was a brief kiss,' she says, 'but I felt so hot all of a sudden.' She and Volodya started to see one another, although they were rarely alone: he would invite a group of friends to the dacha, and it was a rare party that did not include a rendition of his favourite song 'The Dashing Troika This Way Comes', which he performed with great gusto. The lyrics eulogise a bold young coachman who sings to the girl he has been forced to leave behind. His favourite Russian singers were Bulat Okudzhava and Vladimir Vysotsky.

One day an assertive young woman called Lyuda joined the group to hear the performance. After dinner, the boys asked her to wash the dishes but she refused, saying: 'My husband will be the one to do the dishwashing for me'. At that point, Vera felt she would face no competition for Volodya's affections from the new arrival. She knew that he was a shirker when it came to household chores: 'And anyway, she was a brunette and I knew he preferred blondes'.

Vera also discovered that her beau preferred studying to romance. He declined invitations to accompany her to the cinema, saying he had no time for entertainment. 'Despite his charming manner, he always wore a sombre expression on his face,' she said. 'Everybody would burst out laughing while Volodya just sat there, still and emotionless. And he would be amazed at some trifling matter. I would say to him "That's the way it should be done," and he would go, "Really? You must be kidding me!"'

Vera recalls that Volodya's desk at home was positioned next to a sofa in the corner of the Putins' room at the *kommunalka* in Baskov Lane. One day when she called he made it clear that he would prefer to be alone. As he sat writing at his desk, she tried to make conversation: 'Volodya, do you remember the time when . . .' Putin cut her short. 'I remember only things I need to remember,' he snapped. Vera was heartbroken. A proud girl, she felt her feelings for him dissolve at that moment. She walked out and never went back. 'What can I do with a man who treats me this way?' she asked her friends.

Now a married pensioner, Vera says, 'Even to this day, they suggest I write to him to let him know I am still around, but I'm a full-blooded Russian and he knows it. I wouldn't write and ask for help even if I was starving and living under a bridge. Why would he think of me now, when he didn't think of me then?'

THE REASON FOR PUTIN'S preoccupation with study was that he

THEY WERE both prime ministers when this holiday snap was taken: Vladimir Putin with his friend, Italy's then-leader Silvio Berlusconi.

had taken a short walk north of his home along Liteiny Street to the building Leningraders referred to as the *Bolshoi Dom,* 'The Big House', the ugly nine-storey Leningrad headquarters of the KGB. It turned out to be a practice run and so did the next one. It was not until his third attempt that he plucked up the courage to ask a staff officer, 'How can I become a KGB agent?'

He was not disappointed. Though used to dealing with cranks and juvenile dreamers, the officer spoke patiently to the thin, pale-faced 16-year-old and advised him to get a university degree. Putin later recalled that the man also said, 'We don't take people who come to us on their own initiative'. Even so, he was determined to get to university, despite the fact that there were 40 applicants for each of the small number of places and his parents doubted that he was sufficiently academic to get one. Exceeding all expectations, however, Vladimir was admitted to the Faculty of Law at Leningrad State University (LGU) in 1970, to read International Law.

At university, he studied hard and practised his judo. He was involved in numerous tough contests, which he remembers as 'a form of torture'. Anatoly Rakhlin says he was the type of fighter who preferred training: 'Very calm, cold-blooded and clever'. He adds: 'As a fighter he feared no one – he would fight 100kg men. He was very good at changing his grip. It was difficult to guess where he would throw you. His favourite moves were the leg sweep and the shoulder throw.'

In the Leningrad championships, Putin faced the world champion, Volodya Kullenin. He thought he had won when he succeeded in throwing his opponent across his back in the first few minutes, but the referee allowed the fight to continue – the crowd would never tolerate the world champion being beaten so easily. The bout ended when Kullenin twisted Putin's elbow and the referee judged him to have grunted. Since any sort of crying out was construed as signalling defeat, Kullenin was declared the winner. Putin thinks he should have won but adds: 'I'm not ashamed to lose to a world champion'.

After attending a training camp on Khippiyarvi Lake, he travelled to matches at various venues across the Soviet Union, once to Moldavia to prepare for the Spartakiad competition, which was open to all-comers from the USSR. He was devastated in 1973 when his close friend Volodya Cheryomushkin, who had taken up the sport at his insistence, broke his neck diving head-first into the mat during a bout. Paralysed, Cheryomushkin died 10 days later in hospital. Putin, who supposedly lacked the ability to express his emotions, kept himself in check during the funeral but later broke down and wept at the graveside with Volodya's mother and sister.

Thanks to the camaraderie of sport, Putin's reclusive streak became less noticeable. He joined in holiday activities with other students, swimming at a Black Sea resort and cutting down trees in northern Russia (which earned him the very decent sum of 1,000 roubles for six weeks' work). And there were other advantages. Instead of spending years as a conscript in the Russian Army, he took part in exercises run by the Institute for Military Affairs, ending up with the nominal rank of lieutenant. From an uncertain, troubled childhood he was emerging as a young man with prospects. He had learned to balance friendships and focus on his long-term aim of becoming a national hero. He was a hard-working and conscientious student, if not a particularly gifted one.

His 21st birthday came and went and he was concerned that he had still not heard from the very people he was trying to impress, the KGB. His spirits picked up when Maria won a Zaporozhets-966, a little rear-engine car made in the Ukraine, after she had been given a 30-kopeck lottery ticket instead of change at a cafeteria. She could have taken the value of the vehicle – 3,500 roubles – in cash, which would have alleviated the family's poverty for some considerable time, but instead she gave the car to her son.

Putin describes himself as 'a pretty wild driver'. He once hit a pedestrian who jumped in front of his car, apparently with the intention of committing suicide. The man must have been injured but was able to get up and run away. The story got around that Putin had jumped out of his car and chased after him. The allegation brought a furious response: 'What? You think I hit a guy with my car and then tried to chase him down? I'm not a beast.'

In his fourth year of university, a stranger approached him. 'I need to talk to you about your cover assignment,' he said. 'I wouldn't like to specify exactly what it is yet.' Putin knew this was the moment he had been waiting for. He agreed to meet the man in the faculty vestibule but the man was late. Putin waited 20 minutes. Thinking he had been the victim of a practical joke, he was about to walk away when the man arrived, out of breath. 'It's all arranged,' he said, 'Volodya, how would you feel if you were invited to work in the agencies?' Without a second's thought, Putin replied in the affirmative. Had he left even moments earlier, the history of present-day Russia would have to be rewritten.

As explained to him, the KGB deal was that after graduation he would be accepted as a trainee agent with good opportunities for promotion. In contravention of the secrecy he had been instructed to observe, he told his father that he was joining the KGB. His friends were simply informed that he had 'secured a job in the police force', but since his ambition to join the secret service was pretty much an open secret, few were left in any doubt what 'the job' entailed.

Putin graduated as a lawyer in 1974, and the following year attended School No. 401 near the Okhta River, where he was trained in counter-intelligence measures. His friends recall the 'supreme happiness' that lit up his face in those early days, but not everybody was prepared to accept his claim that he worked for the police. One of his closest friends, Sergey Roldugin, a soloist in the Mariinsky Theatre Symphony Orchestra, confronted him about it. 'I'm a cellist,' he said. 'I know you are a spy – I don't know what that means. Who are you? What do you do?' Putin coolly replied: 'I'm a specialist in human relations'.

It was a description that was actually not too wide of the mark: a KGB officer's work was largely about letting go of self and immersing oneself in the other fellow in order to obtain information. To study human weakness, he started examining those around him. One man admits to becoming quite paranoid about Putin constantly questioning him while staring into his eyes. An instructor's report at the end of his first six months shows that Putin had to be told repeatedly that his probing should be far more subtle if it was going to yield results.

Probably the most valuable lesson he learned about the KGB's attitude towards ordinary people was when some of his older colleagues were creating a hypothetical case for the benefit of trainees. When one veteran agent instructing his class at school 401 suggested that a certain course of action should be taken, Putin interrupted him. 'You can't do that,' he said. 'It's against the law.' His KGB colleagues looked at him aghast. 'Our instructions,' one patiently explained, '*are* the law.' The following year Putin started work in the KGB's counter-intelligence department at the Big House on Liteiny Street.

Meanwhile, Putin continued with his judo training. Volodya Kullenin had taken to drink and dropped out of the sport. Putin was sorry to see his decline but in 1976 he replaced Kullenin as judo champion of Leningrad. Kullenin later died of alcoholism, but alcohol was never a serious problem for Putin, despite rumours to the contrary. He recalls getting drunk as a student 'chasing shish kebabs down with port wine', while Vera Brileva says he drank dry wine and champagne with his friends but adds: 'He preferred milk'. Anatoly Rakhlin maintains his desire to win at judo was so strong that he was always sober. And Klaus Zuchold, an East German spy who knew him for almost five years in the 1980s, relates: 'Whenever we drank together, he always made sure he was at least three glasses behind everyone else'. There was even one report that he was seen watering a pot plant with his glass of vodka.

At the Big House, he was talent-spotted by a KGB intelligence officer and sent to Moscow for a year to be trained in foreign intelligence. 'Of course I wanted to go into foreign intelligence,' he says. 'Everyone did. We all knew what it meant to be able to travel abroad.' When he returned to Leningrad, his friends noted that he no longer brimmed with boyish excitement about whatever work it was that he did. He seemed colder and more detached. He moved in a different circle, conversing with academics and foreign businessmen – people who could provide him with the very oxygen he needed: information. Speaking fluent German and passable French and English, he was chosen to show foreign visitors around the city and, for the first time, travelled abroad with Soviet groups to keep foreign agents at bay.

In his memoirs, Putin says his work involved 'dealing with people' but it isn't known how successful he was at recruiting genuine informers. He also admits he disliked the way the KGB was employed to crush dissident art and harass artists. Rather clumsily, he says today: 'The co-operation of normal citizens was an important tool for the state's viable activity'. In other words, Leningraders were encouraged to keep an eye out for unusual behaviour. Interestingly – though under very different circumstances, clearly – U.S. citizens today are encouraged to keep a watchful eye on behalf of state authorities. Walmart runs an 'if you see something, say something' Homeland Security campaign and a recently launched iPhone application, PatriotApp, urges citizens to report similar information to the FBI and other federal agencies.

BACK INTO PUTIN'S life in the summer of 1979 came Lyuda, the girl who had refused to do the washing-up at his family's dacha and who was now a medical student. His parents were pleasantly surprised to learn that he had met up with Lyuda again and was seeing her on a regular basis, especially when – eventually – he brought her home to meet them.

Lyuda took care of him in much the same way as she had always done, telling him what to eat and what to wear, impressing on him the importance of looking smart. She even polished his shoes – no mean feat for a girl who had once refused to wash the dinner plates. Even today, Putin can't say whether he was in love with her or not. She was a trifle bossy, but he decided that quality was desirable in a wife. It was her way of getting things done, and a wife had to get things done if she was going to serve her man.

So he proposed marriage. In her practical, matter-of-fact way, Lyuda accepted and started to plan the wedding. Her parents bought a wedding dress and his parents invested in a new suit for him, along with the necessary rings. The bridegroom visited Leningrad Town Hall to apply for a marriage licence.

No one quite understood why Volodya never actually married Lyuda. Everyone thought they were well-suited and would have had wonderful children. His mother adored her and years later had the nerve

AS ONE of his chauffeurs testifies, he loves to drive fast cars, but has to let others do the job when he's on official business. The same does not apply when he's on the piste: here he rides a high-speed snowmobile

to tell the woman he *did* marry that she would rather have had his first love as a daughter-in-law. But whether it was last-minute nerves or just the fact that he couldn't accept becoming one half of a couple, he called off the wedding, telling the bride-to-be that he was ashamed of himself for not having 'thought it through before it got this far'. 'That was one of the most difficult decisions of my life. It was very hard. I looked like a total jerk. But still I decided it was better to break up now than for both of us to suffer for the rest of our lives. I didn't run away, of course, I told her the truth and that's all I thought I had to do.' His friends were shocked. One of them explains: 'The trouble with Volodya was that he could never express his feelings and from what I've seen of him on television he still can't. He thinks the truth but wraps it up in a myth – that's why he was so well suited to the KGB.'

PUTIN'S NEXT LOVE interest was a young woman with shoulder-length *blonde* hair – a prerequisite according to Vera Brileva – and big blue eyes. He was thin, short and clearly paid little thought to the style or quality of his clothes – not, as Lyudmila Alexandrovna Shkrebneva was later to admit, the sort of man she would have favoured with a second glance on the street. But it was too late now: she had agreed to go on a blind date with him. The main attraction was that Vladimir Putin had tickets to see Arkady Raikin, one of the funniest comedians of his day, at the glamorous Lensoviet Theatre – they didn't have anything like that in her home city of Kaliningrad (the former East Prussian city of Königsberg).

Lyudmila had been born in that dull, militarised Baltic Sea enclave on 6 January 1958. Dropping out of technical college in her third year, she joined Aeroflot as a flight attendant in order to get away. Unlike another flight attendant, Irina Malandina, who went on to marry Vladimir's sometime friend Roman Abramovich, the 22-year-old had no well-connected relative to wangle her a job with an international airline where she could meet better marital prospects.

Lyudmila was on a three-day stopover in Leningrad with another flight attendant when she agreed to make up a foursome. The date was 7 March 1980. The two girls and her friend's current boyfriend met on Nevsky Prospect near the ticket office. Volodya, who had a reputation for always being late, was already standing on the steps. He was poorly dressed – his one good coat was now threadbare – and Lyudmila thought he looked unprepossessing. Interestingly, Putin was to maintain years later that they met when he found himself sitting next to her in the theatre – he did not like to admit that his wife had been a date arranged for him by a mutual acquaintance and that he had secured tickets for both of them without ever having set eyes on her.

The comedy of Arkady Raikin was in total contrast to the quiet, introverted man at her side, but there was something about the young Volodya that made Lyudmila agree to see him again the very next night. And the next. He seemed to be able to get tickets for almost everything. On the second night, it was the Leningrad Music Hall and on the third, the Lensoviet Theatre again. It was a promising start, although never in her wildest dreams could she have imagined that Volodya would one day make her Russia's First Lady.

On those first dates, Putin told his new friend that he worked in the criminal investigation department of the Leningrad police force. He says: 'I told her I was a cop. Security officers, particularly intelligence officers, were under official cover'. Lyudmila recalls she had no qualms about going out with a policeman and was keen to keep in touch. When Putin asked for her telephone number, she told him she had no phone at home but could call him, so he wrote down his number as they were thundering along on the Metro. Lyudmila then returned to Kaliningrad, where she told friends she had met an interesting man, albeit a 'plain and unremarkable one'. It was too soon to talk of love, but she was greatly intrigued. Determined to keep in touch, she called him almost every day from work or a public phone booth.

When friends inquired what her new boyfriend did for a living, Lyudmila told them what Putin had told her: that he was something to do with the police. She discovered the truth after she had given up her job and moved to Leningrad to be near him: 'After three or four months I had already decided he was the man I needed'. Asked why she had reached such a momentous conclusion about the man she had described to her friends as 'plain and unremarkable', she says: 'Perhaps it's that inner strength which attracts everybody [to him] now.'

SINCE EVERYONE in the city seemed to know what they did at the Big House on Liteiny Street, it didn't take her long to determine her sweetheart's true profession. By then, however, she was besotted and as she had no experience of the security forces herself, she thought little of it.

Telling her that 'everyone of our age should do something to improve themselves and broaden their minds', Vladimir persuaded his girlfriend to enrol at Leningrad University. Since he was keen on languages, she chose French and Spanish. Almost as an afterthought, he suggested she also take a typing course – it might be helpful to him in his work – and she agreed. He also encouraged her to study the social graces acquired by some of the wives of his colleagues.

One character trait she found unattractive was his fierce temper if he thought someone was flirting with her – or, indeed, if he considered her own behaviour to be flirtatious. This was one jealous man. As he deemed right and proper, they lived separately, he in a corner of his parents' room at their communal apartment and she in student quarters. It was hardly a passionate start to the romance, but then Putin was not known to be a passionate man. Friends say they consummated their affair only when Vladimir took her on holiday to the Black Sea resort of Sochi.

By then Lyudmila knew she was in love. She was anxious to put their relationship on a permanent footing, but the more hints she dropped, the further he seemed to withdraw from the prospect of marriage. He was, he later admitted, an expert at planning his every move and that applied to romance as well as his career. It was three and a half years before he finally raised the question of their relationship. Putin says his friends had started telling him he should get married, but it is intriguing to note that his decision coincided with a dramatic change in Russian life. Brezhnev had died in November 1982 and Putin's hero Yuri Andropov, head of the KGB, was in the Kremlin. Andropov tackled the economic stagnation and unchecked corruption of the Brezhnev era, but also cracked down ruthlessly on any kind of dissent, all actions that were likely to generate a mood of optimism in devoted young KGB officers like Putin.

How does a man like Putin propose? Clumsily, it turns out. Lyudmila recalls the moment: 'One evening we were at his place and he said: "My dear, now you know everything about me. All in all, I'm not an easy person to be with." And then he described himself as a silent type, sometimes rather abrupt, who might occasionally say offensive things. In other words, a risky life partner. Then he asked: "You must have decided something for yourself in the three and a half years [we have been together]?" All I understood was that we were apparently going to break up. "As a matter of fact I have," I said. He asked me doubtfully: "Really?" At that point I realised we were definitely breaking up. "Well, if so, I love you and propose we get married on such-and-such a date," he said. This came totally out of the blue. I accepted and we agreed to get married three months later. Marriage was not an easy step for me. Nor was it for him,' she concluded, before adding the cryptic remark: 'Because there are people who take a responsible attitude to marriage'.

Other biographers have recorded the date of their wedding as 28 July 1983, when the bridegroom was in his thirty-first year, though I have been unable to find any records which substantiate these claims. However, these were Soviet times, when official ceremonies took place in registry offices rather than in church and records are not always easily obtained.

Whatever form the union took there can be no doubt about the celebrations. There were two receptions – one for family and close friends at a floating restaurant on the Neva River, and another the following day at the Hotel Moscow, which was exclusively for his KGB colleagues, who had no wish to reveal their identities to strangers. For the honeymoon they returned to the location of their first intimate encounter, Sochi, and Lyudmila later surprised their friends by confiding that her husband had made it 'as romantic as romantic could be'.

The newlyweds went to live with his parents who, mercifully, had moved into a two-bedroom apartment on Stachek Prospect in Avtovo, a district of newly constructed apartment blocks in the south of the city. The kitchen windows were so high up that, sitting at the kitchen table, the only view was 'the wall in front of your eyes'. Vladimir Spiridonovich had been given the flat as a disabled war veteran when he retired from the factory in 1977. The newlyweds' room was 20 metres square, little more than half the size of the one in which he had grown up, and the insulation of the walls in the cheaply-built block afforded them little privacy. By Soviet standards of the time, however, they were relatively well off. Vladimir still had the Zaporozhets and he enjoyed driving around the city with his new wife at his side. He has always loved to drive and one of the presidential chauffeurs was later to say: 'He would like to take the wheel of the limousine when we are travelling at high speed in the motorcade to his dacha or to the airport, but he knows he does not

PUTIN and his wife Lyudmila accompany Lyudmila Narusova (second right), the widow of St Petersburg's first Mayor, Anatoly Sobchak, and her daughter Ksenia, to lay flowers on the grave of Putin's mentor in the city's Nikolskoye cemetery.

have the necessary training for terrorist avoidance that we have. It frustrates him though.'

Lyudmila discovered early in their marriage that her husband had other faults apart from his temper. Describing him in an unguarded moment as a 'bona fide male chauvinist', she complained that he expected her to do everything around the home (while this might raise eyebrows abroad, where such behaviour would be considered 'old school', in Russia it remains the norm and is perfectly acceptable). He also told his friend that for a man to praise his wife was to spoil her. 'He has put me to the test throughout our life together,' she was to tell Putin's biographer, Oleg Blotski. 'I constantly feel he is watching me and checking that I make the right decisions.' And giving an unequivocal indication of what was to cause her considerable stress later in their marriage, she added: 'He is extremely difficult to cook for and will refuse to eat a dish if he does not like the slightest ingredient. He never praises me and that has totally put me off cooking.'

But these were the honeymoon days and she was already expecting their first child when he was sent to Moscow for further training at the Yuri Andropov Red Banner Institute in September 1984. Lyudmila moved into a bedsitter on the northern side of Leningrad and carried on with her studies. At Red Banner students were given a *nom de guerre* beginning with the same letter as their surname. Thus Comrade Putin became Comrade Platov. The course included tests for physical endurance and clear thinking. There were night parachute jumps, lessons in how to lose a tail and how to arrange for coded information to be left at dead-letter drops.

Lyudmila visited him once a month and he came home a couple of times. On one of those trips he managed to break his arm. 'Some punk was bugging him in the Metro and he socked the guy,' his close friend Sergei Roldugin says. 'He was very concerned that those who taught and trained him might hold it against him.'

The Putins' first child, Maria, named after Vladimir's mother and known as Masha, was born on 28 April 1985, while her father was on leave. Sergei Roldugin picked up mother and baby from the maternity hospital and, with Putin and his own wife Irina on board, drove to his father-in-law's dacha at Vyborg, where they celebrated the baby's birth.

Putin graduated from the Red Banner Institute in July 1985. While his 'analytical turn of mind' was highly regarded, he received a negative character assessment for being withdrawn and uncommunicative, and for having what was described as 'a lowered sense of danger'. This last characteristic was considered a serious flaw. Agents had to be pumped up in critical situations in order to react well and an inability to feel fear inhibited the flow of adrenalin. 'I had to work on my sense of danger for a long time,' he says.

Now in his early thirties, he was a trained foreign operative and yearned to work outside the USSR against his country's enemies. He devoured information from older KGB colleagues who returned from abroad, not the die-hard Stalinist variety, but those who had experienced a different way of life. 'They were,' he noted, 'a generation with entirely different views, values and sentiments.'

At one point he grilled one of his friends who had worked in Afghanistan about the Soviet occupation, a popular cause in Russia. Putin wanted to know if it was true that his signature was required for missile launchings against Afghan targets. The man's reply stunned him: 'I judge the results of my work by the number of documents that I did not sign'.

These were stirring times. Mikhail Gorbachev had been elected General Secretary of the Communist Party on 11 March 1985, just three hours after the sudden death of Konstantin Chernenko. Almost immediately he introduced *perestroika* (the controversial restructuring programme) to revive the stagnant Soviet economy, and within a matter of months *perestroika* had been joined by *glasnost* (openness of speech), *demokratizatsiya* (democratisation) and *uskoreniye* (acceleration of economic development).

Putin's chance to see things clearly for himself came when he was assigned by a KGB commission to East Germany. It had been clear to him since his early days at Red Banner that he was being prepared for a German posting, because they pushed him to continue his language studies. It was just a question of whether it would be the German Democratic Republic (GDR) or the Federal Republic of Germany (FRG). To make it into the latter, the candidate had to work at Moscow Centre for up to two years. Putin says he decided it was better to travel right away and so, now a fully-fledged KGB man, he accepted the posting without complaint, packed his bags and kissed Lyudmila goodbye.

3

Drama in Dresden

MAJOR V.V. PUTIN'S first KGB posting was as senior case officer at Dresden, a city risen phoenix-like from the ashes following its firebombing by Bomber Command in 1944 (at Stalin's request, incidentally) and now the second most important city in East Germany, even if it was geographically closer to Prague than Berlin. It was an opportune time to be there. East-West tensions ran high over Soviet and NATO missile deployment and nowhere was more central to the ideological struggle than Germany, divided since 1945 into the communist East and the capitalist West.

Putin travelled alone to Dresden in August 1985 to settle into the job and prepare a home for his wife and baby. Lyudmila says he was supposed to go to East Berlin, the most prestigious posting inside the Soviet bloc, but a KGB friend – a Leningrader working in Dresden – recommended him to the station chief there when his own tour of duty was coming to an end. Yuri Shvets, a contemporary of Putin's at the Red Banner Institute, however, claims his posting to Dresden was a punishment for a drinking spree at the institute at a time when the authorities were clamping down on alcohol. There certainly was a purge on drunkenness at that time – not only in the KGB but throughout Russia – though whether Putin was caught up in it remains unknown.

General Oleg Kalugin, a one-time chief of Soviet counterintelligence, was dismissive of both Putin and his posting. 'Any assignment to Eastern Europe, East Germany included, was a sign of someone's failing or lack of abilities,' he says. 'His record in the KGB is zero; he is a non-entity in the KGB.' Little credence can be granted to Kalugin's comment, however, since this is a man who in 2002 was found guilty in his absence of state treason, stripped of his military rank and pension and the 22 state awards he had managed to accumulate before fleeing to the US, where he remains to this day. Since counterintelligence is a different department from the intelligence department in which Putin was employed, Putin is generous in his response: 'He couldn't remember me [because] I had no contact with him, nor did I meet him. It is I who remember him because he was a big boss and everybody knew him. As to whether he knew me, there were hundreds of us.'

THE FUTURE RUSSIAN president was now 32 years of age, and the relief of having a foreign posting instead of the daily bureaucratic grind at the Big House was palpable. 'I had already worked in the agencies for 10 years,' he says. 'How romantic do you think that was?' He soon discovered that life in Dresden was considerably more attractive in a material sense than Leningrad. The stores were stocked with goods and there were few Russian-style lines outside them. The food was so good that he started putting on weight. He drove around in a chauffeured government car, a Russian Lada (known in the domestic market as a Zhiguli), and must have gazed in amusement at bulky East Germans crammed into their tiny Trabants, the little East German vehicle with tail-fins and a two-cylinder, two-stroke engine that put-putted around the city streets like a motor mower. When it came to finding a home, he had no choice: KGB agents were housed in an apartment block in Radeberger Strasse, which also contained members of the East German security service, the Stasi.

Putin was one of eight KGB officers working for Colonel Lazar Matveev, in a grey mansion surrounded by high brick walls, This compound at No. 4 Angelikastrasse stood opposite the Stasi's Dresden headquarters, and overlooked the Elbe River. The new arrival's specialist

GETTING AWAY FROM IT ALL: The man who rarely goes to bed before 2 a.m.
when he's working, takes to a horse and the outback when he needs a break.

field was political intelligence – obtaining information about political
figures and the plans of the Soviet Bloc's enemies, of whom NATO was
considered the most dangerous. One of his first moves was to make
informal contact with the Stasi. Klaus Zuchold, a young Stasi lieutenant,
says that one Thursday morning in the autumn of 1985 Putin turned up
with his predecessor at a sports field where Stasi officers often played
football. He was introduced simply as 'Volodya'.

At the end of the game the agents agreed to meet again socially and
Putin accepted an invitation from Zuchold to be shown the surrounding
countryside. 'Putin turned up in a grey Lada, wearing a large fur hat,'
Zuchold recalls. 'His wife was still in Russia. Together with my wife we
drove out of town and spent most of the day together. That was the first
time we spoke freely. He cracked a couple of police jokes and one about
Jews, which took me and Martina [his wife] a little by surprise. We talked
about history, literature and philosophy. He had a great admiration for
German culture and discipline. He was clearly proud of belonging to the

KGB. That was his life. He showed me his wristwatch, which had an inscription from some KGB bigwig. He loved patriotic stories of Russia's great past and popular heroes.'

Lyudmila joined her husband in Dresden later in 1985, after graduating in Spanish at Leningrad State University. Unbeknown to her, she had been quietly vetted by the KGB and cleared to travel outside the USSR's borders. Putin noted that she was generally pleased with the two-bedroom flat, despite having to lug baby Masha up and down five flights of stairs. For the sake of security the apartments were located close to a Soviet military base, but that did little to relieve the Putins' feelings of alienation in a strange city. 'We sat on our suitcases and dreamed of returning home,' Lyudmila says. 'At the beginning, we were really homesick.'

Practical in all matters, Lyudmila solved the problem by socialising with her German neighbours. She was soon involved in a daily routine with other young mothers and marvelled at their orderliness. They washed their windows once a week and in the morning, before going to work, went into the backyard, stretched a rope between two metal poles and hung their laundry on the line in neat rows with clothes pegs, a ritual that the new arrival found fascinating.

East Germany was a police state run by 'the two Erichs': Erich Honecker, chairman of the Council of State and thus de facto head of state, and Erich Mielke, the Minister for State Security. Honecker had been in charge of building the Berlin Wall which had ringed the Western sectors of Berlin since 1961, while Mielke, head of the Stasi, was credited with creating 'the most perfected surveillance state of all time'. The Stasi employed 97,000 staff in a country of 17 million people, and used the services of a further 173,000 informers. There was one Stasi officer or informant for every 63 people. Mielke, described as a small man with no neck, close-set eyes and puffy cheeks, controlled intelligence and counterintelligence from inside Stasi headquarters at Normannen Strasse in the East Berlin suburb of Lichtenberg.

Putin did not discuss his work at home, so whatever Lyudmila learned about the Stasi she got from her German neighbours. 'There was always a principle at the KGB: Do not share things with your wife,' she says. 'They always proceeded from the premise that the less the wife knew, the better she'd sleep.' It soon became clear that Putin was checking up on her new friends, because he would suddenly suggest she drop one of them from her circle as being 'undesirable'. The information most probably came from the Stasi's files, based largely on the snitching of *inofizielle Mitarbeiter* or IMs, the Stasi's most hated informers against their own family and friends.

At weekends there were drives in the Saxony countryside with friends for sausages and beer. Putin's weight continued to balloon – up almost two stone to 165 pounds. He took up fishing and became something of an expert with rod and reel. He also developed a taste for German beer; his favourite weekend jaunt was to Radeberg, which boasted one of the best breweries in East Germany. Lyudmila fell pregnant again and their second daughter, Katerina – named after Lyudmila's mother, Katerina Tikhonovna, and known as Katya – was born in Dresden on 31 August 1986.

Looking back, Putin describes East Germany as a 'harshly totalitarian country, similar to the Soviet Union 30 years earlier. And the tragedy is that many people sincerely believed in all those Communist ideals'. He was judging the society around him from the point of view of a man whose own country was undergoing a social and economic upheaval, whereas the East Germans were stuck in a Stalinist time-warp. While Lyudmila followed the progress of Gorbachev's *perestroika* on television and picked up snippets about the new mood in Russia from visiting Russians, Putin had far more advanced sources of information through his KGB network. 'We had begun to suspect that the regime would not last long,' he says.

Myths abound about his work in Dresden. Certainly he recruited informants, obtained information from them, analysed it and sent it to Moscow Centre via the KGB headquarters at Karlshorst, outside East Berlin. It was routine spook work and hardly glamorous. He insists it was 'political intelligence' as opposed to 'technical intelligence'. Allegations that he set up a network of agents across the world to indulge in industrial espionage remain unproven. The Stasi, he explains, had copies of everything produced by the KGB's Dresden office and therefore it was impossible for him to have been involved in operations that were unknown to the local GDR security agencies. He further claims that 'a large part of our work was done through citizens of the GDR. They are all on the roster. Everything is transparent and understandable and German counterintelligence knows about all of this.' That may be so, but the question remains as to whether those particular files remained intact in the heavily shredded Stasi archives.

The Prague-based businessman Vladimir Usoltsev, who claims to have been a colleague of Putin's during his Dresden years, rates him as a fairly average spy. According to Usoltsev in his book *Comrade in Arms*, Putin's German was good but not flawless; he hummed pop music in the office and spent a great deal of time browsing West German mail-order catalogues. Indeed, Klaus Zuchold says that Putin once showed off a new stereo system bought during a trip to KaDeWe (Kaufhaus des Westens), an upmarket department store in West Berlin, although Putin categorically denies ever visiting West Germany during his time in Dresden.

Vladimir Usoltsev further claims that a dislike of old-style Soviet bureaucracy led Putin, along with five other agents, to celebrate with two bottles of Russian 'Krim' champagne when the hardline Soviet leader Konstantin Chernenko died. 'We emptied the bottles with great joy and appreciation for Konstantin Chernenko's demise,' Usoltsev writes. 'At least he hadn't tortured us by dying endlessly, as his predecessors [Leonid Ilyich] Brezhnev and [Yuri Vladimirovich] Andropov had done.' The problem with this story is that Chernenko died in March 1985 and Putin did not arrive in Dresden until August of that year. Putin also revered the former KGB leader Andropov, so Usoltsev's claims should be treated with caution.

Usoltsev – whose book casts doubt on Putin's past life as a ruthless secret policeman – is on firmer ground when he likens the existence of KGB officers in Dresden to living in a spaceship on a long-term expedition 'in which recent graduates of the secret service school met with dogged old Chekists. [This was] a world full of stupid work with files, instructive Party circles and human intrigues.' Usoltsev also describes comrade Putin as 'a pragmatist' and 'someone who thinks one thing and says another'. He adds that Putin's intellectual abilities were no more than average, and that since the future president 'was not a great speaker' he was amazed that Putin rose to the highest position in his country.

Even though unofficial contacts with the KGB were strictly forbidden, Stasi officer Klaus Zuchold visited Putin's flat in Radeberger Strasse several times. 'I went to his house, met his wife Lyudmila, and Putin also came to visit me,' he says. 'To my children he was known simply as 'Uncle Volodya'. During those meetings, Putin questioned his German friend on the workings of the Stasi and expressed a particular interest in Werner Naumann, the local head of the Stasi's foreign intelligence department. Zuchold found Putin to be a man of few words. 'He is impenetrable and he mostly lets other people speak,' he says. 'He gives very little away but is clearly very driven and determined to get what he wants: friendly and seemingly very open, luring people into opening-up, but always in control.'

Putin makes no great claims about his time in East Germany. He sought potential KGB informants, principally among foreign students at Dresden Technical University, whom he sometimes picked up in his car and drove to the surrounding moors for a quiet chat. His favourite book at the time was *Dead Souls*, Nikolai Gogol's 1842 classic about the absurdity of what we like to think of as 'reality'.

Eschewing his KGB uniform, Putin on the other hand had come to dress in blue jeans, open-necked shirt and leather jacket, in order to blend, chameleon-like, into student circles. In the evening he dressed smartly to wine and dine foreign visitors to Dresden in the hope of recruiting them. Klaus Zuchold says both the Stasi and the KGB targeted Western businessmen, supplying them with prostitutes, secretly filming them having sex in their hotel rooms and then attempting to blackmail them. He could not recall Putin ever having taken part in such operations.

According to former KGB colleague Vladimir Usoltsev, Putin concealed both his ambition and his tough treatment of others under an image of politeness and obedience that was to serve him well in later years. He presented himself as a member of the Communist Party who had no wish to change the Soviet system. One critical colleague was apparently warned that he'd better keep his complaints to himself and think of his family. Yet in the privacy of a sauna, Putin supposedly told Usoltsev that he had a high regard for the civil rights activist Andrei Sakharov. When Usoltsev raised the question of Stalin's atrocities, he refused to admit what everyone else knew to be true: that Stalin had ordered KGB agents to shoot suspects whether they were proven guilty or not.

PUTIN HAD GROWN into a family man who took his responsibilities seriously. Most mornings he took Masha to a daycare centre adjacent to their apartment block and Katya to her nursery, then brought them both home for lunch with their mother. He was paid in marks and dollars and, by cutting out luxuries and living mainly on government-issued food, was able to put together a little nest egg.

During this time rumours began to circulate that Putin, like many of his KGB comrades, who saw the hand of Zionism in every anti-Soviet activity, was anti-Semitic. A German agent supposedly declared at one of their social gatherings that Putin's mother's maiden name, Shelomova, was Jewish and therefore he was a Jew. Putin, clearly angry, is said to have stormed out of the party. The story is apocryphal – for a start, no German agent would have had access to his personal details. According to Vladimir Usoltsev, Putin was unusually tolerant of Jews and he was known to admire the East German spymaster Markus Wolf, the son of a Jewish writer and physician.

Like many of his contemporaries, Putin was in awe of Markus Wolf, the man on whom John Le Carré modelled 'Karla' in his Cold War novels. As head of the Stasi's foreign intelligence service, the Hauptverwaltung Aufklarung (HVA), he operated a global network of 4,000 agents and was the bane of the CIA, MI6 and the West German agency BND. Wolf excelled in the 'honey trap'. 'If I go down in espionage history,' he writes in his memoirs, 'it may be for perfecting the use of sex in spying.' On discovering there was a shortage of available young men in West Berlin and Bonn, he sent handsome East German agents across the border to romance military secrets out of love-lorn NATO and government secretaries. His most spectacular coup was to place an agent, Gunter Guillaume, in the office of Chancellor Willy Brandt. When Guillaume was unmasked as a spy in 1974, Brandt was forced to resign.

Markus Wolf was later accused by reporters of insulting Putin by suggesting that the bronze medal he had been awarded for his services in East Germany was handed out to practically any secretary who had no gross violations in her record. Putin replied testily: 'Markus Wolf is entirely correct. And there is nothing offensive in what he said. Just the opposite. He just confirmed that I didn't have any gross violations in my record.'

Speaking officially today, Putin acknowledges there is still anti-Semitism in Russia and describes it as 'shameful'. Friends point out that Vera Dmitrievna Gurevich, his favourite teacher, was Jewish; but then, as Klaus Zuchold relates – and Tony Blair discovered during a visit to Moscow – that doesn't stop him from telling the occasional Jewish joke. Though that's not entirely surprising, since Jewish 'Odessan' anecdotes are an accepted part of Russia's popular culture.

It was normal for KGB officers to be promoted while working in a foreign posting. Putin was promoted twice, firstly from senior case officer to assistant head of department, and then to senior assistant head. 'There was nothing higher,' he says. 'Above me was the top managerial level and we only had one boss. So as an incentive I was made a member of the Party committee of the KGB representation in the GDR.' Moscow also showed its appreciation by promoting him to the rank of lieutenant-colonel.

One area of controversy during Putin's time in Dresden was his close friendship with a rising member of the Stasi, Matthias Warnig. Warnig had an enviable reputation among his contemporaries as a top recruiter of spies in the West – men and women who were in a position

THEY RARELY POSE together for the photographers, but Vladimir and Lyudmila made an exception during the then-Prime Minister's visit to India on political business in 2010.

to steal rocket secrets and aircraft technology. According to investigators on the *Wall Street Journal*, he was prepared to share this information with Putin, whom he'd met in Dresden in the 1980s. The newspaper alleged that the episode 'underscores the shadowy interplay between businessmen and former intelligence operatives in today's Russia'.

Warnig was later appointed head of the Russian division of Germany's Dresdner Bank and now runs Gazprom's Nord Stream project, which is building a new gas pipeline under the Baltic Sea from Russia to Germany. The two men remain close friends, although Warnig still denies he knew Putin in Dresden. Representatives at Dresdner, while acknowledging that Putin and Warnig are friends, deny any prior association. Bernard Walter, who headed the bank's East European operations in the early 1990s, says, 'Mr Warnig told me clearly that he met Mr Putin for the first time in his life in 1991, when I sent him to St Petersburg.' The bank also says that close examination of Warnig's past turned up no hint of any association with the Stasi. However, Warnig's declassified 128-page Stasi file discloses that his codename was 'Arthur' and that he began working for the Stasi in 1974, as a member of the brigade named after Putin's former pin-up, Felix Dzerzhinsky, founder of the Soviet state security organisation, the Cheka.

Warnig's file also reveals that he rose rapidly in the ranks of East German intelligence and was awarded a number of medals for his services. In Order No. K 5447/84, 'Leutnant Warnig, Matthias' was awarded the medal For Meritorious Service to the People and the Fatherland. In Order No. K 109/88, 'Oberleutnant Warnig, Matthias' was awarded a number of medals For Meritorious Service in the NVA (National People's Army), the border guards of the DDR, as an activist of socialist labour and for other activities. On 7 October 1989 Hauptmann (Captain) Matthias Warnig was awarded no fewer than nine gold medals by the dreaded Erich Mielke, the head of the Stasi.

'Arthur' submitted reports on the energy business in West Germany, the policies of enterprise management, biotech research, computer technology and dozens of other subjects, mainly to deal with industrial espionage. It was claimed that his career was helped by his alleged relationship with KGB Lieutenant-Colonel Vladimir Putin in Dresden. According to German press reports, the two men collaborated on recruiting West German citizens to work for the KGB, an allegation denied by Warnig.

If further proof of the association between the two men during their murky spying days was needed, it is provided by Lyudmila's friend Irene Pietsch. According to Pietsch, Lyudmila told her some years later that it was much easier to get on with East Germans than West Germans and that especially applied to her husband's friend Matthias Warnig. 'She said that we all grew up in the same system and that Volodya and Warnig worked for the same firm,' Pietsch recalls. 'I asked her what she meant. She said Matthias was in the Stasi and Volodya the KGB. I was quite surprised by her candour.'

EVEN SEEN THROUGH the distorting mirror of the East German

media, the Soviet empire was clearly in danger of imploding. On his first official visit to West Germany, in May 1989, Gorbachev informed Chancellor Helmut Kohl that Moscow was no longer willing to use force to prevent the democratisation of its satellite states. The tanks that rolled into Budapest to crush the Hungarian Revolution in 1956 and in 1968 snuffed out 'socialism with a human face' during the Prague Spring were no longer a viable option. Even so, few East Germans considered the collapse of the GDR to be a real possibility.

Having failed to convey the desperate need for change to the two Erichs, Gorbachev hammered the final nail into their coffin on a visit to East Germany in October to celebrate the 40th anniversary of the founding of the state, when he warned that 'life punishes those who come late'. From that point on, the hotlines between Moscow and East Berlin – usually buzzing with businesslike exchanges between the two Communist allies – fell silent. At a 40th anniversary dinner for the security services, during an interminable rant against the state's enemies Erich Mielke exhorted Stasi agents: 'Execute them – and where necessary without a court judgment'. Erich Honecker also remained intransigent. He told Markus Wolf: 'I will never allow here what is happening in the Soviet Union'. Wolf noted in his diary: 'No enemy could have achieved what we did in terms of incompetence, ignorance, self-aggrandisement and the way we have torn our own roots out of the thoughts and feelings of ordinary people'.

Meanwhile, Wolf's friend Hans Modrow, the softly-spoken, grey-haired secretary of the Communist Party (SED) in Dresden, refused to suppress anti-government demonstrations, which had become a nightly feature of city life. Wolf and Modrow were reputed to have led a clique of reformers inside the SED, although Wolf chastises himself for not having done a great deal more to change the East German system from within. Putin and his fellow KGB agents had seen the writing on the wall. 'We were the young generation of the security service,' Vladimir Usoltsev told *Der Spiegel* magazine. 'It was absolutely clear to us that Soviet power was marching inexorably into the abyss.' Sensitive documents were shipped to Moscow or burned. Lists of contacts and files about Soviet agents went up in smoke. 'We burned so much stuff that the furnace burst,' Putin says.

The unthinkable happened at 6.53 on the evening of 9 November 1989, when a member of the new East German government was asked at a press conference when the promised new East German travel law would come into force. He answered: 'Well, as far as I can see, straightaway – right now'. Thousands of East Berliners surged to the border crossings and demanded to be let through to the West. At 10.30 that night, the border was opened at Bornholmerstrasse – the historic moment that signalled the fall of the Berlin Wall.

On the evening of 6 December the KGB compound was besieged by a baying crowd, which had already ransacked the Stasi headquarters across the road. Putin hurried to his office and was issued with a handgun. He went outside and tried to deflect the protesters' anger by claiming that the KGB building was in fact a Soviet military installation. Someone shouted: 'Then why do you have cars with German licence plates in the car park? What are you doing here anyway?' Putin replied that there was an agreement that allowed the Russians to use German plates. 'And who are you?' another man shouted. 'You speak German too well.' Putin told them he was an interpreter. He then went back inside the building and put through a call for help to the commander of the local Soviet garrison, but was told: 'We cannot do anything without orders from Moscow. And Moscow is silent.'

Moscow did indeed remain silent.

In subsequent years Putin's reaction became famous: 'I got the feeling that the country no longer existed, that it had disappeared'. One report from that fateful night in East Berlin states that the mob did manage to force their way into the building, only to be greeted by the sight of Russia's future president standing at the top of the stairs brandishing a handgun. He addressed them calmly, with a cold half-smile: 'Come up if you wish, but before you get to me six of you will be dead'. This seems unlikely – there were a number of KGB agents in the building at the time and Putin's lone stand sounds like a spin doctor's attempt to turn him into a KGB James Bond. Putin will only say that the Russians 'were forced to demonstrate our readiness to defend our building and that determination certainly made an impression on them, at least for a while'.

In fact, bloodshed was averted when a small group of Soviet paratroopers drove up and the mob dispersed. Putin says the events of that evening severely demoralised him, because: 'They just left'. His dedication at this point wasn't to the Soviet system, whose decay he recognised, but to the KGB as the protector of Russian greatness, Vladimir Usoltsev told *Der Spiegel* magazine: 'He always had a poetic touch – the peculiar pride in belonging to the special corps of defenders of the Motherland, the Chekists'.

The following day Putin carried on with his duties, suffering in silence for what he saw as the wounded pride of the Motherland. His only regret, he says, was that the Soviet Union had lost its position in Europe without even attempting to replace the Communist system in East Germany with something else: 'They just dropped everything and went away,' he says. Lyudmila, who had become quite attached to her East German surroundings (German was by now her second daughter's first language), expressed her sorrow for the secret agents of both countries who had lost their sense of purpose, virtually their *raison d'etre*. One of her neighbours, she says, cried for a week: 'She cried for her lost ideals, for the collapse of everything that she had believed in her whole life'.

Unbeknown to his wife, Putin was still in full operational mode. Like all Stasi officers, Klaus Zuchold was now unemployed. Having sent a copy of Zuchold's file to Moscow, Putin received permission to induct him into the KGB. On 16 January 1990, he visited the German's flat and presented his 12-year-old daughter Cindy with a book of Russian fairytales. When he was alone with Zuchold, he dictated a letter of allegiance to the KGB, which Zuchold wrote and signed. The two men then celebrated with glasses of Sekt, a German wine.

Putin gave his new agent the codename 'Klaus Zaunick' and reminded him that he was sworn to silence, and that there would be serious consequences if he spoke out. The German magazine *Focus* claims that Putin then revealed the identities of some of his top agents in East Germany, but that is almost certainly untrue since, whatever his

PUTIN met with the victim of disastrous wildfires in Voronezh, housed in temporary shelter, to listen to their woes. Environmentalists blamed the fires on a new Forest Code and powerful timber lobbies for dismantling the centralised system of forest protection.

detractors may hold against him, Putin is fiercely loyal. It is more likely that Zuchold was told to be a 'sleeper' until things had quietened down, and then gather information for Moscow on politicians, scientists and business leaders.

A few days later Putin was recalled to his homeland, so his association with Zuchold came to an abrupt end. KGB agents were heading home in droves as the once-mighty Soviet empire shrank before the world's eyes. When the GDR ceased to exist with the reunification of Germany on 3 October 1990, the Putins were already back in Leningrad. Once more they moved in with his parents, who had been allocated a new three-roomed flat on Sredneokhtinsky Prospect near the Okhta River. Apart from a beautiful new daughter, the Putins had little to show for four and a half years in a foreign posting. As a parting gift, their German neighbours had given them a 20-year-old washing machine, which Lyudmila used for the next five years. She was astonished to discover how little things had changed in Leningrad. There were the same long lines of people outside the shops, the same ration cards and coupons, the same empty shelves. 'For a while after we returned home I was even afraid to go to the shops,' she says. 'I would just dart into the nearest shop, buy whatever was most necessary and go home. It was horrible.'

Putin was offered work at the headquarters of the Foreign Intelligence Service (SVR) in Moscow. He turned it down largely because no apartment was included in the offer and his parents were now in their eighties. They had not seen their son in all the years he was away and he was reluctant to leave them again. He had also lost faith in the USSR's ability to survive the shock waves convulsing its empire. Having witnessed one country collapsing around him, he had no wish to repeat the experience at home. Although generally adept at hiding his feelings, he let his friend Sergei Roldugin know that he felt betrayed: he and his comrades had filed reports from Dresden warning about the imminent collapse of the GDR and had recommended what action should be taken, but nobody at Moscow Centre had read their reports.

Markus Wolf, who had fled to Moscow to avoid charges of treason and espionage brought by his West German enemies, found that Gorbachev had thrown him and his fellow agents to the wolves. 'There was no great rush of comradely support from our Moscow friends,' he writes. 'Like us, they had been completely unprepared for what happened.' Wolf was denied political asylum in Russia and after a long legal battle served a short prison sentence in Germany.

Putin was still employed by the KGB but in the 'active reserves', for which he received a nominal retainer. With hundreds of redundant agents flocking back to Russia as Communist regimes went down like dominos in Czechoslovakia, Hungary, Poland, Bulgaria and Romania, it soon became abundantly clear that there was a surfeit of KGB talent on offer to anyone who wanted to hire some well trained muscle. Many became security consultants, bodyguards, night watchmen, even bouncers at the new nightclubs and discos.

Putin's prospects looked bleak. He was heading for 40 and had a family to feed, house and clothe. Friends say he became depressed. Lyudmila took a part-time job teaching German at the university, reluctantly leaving Masha and Katya in the care of their grandmother for several hours a day. It was not a happy existence. Putin invested the little nest egg they had saved in Dresden in a Volga saloon. He told friends he wanted to practice law but if that didn't work out he had a back-up plan: 'Perhaps I will have to drive a taxi.'

As though on cue, he heard that Galina Vasilievna Starovoitova, an important reformist politician and feminist defender of ethnic minorities – and graduate of Lenin State University (LGU) – was looking for someone to drive her around the city. There was little pay attached to the job, but Putin reasoned he might learn something to his advantage from the woman seated in the back of his Volga, since she was already well-known. He volunteered for the post. 'He said he believed in her cause and so he wanted to help,' says Ruslan Linkov, one of Ms Starovoitova's aides.

Putin still needed to earn a living and just when things were at their bleakest one of those fortuitous events that became the hallmark of his career occurred. He was offered a job monitoring foreign students at his alma mater, Leningrad State University, as assistant rector for international affairs. 'I was happy to go undercover at LGU,' he says. 'I wanted to write my doctoral dissertation, check out the university and perhaps get a job there.' So in March 1990 he became assistant to the university president, Stanislav Petrovich Merkuriev.

His sudden reappearance in the law faculty raised some eyebrows, although no one was under any illusions about his true function: it was well known that this post was always held by a KGB officer and that Putin would be spying on the students. Nevertheless, he appointed Valery Abramovich Musin, a specialist in international law, as his academic adviser and drafted the outline of his dissertation. Putin could well have ended up with a career as an international lawyer if one of his friends from student days, now on the university staff, hadn't approached him with an invitation to meet Anatoly Aleksandrovich Sobchak, one of the leading lights in Russia's fledgling democracy movement.

Sobchak, a handsome man with a golden tongue, had risen to prominence with hard-hitting attacks on the Communist elite. Considered unreliable by the Soviet authorities, he had never been allowed to travel abroad, but under Gorbachev his career had blossomed, and the nation listened to his speeches once he was elected a people's deputy. In May 1990, Sobchak had been appointed chairman of Leningrad City Council (Lensoviet). The city was in a parlous state: unemployment was high, crime was rising and everything was in short supply. Although born in Siberia in 1937, Sobchak had taken a law degree at LGU and had later joined the university's staff. He had been one of Putin's lecturers for a couple of semesters, although they had never actually spoken.

Putin bowled along to the chairman's office in the Mariinsky Palace on St Isaacs Square and there Sobchak explained he needed an experienced assistant to act as a buffer between him and the fraudsters and crooks who were everywhere. He was impressed with the fact that the assistant rector spoke good German and some English and was a notably cool customer. Putin had been recommended by Stanislav Merkuriev and, according to the Kremlin property supremo Pavel Borodin, Galina Starovoitova had also put in a good word for him. After a short interview, Sobchak offered to have Putin transferred from the university staff to the council payroll. Indeed, he wanted to know whether Putin could start work as early as the following Monday. The country was falling into disarray and things were happening with great speed.

'Sobchak was already a famous and popular person,' Putin says. 'I didn't like everything but he got my respect.' Putin replied that he would be happy to start on Monday but there was one thing the chairman should know: 'I am not just an assistant to the president,' he said. 'I'm also a staff officer of the KGB.' Sobchak was silent for a moment and then he said: 'Well, screw it. I need an assistant. Frankly, I'm afraid of going out into the reception area. I don't know who those people are.'

Putin got the job and the transfer.

Sobchak's supporters were shocked at his judgment when it became known in democratic circles that Putin was a KGB officer. Questioned about his assistant, Sobchak quipped: 'Putin is no KGB operative, but my former student'.

Things could have gone awry when one of the ghosts from his Dresden past came back to haunt him. Klaus Zuchold, fearing he was about to be exposed, turned himself over to German intelligence in December 1990. Zuchold supplied the Germans with a detailed description of his KGB friend and mentor, Vladimir Putin. He also disclosed the names of four former East German policemen who had spied for the KGB.

Putin denies he was part of operations aimed at setting up a network of East German spies. Today, he finds it 'kind of funny to read all that nonsense in the papers. I'm baffled to read that the Western countries are looking for agents I recruited. It's all baloney.' The most senior spy was an inspector in the Dresden police force known as 'Schorch', whom Putin allegedly ran himself. The inspector was still working for the KGB when he was arrested in April 1993. By then, however, Putin's life had taken a completely different trajectory. Leningrad had been renamed St Petersburg and he had risen with meteoric speed to become deputy mayor of Russia's second city.

4

Trust and Tanks

VLADIMIR PUTIN'S CAREER in politics began in June 1990, when he started working for Anatoly Sobchak at Smolny, the classical 19th-century building on the banks of the Neva, which once housed Leningrad's administrative headquarters. Putin knew about Smolny from his family connections – Maria's brother, Ivan Shelomov, had served there as a naval security officer in the Great Patriotic War. Ivan's nephew quickly distinguished himself as a quiet, efficient and honest technocrat who kept his head down and was happy for his boss to take the credit for his labours. 'Sobchak liked to be the centre of attention and to be talked about,' Putin says. 'It seemed to me that it didn't matter to him whether people were damning or praising him.'

Compared with his imperial surroundings, Putin discovered that the people in Sobchak's outer office at the Mariinsky Palace were 'harsh and rude in the best traditions of the Komsomol' and consisted mainly of officials who had been granted certain business privileges by the Soviet leadership in an attempt to get the economy moving in the early days of *perestroika*. Gorbachev and his Prime Minister, Ryzhkov, permitted resources from 'sacrosanct' State reserves, including oil, to be taken free of charge, or 'without compensation' as they called it.

Members of the Komsomol, the Communist Party's dedicated youth movement, were licenced to set up financial organisations and co-operatives which prospered as restrictions on foreign trade and foreign currency deals were relaxed in the late 1980s. They were the archetypes of the New Russians. By the time Putin arrived in the corridors of power, there were 135,000 such entities throughout the USSR, ranging from tiny hairdressing salons to a prefab dacha enterprise founded by a young entrepreneur named Alexander Smolensky. Everyone wanted a piece of the action and businessmen besieged Smolny demanding favours.

Around this time Putin's employer, Anatoly Sobchak, hired another former law-school student: Dmitry Medvedev, then in his twenties, became the council chairman's legal adviser. The handsome, fresh-faced lawyer with a penchant for Versace jackets and Parker pens sat at a tiny desk in an anteroom, where visitors often mistook him for a lowly secretary. Dmitry Lenkov, a city councillor, who was a frequent visitor to Smolny, describes Medvedev then as 'hardly noticeable… Putin made all the decisions, Medvedev did the legwork'.

Around this time, Putin also met Anatoly Chubais, the ginger-headed economist whose national privatisation programme a couple of years hence would elevate a handful of the co-op impresarios into the super-rich class for which Russia is now famous. Indeed, one of the most successful Komsomol businesses was Menatep, which later morphed into the Menatep Bank, the foundation stone of the empire of Putin's enemy Mikhail Khodorkovsky.

Anatoly Borisovich Chubais was one of a group of young economists who recognised that the Soviet economy was doomed unless it underwent massive change. It did not seem to worry him that millions of people would suffer as a result of Gorbachev's reforms.

After urging his deputies to embark on a programme of 'shock therapy', Chubais was installed as chairman of the city's committee on economic reform. His master plan was to set up a free economic zone inside Leningrad, but the idea was shelved by Sobchak, who saw that the whole of the USSR was fast becoming a free market. He demoted Chubais from head of economic reform to deputy head of the council's executive committee. Putin is careful to distance himself from this controversial figure: 'I never had any direct interaction with Chubais,' he says. 'I never dealt with him closely.'

And that is not unwise. Chubais, after all, has done little to ingratiate himself with his fellow citizens. Discussing the ups and downs of Russian privatisation, politics and the infamous loans-for-shares auctions in a recent interview with *The Financial Times*, for one (in his capacity both as chairman of the Unified Energy System of Russia and as former head of the Presidential Administration) Chubais suddenly launched into a bizarre deliberation: 'You know, I've re-read all of Dostoevsky over the past three months. And I feel nothing but almost physical hatred for the man. He is certainly a genius, but his idea of Russians as special, holy people, his cult of suffering and the false choices he presents make me want to tear him to pieces.'

From his early days at City Hall, Putin's career in the KGB presented certain problems. While he made no secret of his past, some councillors were naive enough to believe that if they threatened to 'expose' him they could elicit favours. Putin regarded such approaches as blackmail and consequently made what he calls 'the hardest decision of my life': he wrote a letter to the KGB resigning his commission. Then, in a move to publicise his actions, he asked a friend, the film director Igor Abramovich Shadkin, to record an interview with him in which he explained he wanted to put his spy past behind him and devote his life to working for the city.

The interview was shown on Leningrad television and provided viewers with the first glimpse of their future president. Meanwhile, Putin's letter of resignation had apparently disappeared somewhere in the KGB system so, despite his best efforts, he was still a ranking KGB officer, confirming the axiom that 'once an agent, always an agent'. Putin's actions stopped the blackmail, however, and he still received his KGB retainer – just as well, because it was actually bigger than his council pay.

IN THE PRESIDENTIAL elections of 12 June 1991 Boris Yeltsin became the first president of the Russian Federation – with 57 per cent of the popular vote, compared with just 16 per cent for Gorbachev's preferred candidate, Nikolai Ryzhkov. Boris Nikolaevich Yeltsin was

AT HOME AMONG STRANGERS: Honorary membership of Moscow's Night Wolves motorbike club was bestowed on Putin by the club's president Alexander Zaldostanov (aka Khirurg) when he joined club members outside Sevastopol during a visit to the Crimea.

born in the village of Butka in the Urals in 1931. In later life when he was drunk he liked to justify his condition by saying that a drunken priest had almost drowned him during his baptism. Those who heard this story again and again were prone to ask who had reminded the priest to pull Yeltsin out of the font. He did have two subsequent brushes with death. As a child, Yeltsin was lucky to survive when a wartime hand-grenade he was dismantling exploded, blowing off two of his left-hand fingers; again, years later, the first President of the Russian Federation narrowly avoided death when he succumbed to typhus.

On 5 November 1991 Yeltsin put Yegor Gaidar, a rosy-cheeked, 35-

year-old former economics editor of the academic journal *The Communist*, in charge of economic policy. Gaidar became de facto premier. The two men could hardly have been less alike. Yegor Timurovich Gaidar was born in Moscow in March 1956, a few weeks after Khrushchev had denounced Stalin's staged cult of personality. Gaidar's father was a war correspondent and his grandfather, Arkady Gaidar, a famous author of children's books, had fought on the Bolshevik side in the Civil War of 1918-22.

When, less than a year later, Gaidar walked into the Gosplan central planning office in Moscow with a presidential decree in his pocket and a policeman at his side, Russia was racked with political division and facing economic ruin. He explained that Russia's biggest problem was the concentration of wealth and power in the hands of acquisitive bureaucrats and their friends. People who argued for such a state, he said, 'have only one purpose – to preserve the status quo. A self-serving state destroys society, oppresses it and in the end destroys itself.'

This was heresy to Gaidar's ideologically correct colleagues at Gosplan, so he called his chum Anatoly Chubais in St Petersburg and asked him to join his team to break what he called 'the vicious circle'. Chubais hopped into his little yellow Zaporozhets and drove all the way to Moscow, with his favourite jazz tracks pumping out from his treasured cassette player.

THE MAYORAL ELECTIONS had also been held on 12 June, and Anatoly Sobchak was returned as the first democratically elected Mayor of Leningrad. Putin had never been and, ironically, had never shown any signs of wanting to be, a politician. He did, however, like working behind the political scenes and had served as chief strategist among Sobchak's supporters during the mayoral campaign.

Sobchak had also run a successful parallel campaign in a referendum to have the city's name changed back to St Petersburg. Out of respect for the blockaded citizens and veterans, Putin himself never insisted that Leningrad should be renamed St Petersburg, but he always called it 'Peter'.

ONE OF THE MOST visible signs of changes taking place in democratic Smolny was that portraits of Lenin, who had lived a Spartan existence in the building in the early years of the Revolution, and the popular Sergei Kirov, who had been assassinated within its walls on Stalin's orders, were taken down; and while most staff replaced them with portraits of Boris Yeltsin, Sobchak chose one of Peter the Great. Putin decided to follow his lead and was invited to choose between two portraits, a romantic painting of the young, curly-headed Tsar or an engraving of a much older Peter when he was laying the foundations of the Russian Empire. He selected the engraving of the autocrat rather than the visionary. And although the Bolsheviks were now in disfavour, he didn't ignore his Sword and Shield days entirely – pride of place was given to a bust of Lenin.

As though in the grip of fever, the 400 city councillors rushed to form a Western-style civic administration, but found they couldn't agree on basic issues, like appointing officials to the various council portfolios. 'We thought we'd introduce the principles of Parliamentary Democracy right at the city level,' Putin says. 'It turned into horror without end.'

Anatoly Sobchak's dream was to make the new St Petersburg the financial capital of Russia; a project that would require an organiser with an abundance of skill and nerve. Putin might be a political novice, but he had a degree in international law, spoke a couple of languages, ran an efficient office and appeared to be almost nerveless, so in June 1991 Sobchak appointed him chairman of the newly formed City Committee for Foreign Economic Relations, with responsibility for attracting foreign investment. The appointment angered some of the councillors and greatly displeased Vladimir Anatolyevich Yakovlev, an ambitious construction engineer who was eight years older than Putin and who regarded himself as the mayor's chief assistant.

Pavel Borodin, former head of the Directorate of Presidential Affairs in the Kremlin (and Yeltsin's pool-playing and drinking buddy), reveals for the first time how Putin's appointment came about. In an interview over tea and cakes in the drawing room of his Park Lane hotel room Borodin, a big, smartly-dressed man who has clearly seen better days, says his daughter Katya was taken ill while studying at the Leningrad State University and her father needed someone in the city to make sure she received proper medical treatment. 'I was given the name of Vladimir Yakovlev, who worked in the Mayor's office,' he says, 'but when I placed the call from Moscow the secretary said Yakovlev wasn't there, just Sobchak and a man called Putin.

'I didn't want to bother Sobchak himself so I said: "Put me through to this man Putin". She did and I explained the problem to him and he said he would take care of it. He was as good as his word. He provided a car to transport Katya to hospital, where he made arrangements for her to be seen and he kept an eye on her progress – even visited her – in the following days. It wasn't because he had to, he was a really nice person – still is. I have liked him immensely ever since that time.'

Borodin says that when he next spoke to Sobchak he heaped praise on Putin, the 'lowly official' who had been so helpful to him and that was why the mayor – to the extreme annoyance of Yakovlev – put him in charge of the Foreign Relations Committee. 'At the time he was just a member of the Mayor's staff, definitely not the No. 2 that some say he had become,' Borodin says. 'I made him that.'

One of Putin's first tasks at City Hall was to deal with an act of defiance by a group of Communist die-hards who persisted in flying the red flag of the Communist International on a metal flagpole on the roof of the House of Political Enlightenment in full view of Smolny. Whenever Putin had the flag removed, the Communists would hoist up another one until they ran out of red flags. Instead of calling it quits, they produced one that was a sombre shade of dark brown, a colour normally associated with the far right. Putin's patience snapped. He ordered a crane and ended the game of tug-of-war by personally supervising the cutting down of the flagpole with a blowtorch.

Such distractions were not welcome in Putin's orderly world. Regrettably for all around him, Anatoly Sobchak was in such a hurry to achieve his aims that he revealed a worrying authoritarian streak. Deputies winced whenever he rose to speak in the assembly chamber at Mariinsky Palace, treating his audience to a 45-minute lecture, as though they were students at LGU. His efforts to force through decisions were seen as an attempt to seize dictatorial powers and many of his decisions were challenged in the courts. Indeed, Boris Yeltsin noted in his 1995 memoirs that in dealing with the city council Sobchak had ditched his old liberal image and turned into 'a harsh authoritarian administrator'.

Putin was an easy target for Sobchak's detractors. There were pointed suggestions that he was a KGB plant or that he had used some sort of underhand method to get the job; otherwise why would an anti-Communist democrat have taken a known KGB officer into his inner sanctum? It seems clear that, in hiring Putin, Sobchak had decided to fight fire with fire in order to neutralise the Komsomol businessmen, the criminal elements and, indeed, the many councillors who plagued him for favours. The two men had grown fond of one another during the election campaign and had formed a genuine alliance, with Sobchak as ruler of an emergent St Petersburg and Putin his strong right arm.

Meanwhile, the USSR was falling to pieces. Putin believed – correctly as it turned out – that by carrying through a policy of unilateral disarmament, Gorbachev was contributing to the collapse of the Russian empire. The chief cause of Communism's downfall, however, was Gorbachev's belief that an edifice built on fear, terror and corruption could survive blows from the twin battering rams of *perestroika* and *glasnost*. Most of the approved *nomenklatura* members in Russia and its Eastern European satellites knew that attempting to reform the system would expose its basic flaws and bring it crashing down. When Gorbachev was awarded the Nobel Peace Prize in 1990 for his part in allowing the mostly peaceful revolutions that took place across the Eastern Bloc, one Soviet minister caustically commented: 'We must remember this certainly was not the prize for economics'. Even in their death throes, a backlash from the forces of Soviet conservatism was inevitable.

Putin was holidaying with Lyudmila and the children at Kaliningrad – her home town – on 18 August 1991, when eight hardline government members opposed to *perestroika* – led by Gorbachev's disloyal deputy, Gennady Yanaev, and supported by the KGB boss, General Vladimir

HIS FRIENDSHIP with Russia's leading film director, Nikita Mikhalkov,
led to Putin's association with a number of international film stars,
including Leonardo DiCaprio (pictured with him above) and Jack Nicholson.

Kryuchkov, as well as elements of the armed forces – attempted a *coup
d'etat*. They formed themselves into an emergency committee and
dispatched censors to control newspapers and television stations. The
KGB placed Gorbachev under house arrest at his holiday villa at Foros
in the Crimea when he refused to resign as General Secretary. All TV
stations were ordered to show a performance of *Swan Lake*, a dead
giveaway to the public that something nasty was going on.

Anatoly Sobchak was in Moscow when news of the coup reached
the capital on the morning of 19 August. He drove to Yeltsin's dacha
deep in the birch forest at Zavidovo, where it was agreed to call an
emergency session of parliament. By now, *Swan Lake* had served its
purpose and the plotters were using TV to announce a State of
Emergency. Vice President Yanaev issued a statement that Gorbachev had
been removed from office 'for health reasons' and that he, Yanaev, was
now acting president.

Fearing arrest, Sobchak headed for Sheremetyevo airport to fly back to St Petersburg and rally the city against the plotters, while Yeltsin kissed his tearful wife and daughters goodbye and made for the White House, the gleaming white marble parliament building near the embankment of the Moscow River, to issue a passionate appeal for support to the citizens of Russia. Both men were indeed on a list of 69 Russian leaders to be arrested and Kryuchkov's agents from the crack Alpha Group had surrounded the dacha. Its commander waited in vain for orders from the emergency committee to move in and arrest the occupants, so they got away.

Kryuchkov's rival, General Oleg Kalugin, defied his KGB masters by leading crowds to the legislature, which had now been surrounded by the Alpha Group and the tanks of the Tamanskaya military division. He induced Yeltsin to address the crowd. As TV footage later showed, the portly, snowy-haired figure, wearing a heavy bullet-proof vest under his brown suit, mounted the hull of one of the tanks and called on the populace to offer the sternest resistance to the coup. It was a dramatic gamble and it worked for Yeltsin, although Kalugin was put on trial in absentia in 2002 and found guilty of spying for the US, where he now lives in exile.

The troops faltered in the face of such a patriotic outburst and defected to Yeltsin's side. As thousands of Muscovites threw up barricades in front of the White House with trees, trolley buses, building materials, even old bathtubs, the tank commanders swung their guns away from the building and pointed them at the Alpha Group. The situation was critical, although James H. Billington, an American academic who was in Moscow throughout the coup, found that the atmosphere around the White House was now 'more carnivalesque than revolutionary'.

Over in St Petersburg, the KGB had orders to arrest Anatoly Sobchak when he touched down at Pulkovo airport. 'To their great surprise, when they arrived, they found the plane guarded by armed police units,' Alexander Rahr writes in his biography of Putin. 'Putin had returned from vacation and, learning of Sobchak's impending arrest, decided to defend him by all means possible, thus openly turning against his former employers.' According to Rahr, Putin put Sobchak in his car and drove him at breakneck speed into town, where crucial talks were held with the heads of the city's KGB and military.

While it is true that an armed bodyguard met Sobchak at the airport, Putin actually had nothing to do with it – on 19 August he was still in Kaliningrad. Sobchak's real saviour was one of his close friends, Arkady Kramarev, the Leningrad commander of the Interior Ministry forces. Escorted by Kramarev's special units, Sobchak drove to general staff headquarters in Palace Square to confront the pro-coup military commander, General Viktor Samsonov, whose tanks were rumbling along the highway towards central St Petersburg from their barracks at Pskov. The general was astonished to see Sobchak – he was supposed to be under arrest – and he said little as the mayor berated him in front of his staff, a clutch of KGB officers, the local Communist Party chief, Boris Gidaspov, and Arkady Kramarev.

Sobchak demanded to see Samsonov's orders; Samsonov had none. Although the coup leaders in Moscow desperately wanted him to occupy the Mariinsky Palace, they had refused to issue the relevant orders, just as they had declined to order troops to storm the iconic home of the Supreme Soviet, the White House. Sobchak warned Samsonov that the coup was 'illegal and illegitimate' and the coup plotters would be tried as criminals. Samsonov wavered. He agreed to keep his troops out of the city, but only for the time being.

The next 36 hours were critical to the future of St Petersburg, a city steeped in armed conflict and indeed, for all of Russia. Sobchak hurried to the Mariinsky Palace, where the members of the Lensoviet and his mayoral office were located. In the late afternoon, he addressed the councillors who had rallied around the new chairman, Alexander Belyaev, and his speech was broadcast over the public address system to thousands of people gathering at St Isaac's Square.

That evening, Acting President Yanaev held a press conference in Moscow. His hands shook and he had difficult speaking, suggesting either a lack of conviction in his cause or a surfeit of vodka (giving rise to the coup's unofficial title, the 'Vodka Putsch'). Reporters jeered at his inept performance. Later that night Anatoly Sobchak appeared nationwide on independent TV's Channel 5, whose president Boris Petrov was opposed to the coup. Appearing calm and eloquent, the mayor denounced the emergency committee and called on the public to rally in Palace Square at 10 a.m. on the 20th.

Meanwhile, barricades had been set up outside the Mariinsky Palace in case the tanks unexpectedly turned up under cover of darkness. Members of the co-operatives, which faced certain extinction if the old guard were returned to power, rushed photocopying and fax machines to the palace to print and distribute leaflets opposing the coup. Television sets and food supplies were brought in. The mafia offered guns. Lev Apostolov, a 19-year-old student, went straight to Nevsky Prospect and joined in a demonstration against the putsch. He and six friends were assigned to patrol Bolshaya Morskaya Street and build a barricade beside the Barrikada cinema. 'We were given armbands and told not to jump on tanks if they appeared,' he says.

On the morning of 20 August, up to 300,000 people amassed in Palace Square and the surrounding streets at Sobchak's behest. Demonstrators waved banners proclaiming 'Down with Fascism!', 'No to the military coup!' and 'Better death than slavery!'

Had Putin been the KGB's man inside city hall, the coup would have been the time for him to defect. He did the opposite. As soon as the coup began he decided to throw in his lot with the democrats. 'I got back to Leningrad on the 20th,' he relates. 'Sobchak and I practically moved into the city council. Well, not just us two – a whole bunch of people were camped out there.'

Putin says it was dangerous to drive out of the council compound but Sobchak was determined to spread his message among the workers. Wherever he went, support was virtually universal. They drove to the Kirov Works in the south-west of the city where they were welcomed. 'But we were nervous,' Putin recalls. 'We even passed out pistols, although I left my service revolver in the safe.'

At some point during the day, Putin negotiated with senior officers in the Big House, including his friend Viktor Cherkesov, for the local

KGB to remain neutral. He also sensed that this would be a good time to sever his official KGB links. He submitted a second letter of resignation, which was later accepted after Sobchak had a word with his divisional commander.

By 21 August, most of the coup leaders had fled Moscow. 'That whole night was very tense, full of rumours,' Lev Apostolov says. 'In the morning came the announcement that the putsch had failed, and they played Bob Marley on the speakers. I remember that the democrats in City Hall behaved with great dignity and calm. Sobchak gave a splendid speech – Fascism shall not pass, things of that sort.'

Putin says that once he saw the faces of the coup plotters on TV, 'I knew right away that it was all over'. Gorbachev was freed from his Crimean detention and, although he was restored as General Secretary of the Party, his influence had been fatally compromised. Almost unanimously, the centres of power throughout the USSR swung behind Boris Yeltsin, who took over one USSR ministry after another. The people's tribune was photographed standing behind Gorbachev and giving the Churchillian V-sign. People took to the streets, tearing down statues of Lenin, hammer-and-sickle symbols and even the statue of Felix Dzerzhinsky outside KGB headquarters. Lenin's Mausoleum closed indefinitely.

Gorbachev was jeered by many of the deputies when he attended a session of Parliament on 23 August. He was forced to dismiss his entire cabinet and the following day he resigned as General Secretary. Ukraine, Belarus, Estonia and Latvia declared independence. Anatoly Sobchak was called in to help draft a new Constitution, providing Yeltsin with plenty of presidential muscle to deal with his enemies. On 6 November 1991, he issued a decree banning the Communist Party throughout the Russian Federation. When it became law a year later (temporarily, as it happened), Putin slipped his Party membership card into his desk drawer.

To this day, he refuses to condemn the infamous August coup, describing Kryuchkov as 'a true believer in Communism', and the conspirators' motives in wishing to preserve the Soviet Union as 'noble', although he is quick to add that the events tore his life apart. 'Up until that time, I didn't really understand the transformation that was going on in Russia,' he says. 'But during the days of the coup, all the ideals, all the goals that I had had when I went to work for the KGB collapsed. Of course it was incredibly difficult to go through this. After all, most of my life had been devoted to work in the agencies. But I had made my choice.'

5

Tricks of the Trade

THE SIGNIFICANT RISE in Putin's political position alongside Sobchak meant that he now had to hire a secretary. He found one in Marina Yentaltseva, who initially thought she had blown her chances when Putin spotted her putting on lipstick before her interview. 'He pretended he hadn't noticed a thing,' she says, 'and I never put my lipstick on at work again.'

Next, his employers paid for him to have English lessons two days a week, as English was the *lingua franca* of the commercial world, and he was now required to mix with international businessmen.

At this time, St Petersburg's foreign trade was dominated by state monopolies and huge government-authorised companies like Lenfintorg (Leningrad Finance and Trade). The usual aids to mercantile intercourse between nations such as a customs service, independent banking facilities, currency exchanges and a stock market simply didn't exist. Starting virtually from scratch, reformers like Putin had to create an environment in which Russians could do business deals with the market-based West.

MANY OF THE people on Putin's committee at that time have remained with him throughout his career. Dmitry Medvedev, his nominee and successor as president; Alexei Miller, CEO of Gazprom; Igor Sechin, Kremlin chief of staff, and chairman of Rosneft, and

Vladimir Churov, chief of Russia's Central Electoral Commission, the main elections organiser. 'Dima' Medvedev advised Putin on the registration of foreign joint ventures in which the city participated (a practice that was later discontinued as representing a possible conflict of interest). A senior banker who worked closely with Medvedev at Smolny notes: 'The work he was doing for these guys as a legal adviser solidified his relationship with Putin'.

Medvedev too had been raised in St. Petersburg, but unlike Putin he came from an academic family. His mother Yulia taught Russian and literature at the Hertzen State Pedagogical University, while his father Anatoly was a physics professor at Leningrad State Polytechnic. As a schoolboy, Dmitry Medvedev worked on a construction site in order to pay for blue jeans and foreign records; he had saved for months to buy Pink Floyd's anarchic album 'The Wall', and listened to lectures on the evils of Stalinism by historians who were finally free to express their opinions.

Albert Stepanov, a tall, slim bureaucrat who spent the best years of his life in the service of his country, remembers Putin in those early days. 'He was very self-disciplined,' he says over dinner at the Sovietsky Hotel in Moscow. 'He put himself under great pressure – he'd be in his office until around 10 at night and was a bit of a machine. His one fault was that he was always late. For him, the clock does not exist. That made him rather a hard taskmaster and there was very little socialising. We didn't go out for beers or anything like that, although I did go to his home on a few occasions to take his daughters to their music classes.'

One consequence of the failed August coup was that Sobchak moved his office from the Mariinsky Palace to Smolny. Putin's life became so hectic that he made Albert Stepanov his trusted signatory. 'There were lots of papers to sign – about 10,000 in four years – and he couldn't sign them all,' Stepanov says. 'And anyway, his signature was a squiggle that no one could decipher – as president, he's had to work on that – so I was given a letter by him authorising me to sign on his behalf. I still have it.'

Ironically, Sobchak's trust in Putin was such that he refused to sign any document unless it already bore Putin's signature. Sobchak was frequently away from the office on business trips and on one occasion had signed three clean sheets of paper and left them with Putin in order to clear up various administrative matters while he was away.

That same evening a couple of Putin's KGB colleagues visited him. They said it would be very handy for them to have Sobchak's signature on a certain document. Could they discuss with Putin how it might be obtained? Putin realised that he had to act quickly to head off a potentially compromising situation. He took out a folder and showed the agents the blank sheets of paper with Sobchak's signature to prove that the Mayor trusted him completely. Then he said to them: 'What do you want from me?' The KGB men backed down. 'No more questions,' they said and left his office with an apology.

These were heady times. After 70 years of Communist dictatorship, newspaper columnists were giving readers the benefit of their uncensored opinions, political prisoners had been freed from the gulags, Russians could get a passport to travel abroad, voters could choose from a dozen political parties, and 89 regions and ethnic republics of the Russian Federation had gained their independence from direct Kremlin rule.

If Putin had reservations about this sudden outbreak of liberty, he kept them to himself. Nothing, however, could disguise the fact that despite the Herculean efforts of Yeltsin's young reformers, Russia was almost broke. The previous Soviet government had run up foreign debts of $72 billion and there was virtually no money with which to pay the interest. The nation's storehouses contained just two months' supply of grain. Producers refused to sell their crops to the state at regulated prices. The shelves in most shops were bare and there was no money to replenish stocks with imported food. So Yegor Gaidar took the necessary steps to abolish price regulation and allow free trade.

IN A WAVE OF 'shock therapy' measures, Gaidar slashed subsidies to inefficient state industries, cut the armed forces budget and temporarily lifted import restrictions. From midnight on 2 January 1992 prices were allowed to find their own level. They went up and up, wiping out

PUTIN's favourite holiday resort of Sochi will benefit not only from the Winter Olympics in 2014, in the same year it will also be the venue for the first Formula One event in Russia under the terms of a six-year agreement with racing boss Bernie Ecclesone (pictured centre) and oligarch Oleg Deripaska.

people's life savings but stimulating trade. There were mass protests from the old guard. Boris Yeltsin's vice president, Alexander Rutskoy, a former general in the Red Army and veteran of the Afghan war, denounced Gaidar's policies as 'economic genocide', heralding the start of a roller coaster ride for the Yeltsin government. Bowing to pressure, Yeltsin sacked Gaidar and replaced him as prime minister with the conservative Viktor Chernomyrdin, former head of the state oil and gas colossus Gazprom.

In June Yeltsin visited the United States and Canada and caught the public imagination with his deep rumbling baritone, electric blue suits and impassioned speeches on behalf of his embattled regime. The Americans impressed on him that it was absolutely vital to keep the reforms going if he was to activate desperately needed loans from the

International Monetary Fund (IMF).

Yeltsin needed no prompting. During his term as prime minister, Gaidar had convinced him that only the speedy transfer of state assets into private hands would break the Soviet stranglehold on the economy and prevent a Communist revival. At their headquarters in a Stalinist skyscraper at No 21 New Arbat, Anatoly Chubais and his St. Petersburg economist chum Dmitry Vasiliev, small of stature but big on ideas, worked out an ingenious voucher scheme that would privatise thousands of state-owned companies.

In August 1992, on the first anniversary of his moment of glory outside the White House, Yeltsin, who had little idea of economics, announced that every Russian citizen born before 2 September that year would be issued with a voucher nominally valued at 10,000 roubles ($25) which could be traded for equity in a large number of small and medium-sized businesses. Millions of Russians paid a small registration fee to receive their vouchers but then sold them to speculators and the so-called 'red director corps', the managers who ran state-owned factories.

The first Soviet enterprise to be privatised was the Bolshevik Biscuit Factory, a symbolic choice, which went under the auctioneer's hammer in a vast exhibition hall on the Moscow River on 9 December. The factory's managers and employees retained 51 per cent of Bolshevik's stock, so would-be tycoons armed with sack-loads of vouchers competed against one another for the remaining 49 per cent. Even so, the sale of Bolshevik Biscuits raised just $654,000, which made it an absolute bargain for the stockholders.

Up to 600 plants a day were sold off at bargain prices – even the shipyard in Komsomolsk-na-Amure, which had once been a secret installation producing the country's nuclear submarines.

It was an inauspicious start, but the public soon got the hang of it. The first phase of privatisation picked up speed in 1993, continued through 1994 and finally ran out of steam at the start of 1995. Not counting small businesses such as retail shops, more than 18,000 companies had been privatised and Chubais had succeeded in turning 40 million ordinary Russians into stockholders.

On the first anniversary of Vladimir Putin's appointment as Chairman of the Foreign Relations Committee, there was a small celebration at Smolny. 'Everybody got a baseball hat and a T-shirt with his name on it and a nice message about him,' says Albert Stepanov. 'He came in and had some cake and admired the T-shirts. Now a lot of people in his position would not have allowed [such informality].'

With Putin's post came membership of a small group of men who met regularly at a house on the shores of Lake Komsomolskoye (named after the Komsomol), some 60 miles north of the city. The group called themselves *Ozero* (meaning 'the lake') and Putin took Igor Sechin and Dmitry Medvedev along with him. 'Sechin used to sit in Putin's outer office as a very junior factotum,' says a senior British diplomat. 'People who knew him in his St Petersburg days are astonished at the power he now wields.' Though he knew about these gatherings, Sobchak himself never attended and his three lieutenants – who were one day to run the whole country – were able to discuss the running of his city with complete freedom.

The flood of Westerners pouring into St Petersburg included American capitalists, Christian idealists and ruthless carpetbaggers determined to cash in on the open economy of the New Russia. The National Democratic Institute, a non-profit-making organisation partly funded by the United States Government, sent former presidential candidate Walter Mondale to lecture on such topics as how to draw up a budget. One of the institute's members, Michael McFaul, told the *Wall Street Journal* that Putin decided the American efforts were 'all bullshit'. He wanted US dollars, not Wall Street jargon – and assigned Igor Sechin to organise the seminars.

One night over dinner McFaul was startled when Sechin addressed him in Portuguese, a language he had learned in order to do research in Angola in the 1980s. Sechin explained he had also been in Africa at that time. 'I worked for the KGB, but now we're all democrats,' he said. Indeed, Sechin had acted as an interpreter with Soviet trade and diplomatic missions to Angola and Mozambique but, according to a number of allegations, he was actually a GRU military intelligence agent involved in arms sales.

At Smolny, Igor Sechin was certainly aware of Anatoly Sobchak's weakness as a free-spending party animal, and of his connection to the Kovalchuk brothers, Mikhail and Yuriy, who arranged 'entertainment' for the mayor. The brothers remain in touch with Putin to this day – indeed, Yuriy is his neighbour at the Karelian Isthmus near St Petersburg, where both own dachas on the eastern shore of the Komsomolskoye Lake, and the pair are partners in a local property-owners' condominium called Ozero.

With money in short supply in St Petersburg in those early days, as in many parts of the country, workers suffered severe delays in receiving their wages. Some were paid in manure or hacksaws – even coffins – instead of cash. Putin was given the responsibility of seeing what could be bartered rather than bought. 'There was a terrible shortage of flour, so there was little bread in the shops and he had to work on that,' Stepanov says. 'In those days, numbers were more important than words.' Putin was a master of the numbers game (a point confirmed by Deputy Press Chief Dmitri Peskov, who explained during a private meeting in the Kremlin that Putin could tell you the exact quantity of grain produced and exported for any of the past several years). But, ultimately, his efforts involved him in scandal.

Food shortages reached such a crisis point that St Petersburg was forced to break into its strategic reserves of canned rations. A group of Russian businessmen approached Putin with a deal that would cause him endless grief: the group promised that if they were allowed to sell goods – mainly raw materials – abroad, they would import food and distribute it in the city. Putin agreed. 'We had no other options,' he says. He obtained permission from the relevant government department and signed the contracts. The scheme began well, but it was soon noticeable that some of the firms were failing to honour the main condition of the contract regarding the delivery of foreign food. Putin observes: 'They reneged on their commitments to the city'.

A number of council deputies from that time, including the fiery Marina Salye, one of the leaders of the pro-reform group Radical Democrats, seized on this failure and demanded that Sobchak dismiss his assistant. The main allegation against him was that he had issued licences to crony companies to export non-ferrous metals valued at $93 million, in exchange for food aid from abroad that never arrived; and that he had also understated the value of these exports. Sobchak resisted the demands and was further subjected to calls for his own resignation.

Dmitry Medvedev and Putin's former academic adviser Valery Musin, who were both legal advisers to the committee, helped Putin fight off the accusations. Today, he denies that 'a single gram of any metal' was exported. He claims that some of his opponents wanted one of their own – and not 'a meddlesome KGB agent' – in the post in order to make money for themselves.

Indeed, graft, fraud and corruption – coupled with mafia-style contract killings – flourished to such an extent that St. Petersburg became the crime capital of Russia. Front offices were set up to hide dodgy business deals. Pyramid-selling (or Ponzi) schemes fleeced people of their life savings. The Russian mafia gained notoriety throughout the Western world, where gangsters like the Tambov mob from St Petersburg invested their ill-gotten loot.

Putin now believes that the city council should have worked more closely with law enforcement agencies to stamp out these practices. The difficulty was that no one knew who could be trusted and who was on the take. Critics labelled Sobchak's regime a kleptocracy, with him and Putin suspected in some quarters of shady dealings, although nothing has ever been proven.

The spotlight fell on the issuing of export licences for Russian timber, previously a lucrative source of bribe money. It was claimed that Putin found a legitimate – some might say ingenious – way to accept such financial perks: he set up a consultancy which offered 'advice and direction' to those with whom he was dealing on behalf of the city. Now that he was no longer receiving his KGB retainer, any resulting fees – should they have been offered – might have provided him and Lyudmila with a welcome boost to a modest council salary.

An Englishman, who met Putin when he went to the council office to obtain a licence for a cargo of timber he was exporting to the United

Kingdom, discovered how the system worked. Not only did he get his licence from the mayoral assistant, he says, but the 'consultancy' helped him find a car ferry to transport his cargo across the North Sea to Hull. 'He saw nothing wrong with such an arrangement,' says the Englishman. 'After all, he was declaring his "bonuses" and paying tax on them, unlike predecessors who had accepted brown envelopes containing bundles of cash for doing what the city was already paying them a wage to do.'

Putin denies that his committee granted export licences to anyone but leaves scope for speculation about how such licences were obtained. 'We did not have the right to grant licences,' he says. 'That's just it: a division of the Ministry for Foreign Economic Relations issued the licenses. They were a federal structure and had nothing to do with the municipal administration.'

The flamboyant Georgian billionaire Badri Patarkatsishvili claimed he met Putin in St Petersburg while seeking protection for his operations. He says that Putin provided a 'roof' for his businesses, although he never explained what that entailed. His future partner Boris Berezovsky was uncharacteristically flattering about the man whose bitter enemy he would become. He told *Vanity Fair* in October 2008 that Putin helped him set up a car dealership in St. Petersburg in the early 1990s and impressed him by neither asking for nor accepting (so presumably one was offered) a bribe.

Even so, there can be no doubt that the Putins were prospering at this time. They lived in a handsome state-owned dacha in the Zelenogorsk district, 50 kilometres north-west of central St Petersburg, and bought a small but comfortable apartment on Vasilievsky Island with pleasant views.

IN 1991 PUTIN was reunited with his German friend Matthias Warnig when Dresdner Bank opened an office in St. Petersburg. Warnig was encouraged by his head office to help Putin drum up foreign investment. The bank underwrote some of his trips to Germany, but neither he nor Warnig has ever been accused of impropriety. Two years later, Putin's committee assisted BNP/Dresdner (a joint venture between Banque

Nationale de Paris and Dresdner) to open a branch in the massive former German embassy in St Isaac's Square. Deutsche Bank and Credit Lyonnais soon followed suit. Denmark, South Africa, Norway and Greece all opened new consulates to stimulate trade with their nations and the United Kingdom expanded its consulate into an impressive building adjacent to the Smolny compound.

Putin's committee also created investment zones offering tax breaks and other incentives to foreign companies. Coca-Cola was invited to build a bottling plant at Pulkovo Heights on condition it installed high-capacity power lines and communications cables. Gillette, Wrigley, Otis Elevator, Ford, Kraft-Jacobs, Cadbury-Schweppes and Caterpillar all set up factories in the same zone or in the surrounding districts. As far as Petersburgers were concerned, Putin's most valuable contribution was not locally-produced Coke or chewing gum, but the completion of a fibre-optic cable to Copenhagen, a project that had started in the Soviet era but was never completed, and which now provides the city with a world-class international telephone service.

Sobchak made frequent trips to Germany, with Putin acting as interpreter. Chancellor Helmut Kohl impressed Putin with his knowledge of Russian history and contemporary life. 'He said that the Germans were not only interested in the Russian market but in becoming worthy partners with Russia,' he says. At different times, he also met the British prime ministers Margaret Thatcher and John Major. When the mayor decided to introduce legalised gambling to St Petersburg, Putin was sent to Hamburg, Germany's leading gambling city, to check out the links between prostitution and the city's casinos. He came away with the conviction that the government should establish strict control over the gaming industry.

Despite his boss's difficulties with his fellow councillors, Putin's reputation for getting things done served him well with the city legislature. The deputies created a municipal entity, Neva Chance, controlling 51 per cent of the stock in the city's new casinos, from which it was hoped to receive big dividends. Even though the FSB (the main agency to replace the KGB), the tax police and the tax inspectorate were

THEY MET on a blind date in Moscow when he was a novice secret agent, but airline stewardess Lyudmila Shkrebneva could never have imagined that Vladimir Putin would one day make her Russia's first lady.

assigned to supervise gambling operations, the casino owners diverted the money from the tables and claimed to be operating at a loss. There were no profits, hence no dividends. Putin admits to a certain amount of naivety. 'They were laughing at us and showing us their losses,' he says. 'Ours was a classic mistake made by people encountering the free market for the first time.'

It was not a case of all work and no play. On one of his trips to Hamburg, Putin took Lyudmila and another couple who were travelling abroad for the first time to an erotic show. He would rather have paid a visit to the Star Club, where his beloved Beatles had cut their musical teeth but 'they talked me into it'. The group quickly discovered that the show was not so much erotic as crude, so much so that Lyudmila's female friend stood up from their table during the performance and, with her eyes fixed on the stage, dropped down in a dead faint. Putin took the executive decision to lead the shocked lady – and their friends – towards the door as soon as she came around.

Marina Salye returned to the attack with allegations that Putin gathered information on the sexual proclivities of Sobchak's rivals for possible use against them. However, Vatanyar Yagya, who worked closely with him on the Foreign Relations Committee, denied that he ever acted in KGB style. 'He always supported democratic principles, respected people and talked calmly,' he says. 'He always thought about the interests of Russia and St Petersburg.'

With Igor Sechin at his side, he developed the brusque, no-nonsense style that would become the leitmotif of his presidency. 'He was the first to arrive at receptions and the first to leave,' says one foreign diplomat quoted by biographer Andrew Jack. 'He shook hands and he never said anything.'

The *Wall Street Journal* recounts the experience of a foreign property developer who called on Putin to appeal for exemptions from Soviet-era tax provisions. As he explained that the taxes were preventing investment in some downtown real estate, Putin interrupted. 'Look,' he said, 'to stay in power, we need jobs. In order to get jobs, we need investment. I understand all this, so I'll help you. Now get out of my office.'

Graham Humes, a Philadelphia investment banker, received a much more sympathetic hearing when he arrived in the city in 1993 to turn gifts of American butter into financial assistance for small Russian businesses through a non-profit organisation called CARESBAC. The idea was that shipments of surplus frozen butter would be sold on the St Petersburg commodity exchange and the proceeds – estimated at $9 million – invested in the city. At a meeting with 'several very grumpy, self-righteous, old men in Moscow', Humes was informed that his operation was in breach of a new Russian law and that the proceeds from the sale of butter – already amounting to more than $2 million – would be forfeited.

Back in St Petersburg, the United States consulate commiserated with Humes but said there was nothing it could do, so he took the problem to Putin in his sparsely furnished room at Smolny. 'Putin listened intently,' he says. 'He then said he did not think there was such a law but as a lawyer he would check for us and call us back.' Putin was surprised to discover that the grumpy old men in Moscow had been right and the butter scheme would need an exemption if it were to go ahead. He prodded Sobchak into raising the matter with Prime Minister Chernomyrdin during a visit to Moscow. Humes was in Putin's office when Sobchak called from the capital. He was shouting so loudly that Putin held the phone at arm's length and said: 'I think we can both hang up our phones – I can hear you fine without'.

The matter was resolved when Chernomyrdin paid a visit to Smolny a few months later and Putin presented him with the draft of a decree exempting the butter project from confiscation. Chernomyrdin signed the paper and within weeks Sobchak cut a ribbon to open a new dental clinic, funded by $1.5 million from Humes' organisation. 'I found Putin to be professional and skilled in political tactics, enabling him to dance around the old apparatchiks in order to achieve a St Petersburg opening for foreign capital to benefit fledgling Russian businesses,' he says. Asked about kickbacks, Humes replied: 'Not one Russian connected with his office ever suggested any variant of our negotiations which might have diverted money from the dental clinic. Russian friends of ours said then, and affirm today, that Putin has earned widespread respect for working for the best interests of the city and for maintaining a low profile. Unlike Sobchak, he has never appeared to benefit personally from the job.'

Meanwhile, relations between Sobchak and the city councillors had reached a nadir in 1993, when he began moves to have the council disbanded; later that year it was dissolved by decree from Moscow. In the parliamentary elections of December 1993 he successfully led one of several competing reform parties. The following March Putin became

ALWAYS HAPPY when Silvio Berlusconi is around: Both men donned fur hats and coats when Putin invited his friend to dine outdoors at his country residence on a bitterly cold night.

First Deputy Mayor of St Petersburg (there were two other deputies, Vladimir Yakovlev and Alexei Kudrin) while retaining his foreign investment role. His new duties included overseeing the city's law-enforcement agencies and the media.

Sobchak was frequently out of town. He employed Richard Torrance, a New York PR man, to arrange speaking trips to the United States. Putin accompanied him on two such trips but often stayed behind to assume the responsibilities of acting mayor. Sobchak was a lover of culture and the arts and is credited with restoring St. Petersburg to its imperial glory. Much of the restoration work was supervised by Putin and his fellow mayoral deputy, Vladimir Yakovlev, during this time. One of the relics to benefit was the old Astoria Hotel in St Isaac's Square, where Putin's grandfather Spiridon had demonstrated his culinary skills back in Tsarist times. Putin also developed a love of the theatre, especially opera and orchestral concerts, and befriended Russia's most famous conductor, Valery Gergiev. Nights at the opera, Lyudmila has said publicly, put the romance back into their lives.

Many of the improvements to the fabric of St Petersburg life were cosmetic. Crime rates remained embarrassingly high and headline writers were now calling it 'Chicago on the Neva'. While Moscow prospered during the early years of Russia's open economy, with new high-rise building reshaping its skyline and luxury shops and restaurants opening in its downtown streets, St Petersburg remained firmly in second place. Every major hotel group spurned the city's overtures to build there and Crédit Lyonnais, Honeywell and other companies which had initially set up shop in St Petersburg decamped to the newly fashionable capital.

Throughout this period Anatoly Sobchak was subjected to smear campaigns about his private life. There were rumours that he had dipped into city funds to buy an apartment for himself and procured other state-owned properties for relatives, including an artist's studio for his wife, Lyudmila Narusova, a member of the federal parliament. For the last year and a half of Sobchak's term, Putin stood by him while he was under investigation, although he points out that in some cases the mayor was a witness rather than a suspect.

'[Putin is] basically a conformist, loyal to the team of which he is a member,' says Alexander Sungurov, a democratic deputy in the St Petersburg city council at the time. 'When he was on Sobchak's team, he was loyal to Sobchak.'

Meanwhile, powerful forces were gathering to mount an assault on the bastions of Russian industry: an assault that one day would present Putin with his greatest challenge.

6

The Oligarchs

VLADIMIR PUTIN'S extraordinary journey to the Kremlin began as
far back as November 1992, when the Constitutional Court repealed
Boris Yeltsin's ban on the Communist Party, enabling Party members to
mobilise their forces in the Supreme Soviet and contest future elections.
Yeltsin's problem was that only about 300 of the thousand parliamentary
deputies could be described as democrats. The majority were dyed-in-
the-wool Communists or ultra-Nationalists who rallied behind Vice
President Rutskoy and the Speaker of the House, Ruslan Khasbulatov.
Rutskoy fixed a large map of the USSR to the wall of his office and
provocatively told visitors: 'That's the past, but it's also the future'.

Yeltsin's confrontation with his parliamentary enemies was playing
havoc with his health. He was drinking heavily, which brought on bouts
of depression, high blood pressure and a recurrence of heart trouble. The
situation reached flashpoint in October 1993, after Yeltsin dissolved
parliament and called new elections. Two hundred of his political
opponents, supported by several hundred heavily armed men, barricaded
themselves in the White House. Alexander Rutskoy and his confederate
Ruslan Khasbulatov sent armed gangs into the street to attack police
trying to restore order among hundreds of demonstrators chanting: 'All
power to the Soviets'.

The rebels looted the office of the Moscow mayor, Yuri Luzhkov, in
a skyscraper opposite the White House and stormed the state-owned

Ostankino television tower in a fierce, bloody battle that was televised live on the Channel 1 network. Yeltsin called in the tanks. On his command, they blitzed the White House, setting the upper floors ablaze and killing 150 people. Through the smoke, several figures stumbled into the open waving a white flag. Rutskoy, Khasbulatov and their followers were herded into buses and driven away.

Yeltsin was at his most eloquent when he addressed the nation. 'The nightmare of those dark days is now behind us,' he said. 'Nobody has won, nobody has scored a victory. We have all been scorched by the lethal breath of fratricidal war. Our people, our fellow countrymen, have perished. No matter what differences existed among us in our political views, they are all Russia's children. This is our common tragedy. This is our huge grief. Let us remember this insanity, so that it will never happen again as long as we shall live.'

Later that year Yeltsin brought in a new constitution granting him stronger presidential powers, but he couldn't stop the runaway locomotive of economic chaos. In 1994 share prices plunged, inflation ran out of control and the government did not have the money to pay wages and pensions. By the following year Russia was in deep crisis. 'A good communist,' the German dramatist Bertolt Brecht maintained, 'has many dents in his helmet. And some of them are the work of the enemy.' The same could be said of Boris Yeltsin's Russia: the vast majority of blows against the fledgling democracy had been struck not only by die-hard Communists but also by Yeltsin and his cronies, through multiple acts of greed and corruption which would ultimately rebound on them.

With its evocation of corruption and dread, Brecht's masterpiece *The Threepenny Opera* offers an allegory about such men. Brecht poses the question: 'Who is the greater criminal; he who robs a bank or he who founds one?' Parallels between post-Soviet Russia and the Weimar Republic of the 1920s that gave birth to Brecht's critique of the capitalist system are striking: hyperinflation, civil unrest, political extremism and the unseating of numerous prime ministers.

While the vast majority of Russians struggled with rising prices, acute shortages and unpaid wages, they had been infuriated by the enrichment of a handful of insiders through the voucher system. Their fury led to an abiding suspicion of democracy and a loathing for a free-market system in which most of them were too poor to participate. This was the power base on which a new Communist challenge would be built, while at the opposite end of the scale was the new breed of tycoon soon to be christened 'the oligarchs'. It was these opposing forces that would decide Russia's destiny.

The sharpest and most controversial of the oligarchs was Mikhail Borisovich Khodorkovsky. 'Misha', as his family calls him, was born on 26 June 1963 to a Jewish father and Orthodox Christian mother. He grew up in a standard two-room Moscow apartment, and although his parents were not particularly religious, young Misha was considered Jewish by the neighbours. Anti-Semitism turned him into a fiercely combative little boy who took great pains to succeed in everything he did. He was so self-disciplined that his nickname was 'Toy Soldier'.

The abject failure of the Communist economic and political system was abundantly clear to anyone living in the Brezhnev era. Khodorkovsky took it as a personal challenge. 'We as citizens were denied true voting rights, the right to create political parties, or to participate in public life,' he says. 'Not only did we not have these rights, we would definitely have ended up in jail or in a mental hospital if we had tried something like that.'

Both of Khodorkovsky's parents were chemical engineers and he embarked on a chemical engineering course at the Mendeleev Institute of Chemical Technology. He quickly made his mark. Few of his fellow students had his drive, intelligence or daring; women fell for his charm and dark good looks. He sought membership of the Komsomol as the quickest route to success and by the end of his second year had been promoted to branch secretary.

Around the same time, he got married and soon had a son as well as wife and son to support. Every morning at 6 a.m., he queued up to buy baby food with state-issued ration cards. 'Today's young people do not remember what life was like for us in the Soviet Union before the start of *perestroika*,' he says. 'I sometimes find it difficult to explain that rising prices for goods are not the most frightening thing in life. It is worse when you walk into a store and there is simply nothing there to buy.'

As a trusted Komsomolite, Khodorkovsky was permitted to travel abroad. He followed the Moscow-Paris axis to France, where he discovered the delights of capitalism and the free market. It changed his view of the world around him. Khodorkovsky was in charge of the Mendeleev Institute's canteen and bar and his first co-operative venture, in 1986, was to open a student cafe in the local Komsomol bureau with another young official, Alexei Golubovich, whose parents held senior positions in Gosbank, the state bank that administered all of the country's payments, including salaries, state subsidies and pensions.

Well-connected patrons were essential to any would-be impresario and Khodorkovsky schmoozed his way into favour with such people. His next move was to set up a co-operative to import computers, which were modified for Russian use and sold at a huge mark-up. He also recruited a team of programmers from among the institute's student population to service the IT networks of state enterprises and government ministries. This operation was called the Centre for Inter-Industry Scientific and Technical Progress, known by its Russian acronym as 'Menatep'.

By now, Khodorkovsky sported an impressive moustache and dressed in jeans and polo-neck sweaters. He had been given the added responsibility of vetting new employees at the Mendeleev Institute. One applicant – a beautiful young laboratory assistant named Inna – was invited to work with him in the Komsomol bureau. They had an affair and his marriage broke up. He married Inna two years later.

At the same time – 1988 – Khodorkovsky turned Menatep into a bank which sought deposits of government funds controlled by Communist Party apparatchiks. As one of the bank's executives explained to David E. Hoffman, the *Washington Post's* correspondent in Moscow, Khodorkovsky would have a sauna with one of his chums at the Finance Ministry, which would deposit 600 million roubles in Menatep. This money would be put into dollars or high-yielding rouble bonds and Menatep would collect the exchange-rate gains and the interest. When the ministry asked for its money back, inflation would have eroded its

ON AN EXPEDITION to the Ubsunur Hollow Biosphere Preserve. Inspecting a
snow leopard's habitat.

rouble value and Khodorkovsky would be left with a substantial profit.
All of which, of course, is perfectly legal.

Recognising the threat to his businesses posed by the attempted
Communist coup of 1991, the embryonic tycoon had dashed to the
White House to support Boris Yelstin. 'It's true to say that 1991 made me
a confirmed supporter of democracy and the market economy,' he says.
Practising what he preached, he and his partners took full advantage of
the opportunities offered by Anatoly Chubais during the voucher years
to acquire shareholdings in dozens of different industries, including
textiles, chemicals, metallurgy, fertilisers, glassmaking and food
processing. When they were accused of plundering state assets for a
fraction of their true value, he pointed out that the risks were high and

that many of these businesses, including his food processing operations, had to be closed down.

'I played according to the rules of that time,' he says. 'Of course those rules could have been better. Then we could have avoided some of the current problems. But nowadays, it's like going to someone who bought an apartment back in 1994 when prices were very low and saying to him: look at what that apartment is worth today – there must be something crooked here. And if they apply today's laws to the time when all this was happening, then of course it's perfectly possible for them to accuse anyone. That's the danger: they're trying to use that time when the legal system was completely chaotic to formulate accusations today.'

Inevitably, Khodorkovsky's brilliance attracted the attention of the Yeltsin administration. In 1993, he offered his services to the President. It was a shrewd move. Yeltsin appointed him deputy oil minister in the Department of Energy, an appointment that would bring him the promise of untold riches along with the heady smell of crude oil.

The most voluble of the oligarchs was the hyperactive maverick Boris Berezovsky. Seventeen years older than Khodorkovsky and desperate to make up for lost time, he had followed the path to oligarchdom like a hunting dog on the trail of a wounded stag. Born in Moscow on 23 January 1946, Boris Abramovich Berezovsky was the only child of an engineer at a brick factory, and a nurse at the Institute of Paediatrics. Although he describes his childhood as 'absolutely fantastic', he admits his father was laid off during Stalin's anti-Semitic purges and there were times the family didn't have enough food.

Berezovsky studied science in the computer technology department at the Moscow Forestry Engineering Institute. After graduating, he moved to Moscow State University and the prestigious Academy of Sciences and took a PhD in mathematics and physics. 'He was an outstanding organiser and problem solver,' says fellow student Alexander Mandel. 'He always had fat notebooks and a big intellect.'

Berezovsky's first research position was at the prestigious Institute of Control Sciences. He wasn't a brilliant scientist, but he was an indefatigable networker, constantly giving speeches and organising seminars and foreign trips. Even so, he struggled to provide a decent standard of living for his wife and two children. As the Soviet economy staggered towards free-market capitalism, he set up a business selling computer software and succeeded in persuading a Soviet committee to order 30,000 state institutions to buy his programs.

Berezovsky operated on the old Onassis principle that everyone has his price, although he adds with a touch of sensitivity: 'It is impossible to buy feelings. All the rest it is possible to buy.' Berezovsky entered Russia's highly volatile (and dangerous) car trade in 1989, importing Mercedes-Benz cars which he drove back to Moscow one at a time from trips to Europe and resold at a huge profit. He founded his own company, Logovaz, taking 'logo' from Logosystem, a Turin-based Fiat supplier, and 'vaz' from Avtovaz, makers of the Zhiguli on an imported Fiat production line at Togliatti on the Volga in central Russia. (In fact, the car took its name from the hills on the west bank of the river.)

Avtovaz loaned Berezovsky $5 million to import a fleet of 846 Fiats. The deal failed to return a profit, but it taught him a lot about the motor trade and consolidated his relationship with the company. The director of the plant, Vladimir Kadannikov, agreed to supply Berezovsky's expanding empire of car showrooms and dealerships with no fewer than 35,000 Zhigulis for a deposit of just 10 per cent, with the balance to be paid over the next two and a half years.

This remarkably generous deal was similar to many others made in post-Soviet Russia, which had the advantage of separating the profit centre – in this case, the sale of the cars – from the cost centre – the Avtovaz factory that bore all of the overheads for producing them. Tax loopholes enabled dealers to buy Zhigulis for almost $3,000 less than their retail price. The plant might be antiquated and the workers might not get paid, but the entrepreneurs at the sales end would make a fortune.

Berezovsky was soon the biggest Zhiguli dealer in Russia. He opened a club in the lavishly renovated Smirnoff mansion in central Moscow, where he entertained important clients, useful politicians and potential partners. He was rightly proud of the club's décor, which had matching silk upholstery on the walls and chairs, and a display of Chinese porcelain on the sideboard. He had only to tap a bell to summon a white-jacketed waiter to refill his glass of St Emilion or Chateau Latour. George Soros, the American financier who broke the Bank of England (and made billions of dollars' profit) on Black Wednesday 1992, was lured into Berezovsky's orbit with promises of lucrative investment opportunities. After they had fallen out, Soros wrote: 'His anger gave me the chills – I literally felt he could kill me'.

But it was Berezovsky who was the marked man. Just after 5 o'clock on the evening of 7 June 1994, a car bomb exploded as his Mercedes 600 pulled out of his clubhouse. His driver was decapitated by the blast, his bodyguard lost an eye and Berezovsky was lucky to stagger out of the wreckage with minor injuries. No one was ever arrested for the attack; the bombers were most probably contract killers hired by one of his business rivals in the car trade.

Berezovsky and the other new Russian tycoons were now a small but potent force in Russian life, the New Russians, or new business class. Another mansion – on Sparrow Hills on the right bank of the Moscow River – was designated neutral territory, where Berezovsky, Khodorkovsky, Smolensky and a young newcomer named Vladimir Potanin (but not Vladimir Gusinsky, who was in dispute with most of the other tycoons and was therefore blackballed) could discuss business and show off their wealth. They pledged to stand together in an alliance against their growing number of business enemies, but internecine squabbles would inevitably set them at each other's throats. And there was an even bigger menace: the Communists still hadn't quit after Boris Yeltsin's 'shock therapy' had turned ballistic in October 1993.

The Reds were threatening a sensational comeback under an aggressive new leader, Gennady Zyuganov; a thickset, balding, 51-year-old former physics teacher and Communist Party propagandist. Yeltsin was also opposed by the neo-fascist Vladimir Zhirinovsky, who openly advocated a return to authoritarian rule. For the men sipping iced vodka on Sparrow Hills, a Communist victory would mean triumph for the Red Directors, and a return to nationalisation, while most of them would face charges of fraud and corruption. It was Berezovsky who galvanised them into action on Yeltsin's behalf to protect their empires and their lives.

The tycoon had gained entrance to the Kremlin's inner circle at the end of 1993 through Valentin Yumashev, a former journalist whom Yeltsin treated as the son he never had. The bond between the two men had been sealed in 1990 when Yumashev spent weeks with Yeltsin ghosting his first book of memoirs *Against the Grain* (a title which drew its inspiration from Yeltsin's early life as a master craftsman).

For someone from the sciences, Berezovsky was remarkably media-savvy. He had bought a popular weekly magazine, *Ogonyok*, where Yumashev was one of the editors. He persuaded Yumashev to introduce him to Yeltsin's Cerberus-style gate-keepers, the liberally inclined chief of staff, Viktor Ilyushin, and the ferocious chief of security, General Alexander Korzhakov.

Korzhakov had stuck to Yeltsin after he quit the Communist Party in 1990 and developed his own political machine, which propelled him into the chairmanship of the Supreme Soviet, and from there into the presidency. For his loyalty, Korzhakov had been promoted to general and given control of the Federal Bodyguard Service (FSO), the agency which supplied bodyguards to federal bureaucrats, but which Korzhakov had drilled into a private army. 'Korzhakov was much heavier on muscle than grey matter and about as Neanderthal as they come,' says a senior British diplomat. 'He was close to the boss and was very loyal for a long time. He became one of Yeltsin's prime drinking companions.'

As an unreconstructed hard-liner dogmatically opposed to democracy and the new-fangled market economy, Korzhakov was the natural enemy of men like Berezovsky. It didn't require much grey matter to deduce that the oligarch's prime target was Boris Yeltsin. Indeed, Berezovsky intended to privatise the presidency, thus making himself inviolable, while protecting his newly-acquired wealth. That he was successful in these objectives is beyond doubt, but his belief that he had an inalienable right of access to the presidential suite, irrespective of who might occupy it, would ultimately bring about his downfall.

Berezovsky's chance to inveigle his way into Yeltsin's favour came when he learned that Valentin Yumashev had just completed the second volume of the president's memoirs, *Notes of a President*, and that he was looking for a publisher. There would have been no shortage of Russian houses willing to bring out the innermost thoughts of the most powerful man in the country, but Berezovsky's typically bold plan was to print a million copies in Finland and pay Yeltsin 'royalties' from foreign sales into a London bank account.

Yumashev recommended the deal to the group known as 'the Family' – Yeltsin's wife Naina and two daughters, Yelena and Tatyana, plus a handful of trusted cronies including Yumashev himself – and it was accepted. Korzhakov claimed that Yumashev presented the business of publishing the book as 'a great feat, implying that only Boris Abramovich was capable of such an act'. The result was a handsome volume, but even more satisfying was the $16,000 in cash that Yumashev brought to the President's office every month – Yeltsin's interest on the $3 million 'royalties' that Berezovsky had lodged for him at a branch of Barclays Bank in Mayfair.

According to Korzhakov, Yumashev did 'everything he could' to connect Berezovsky with the Family. There was nothing the embittered general could do to prevent Yeltsin making Berezovsky a member of the President's Club, where the Family and their guests swam, played tennis and disported themselves in luxurious surroundings. Korzhakov gave Chrystia Freeland, the *Financial Times* correspondent in Moscow, a vivid insight into Berezovsky's thick-skinned approach to networking. He was having a shower after a game of tennis when he was joined by the pushy tycoon, who started a conversation above the roar of the water jets. 'I can't hear half of what he's saying, but he keeps on shouting,' Korzhakov recalled. 'Berezovsky never did sports. He came to the club to prevent other people from doing sports; to approach the necessary people with his questions, his affairs, his issues.'

His chutzpah was extraordinary. Resembling a slightly taller version of Danny DeVito, he bobbed and weaved among Russia's political elite, offering opinions and dispensing favours. He spotted that the quickest route to the President was via his younger daughter, the shy and timid

Tatyana ('Tanya') Dyachenko, former wife of businessman Leonid Dyachenko. As Korzhakov says, 'If Tanya Dyachenko gave him her direct telephone number, what could anybody do to stop him?' Berezovsky lavished gifts upon her, including a Niva – a type of Russian Jeep – and a Chevrolet Blazer (although she could not recall receiving either vehicle). He consolidated his position by becoming the Family's financial adviser in such matters as arranging the purchase of a house for the Yeltsins to use at Cap d'Antibes, where he also had a holiday mansion.

Berezovsky floated the idea to Viktor Ilyushin and Alexander Korzhakov that the state-run television station Channel 1 should be 'the President's channel', relaying pro-Yeltsin propaganda to its 200 million viewers across 10 time zones. Channel 1 was part of Ostankino, a hotchpotch of TV studios and programmes that the Communists were trying to take under their wing. Although suspicious that Berezovsky intended to turn this cumbersome giant into his own network, Ilyushin and Korzhakov could do little other than support the idea. At the time, the only private network in Russia was Vladimir Gusinsky's NTV, which held roughly 15 per cent of the market share. And Gusinsky was not only Berezovsky's enemy, he could not be relied on to support the President.

KNOWN AS 'GOOSE', Gusinsky was a Russian theatrical director whose only claim to fame was that he had directed the opening and closing ceremonies at Ted Turner's 1986 Goodwill Games in Moscow. Born on 2 October 1952 (five days before Putin), he was driving a taxi when first *perestroika* and then Chubais' voucher system introduced him to the infinite possibilities of free enterprise. He made millions of dollars by teaming up with Moscow's Mayor Yuri Luzhkov, then an old-style Soviet bureaucrat, to renovate state-owned buildings and sell them on at a vast profit in the capital's booming property market.

As his fortune grew, Gusinsky launched the liberal newspaper *Sevodnya* and a bank called Most (Russian for 'bridge'). On 10 October 1993, just a week after Yeltsin declared war on the Communists, he launched NTV with the slogan 'News is our profession', poaching well-

RUSSIAN President Vladimir Putin (centre) visits the apartment of submarine
officer Vitaly Shebelev and his wife Polina in Vilyuchinsk (Kamchatka).

known presenters Tatyana Mitkova and Mikhail Osokin, as well as
managers, directors and technicians, from the ossified Ostankino
network. 'I just wanted to be No 1,' he explains.

Despite its near-monopoly, Ostankino was costing the state $170
million a year to run, whereas its advertising revenues produced just $40
million. Berezovsky's suggestion was that Yeltsin grant the Channel 1
licence to a new company in which 51 per cent would belong to the state
and 49 per cent to private investors, controlled by him. Yeltsin agreed to
the proposal as much from a desire to keep it out of Communist hands
as to enrich Berezovsky and his partners: Khodorkovsky, Alexander
Smolensky and the Ukrainian physicist-turned-banker Mikhail Fridman
among others.

At the same time, Avtovaz Bank, controlled by Berezovsky, was
involved in a titanic battle with Gusinsky's Most Bank for the right to
handle the overseas earnings of Aeroflot. The Russian national airline

had been privatised but the majority of its stock – and therefore control of its assets – remained with the state. Once the largest airline in the world, it was now in dire straits, often running short of money to buy fuel and pay its staff. Tarmacs across the country were littered with obsolete aircraft, which had been cannibalised for parts to enable other planes to take off.

Although the state was expected to provide the funds to keep Aeroflot solvent, the cash from tickets sold abroad for hard currency – estimated at between $80 million and $220 million at any given time – never flowed back into the system. Instead, it was siphoned off by middle-men and disappeared into hundreds of secret foreign bank accounts. Much of the money went into a company called Andava, founded by Berezovsky.

At the same time, there were whispers in the Kremlin. According to Korzhakov, Berezovsky 'would regularly report what Gusinsky said about the president, and where, how he cursed him, what name he called him, how he wanted to deceive him.' Knowing Yeltsin feared Yuri Luzhkov as a potential presidential rival, Berezovsky played on his paranoia by claiming that Gusinsky and Luzhkov had drunk a toast to the day when the mayor would become president.

Korzhakov claims he finally refused to act as a conduit for such tittle-tattle, so Berezovsky turned to Tatyana Dyachenko. When he took control of the Aeroflot's accounts a short time later, he appointed Valery Okulov – previously one of the airline's pilots – as head of the national carrier. It was no coincidence that Okulov was at the time married to the attractive Tatyana.

BY FAR THE BIGGEST event of 1994 was the outbreak of the First Chechen War. Chechnya, once part of southern Russia, had declared its independence three years earlier but Moscow had sought, without success, to stage a referendum in Chechnya on whether the breakaway republic should stay in the Russian Federation. The separatist leader Dzhokhar Dudayev's power was increasing and Moscow was seen to be dithering. Yeltsin was loathe to send in the Russian armed forces to crush the rebellion, but a series of unedifying incidents drove him into the belligerents' camp.

On 31 August that year he attended a ceremony in Berlin to mark the final withdrawal of troops from a unified Germany. Live television images of him grabbing the baton from a band leader and drunkenly conducting the orchestra were flashed around the world. Then on 30 September, on a return flight from the United States, he failed to get off the plane in Ireland to see the waiting Taoiseach, Albert Reynolds. Once again, television pictures recorded the occasion; but instead of the Russian President, they showed only the steps of the aircraft and an empty doorway. Once again, many people assumed that he was drunk. The Deputy Prime Minister, Oleg Soskovets, finally got off the plane to meet Reynolds and was later quoted by *Tass* as saying that Yeltsin was in good health, when in fact he had suffered a heart attack during the flight.

Yeltsin was now assailed by one crisis after another. On Black Tuesday, 11 October 1994, the rouble lost 27 per cent of its value in an unexpected meltdown on the currency markets. Yeltsin was an ignoramus in matters of economics. Blaming the liberals in his government for the collapse, he moved closer to his drinking companion General Korzhakov, who had formed a hawkish group within the Kremlin labelled 'the party of war' by its liberal opponents. Its members included Soskovets, a veteran of the Soviet military industry, whom Korzhakov had secretly marked down as a future president.

Realising the advantage of having his own uncritical television network in these trying times, Yeltsin signed a decree on 29 November, dismantling Ostankino and replacing it with ORT (Russian Public Television). There was no auction, as required by law, not even a token one. Berezovsky was initially appointed chairman of an oversight board but later consolidated control in his own hands.

The following month, the President sent forces into the Chechnyan highlands at the behest of the 'party of war'. Gusinsky's NTV focused on the horrors of the conflict, and support for the war evaporated among the electorate. In less than 18 months, more than 30,000 people,

IT HELPS to get out of the Kremlin once in a while. Putin, here with Civil Defence Minister Sergei Shoigu (centre), savours local food and entertainment on a visit to Tuva, where Tuvan throat singing is the specialty.

including 5,000 Russian soldiers, would be killed in that savage conflict. Yeltsin's poll ratings dived into single digits, while the Communist leader, Gennady Zyuganov, was polling 30 per cent.

On 20 February 1995 ORT severed all links with the middlemen who had been making huge profits selling advertising time on Channel 1. 'This was my personal idea,' Berezovsky says. 'It caused wild surprise.' As payback, ORT's popular new Director-General, Vladislav Listyev, was gunned down by two assassins at the door of his Moscow apartment. Though only 38 years old, Listyev was Russia's Larry King figure and his Field of Miracles game show had been a national hit.

Yeltsin drove to the ORT studios and denounced 'this cowardly and evil murder' in a live broadcast. In homage to the dead man, every television station then closed down for twenty-four hours. Berezovsky fell under suspicion: the special police were ordered to arrest him and went to his home. When they arrived, FSB operative Alexander

Litvinenko (later poisoned in London) emerged from the house waving a gun, and told the special police (OMON) that their services would not be required because the FSB were going to pick Berezovsky up for questioning. Berezovsky would be forever grateful to Litvinenko for saving him from arrest and the two later worked together. After an investigation, the FSB decided that Listyev's murder and the bomb attempt on Berezovsky's life eight months earlier were the work of the Kurgans, a gang of mobsters who had penetrated Moscow's police department.

The oligarchs simply bought more armoured Mercedes and surrounded themselves with more bodyguards. They licked their lips at the prospect of further financial killings. One of the Sparrow Hills clique had an idea which would turn the locomotive of economic chaos into a richly-endowed gravy train.

7

The Gravy Train

VLADIMIR PUTIN has done little to disguise his personal loathing of the oligarchs, who continue to capture the attention of the world's media. The resentment stems from the looting of the jewel box of Russian industry in 1995/6, under the collaborative eye of his one-time colleague on the St Petersburg Council, Anatoly Chubais. A dozen tycoons were able to pull off what has been called 'the Sale of the Century' (or more precisely 'the Biggest Heist in History') because Boris Yeltsin desperately needed a massive injection of cash to keep the economy going if he were to have any chance of winning the 1996 presidential election.

The architect of the scheme that was to save his skin was Vladimir Potanin, a short, pug-nosed, 34-year-old son of the *nomenklatura,* whose private company, Onexim Bank, had been gifted accounts worth $300 million by obliging officials at the crumbling state-owned Bank of Economic Co-ordination. On this occasion, Potanin rolled up at the Kremlin, flanked by two other powerful bankers, Mikhail Khodorkovsky and Alexander Smolensky, and delivered his pitch to the Cabinet at a meeting chaired by then Prime Minister, Viktor Chernomyrdin. Potanin's idea was a 'loans for shares' scheme. He proposed that a group of Russian tycoons would give a huge loan to the government, which would put up a controlling interest in strategic state industries as collateral, and transfer the right to manage those entities to the lender.

The scheme was attractive to the cabinet for a number of reasons.

The State Property Committee, which had been ordered to generate 8.7 trillion roubles in privatisation receipts, had so far managed to make only a tiny fraction of that amount. So when the oligarchs' banks offered the government loans totalling 9.1 trillion roubles (then £1.12 billion) in return for shares in state-owned companies, Yeltsin gave it his blessing, provided it could be dressed up as a pawning of state assets rather than outright disposal. As prime minister and later president, Vladimir Putin would come to abhor this scheme as much as he disliked most of the men who participated in it; yet without it, it is widely believed that Russia would almost certainly have returned to Communist rule.

THE BIG STATE enterprises that dominated the oil and gas, minerals, telecommunications and military sectors were still in the hands of the red director corps, many of whom were skimming profits and stashing the money in offshore tax havens. Chubais saw the 'loans for shares' scheme as the lever that would prise these assets from their hands forever, thus annihilating the Red Directors, whose leading advocate in the Kremlin was his chief rival, Oleg Soskovets. For Chubais, the disaffected son of a die-hard Communist, the end justified the means. 'I had a choice between the Communists coming to power, or robber capitalism,' he later explained. 'I chose robber capitalism.'

Throughout that summer, few details of the scheme leaked from the State Property Office or the oligarchs' secretive world while the mechanics of the operation were put into place. Putin was still in St. Petersburg and would have known little about it. His hostility towards the oligarchs started only after the underhand manner in which they had secured these assets became clear.

By 30 August everything had been agreed among the conspirators. Boris Yeltsin signed a decree under which the State Property Committee sanctioned a series of auctions at which the banks would offer low-interest loans to the government in exchange for shares in 12 valuable state enterprises. It was understood that if the government failed to repay the loans, the lenders would have first refusal to acquire these shares in a second series of auctions to pay back the loans, while retaining 30 per cent of the proceeds as commission. As the chances of the loans ever being repaid were minimal, the long-term effect of this arrangement was to hand over the commanding heights of the economy to a handful of speculators at bargain basement prices.

Chubais had cleverly created the two-phase system to ensure maximum support for Yeltsin throughout the 1996 re-election campaign. The oligarchs would get their first hold on each factory prior to polling day, but the auction that would enable them to consolidate their ownership would take place only after the election. The oligarchs were quite happy with this: their own banks were in charge of the auctions and they would effectively be the only bidders through secret shell companies or affiliates of the state-owned enterprises themselves. They simply couldn't lose if everything went according to plan.

Bold as brass, Alfred Kokh assured reporters that the auctioneer's function was largely technical and did not give the bidder 'any additional advantage'. Chubais was just as disingenuous as his colleague. 'As you may know,' he told journalists, 'we don't predetermine the buyer.' The procedures for the auctions would be 'free and competitive'. Yet it is a fact that the vast majority of the enterprises auctioned between 3 November and 28 December 1995 went to banks that had organised the auction or their intermediaries.

On 17 November Vladimir Potanin seized his prize, a 38 per cent stake in the Arctic mining colossus Norilsk Nickel, one of the world's biggest producers of nickel, platinum and cobalt. It had just reported profits of $1.2 billion – more than the entire amount raised in loans to top up the government treasury.

Khodorkovsky's target was Yukos, then Russia's second largest oil and gas producer. The Deputy Energy Minister had spent weeks courting the company's Red Directors and was confident he had them in his pocket. He also knew that John Browne, the intrepid chief executive of BP, was champing at the bit to get into the massive Russian oil and gas market. As a first step, Browne had set up a joint venture with Yuri Luzhkov to build a chain of BP service stations around Moscow. This had proved commercially successful and had also made the BP brand

SHOWING OFF Russia's new high-speed train, which cuts the time for the 650 km journey from Moscow to St Petersburg to just 225 minutes.

known to the country's top decision-makers, including Boris Yeltsin, who took an interest in all of Luzhkov's schemes.

In order to prevent BP or any of the other super-majors bidding against him – and therefore pushing up the price – Khodorkovsky successfully lobbied the State Property Committee to have all foreign companies excluded from the auction. Thus Menatep Bank became the official auctioneer for Yukos, as well as the chief bidder.

The Yukos auction was held on 8 December 1995. Up for grabs was 45 per cent of the shares in a 'loans for shares' deal, as well as another 33 per cent in an investment tender that committed the bidder to sinking $200 million into the company. The starting price was a $150 million loan for the shares and $150 million for the investment tender.

Khodorkovsky entered his bid through one of his front companies, Laguna, but there was a problem. Three other bankers – Vladimir Vinogradov of Inkombank, Mikhail Fridman of Alfa Bank and Valery

Malkin of Rossiisky Kredit – had joined forces to prepare a rival bid. They were unable to raise the $350 million deposit in cash, but offered $82 million in cash and the remainder in short-term government bonds (GKOs). Kokh and Chubais, however, rejected the GKOs – saying, in effect, that the Russian Government would not accept its own bonds – and insisted they produce the full amount in cash. Fridman's associate Pyotr Aven, president of Alfa Bank, tried to talk to Chubais, whom he had known for years, in order to persuade him that this decision was unjust. But Chubais would not see him or even talk to him on the telephone. There was nothing the three bankers could do to prevent Khodorkovsky walking away with his prize.

His Laguna front company paid $159 million – just $9 million over the starting price – for 45 per cent of Yukos shares and he won the investment tender for another 33 per cent by offering just $125,000 above the starting price of $150 million. In total, a majority shareholding cost him the knockdown price of just over $309 million. Yukos was soon valued on the Russian stock market at $15 billion. The *Economist* estimates that Khodorkovsky made more money more quickly than almost anyone in history.

Khodorkovsky disputes claims that the Yukos purchase was crooked. 'Oil production was falling by 15 per cent a year, debts to contractors amounted to about $3 billion, wages were six months in arrears and employees were either grumbling to themselves or complaining out loud,' he says. Alfred Kokh comments mysteriously: 'All sorts of things become possible when such an oil company joins forces with a large bank'.

On the same day as the Yukos auction a consortium led by Vladimir Potanin picked up 51 per cent of the shares in another oil company, Sidanco, for a mere $130 million. It wasn't long before Potanin received an approach from BP, looking for part of the action. Excluded from the auctions, John Browne bought a 10 per cent stake in Sidanco for $571 million, an offer Potanin couldn't refuse. The deal was signed at 10 Downing Street in front of Prime Minister Tony Blair.

Meanwhile, Boris Berezovsky was in danger of missing out on the bonanza. At the eleventh hour he persuaded Anatoly Chubais and

Alexander Korzhakov – an astonishing feat considering their diametrically opposed views – that he needed a regular cash flow to support his ailing, pro-Yeltsin television company ORT. Korzhakov admitted: 'I am not very good at economics', but he 'put in a word for Berezovsky' despite his animosity towards him, while Chubais and his cohorts knew exactly what to do.

On 11 October the State Property Committee obligingly ordered the auction of a controlling stake in Sibneft, the seventh largest oil producer in Russia. Sibneft (short for 'Siberian oil') had been created two months earlier by the vertical integration of the country's largest oil refinery at Omsk, the Siberian oil producer Noyabrskneftegaz, the exploration outfit Noyabrskneftegasgeophysica and the marketing company Omsknefteprodukt.

When it went up for auction in December, Chubais' economists valued the stake at a minimum of $100 million but Berezovsky could put up only half that amount. 'This is Roma, my new partner,' he said, introducing an unknown oil trader named Roman Abramovich to George Soros' associate Alex Goldfarb at the Logovaz clubhouse. 'He's a wonderful guy – we need more like him!' Abramovich was a shy, unshaven, 29-year-old in sweater and jeans, but he had access to $50 million – so for just $100 million, Berezovsky and Abramovich, acting as a team, acquired a controlling interest in Sibneft at auction later that month. Eight years later, the value of the company would have risen to $15 billion when Berezovsky was forced by Vladimir Putin to sell out to his partner.

Chrystia Freeland concludes in *Sale of the Century*, her exposé of the 'loans for shares' scam, that 'Russia was robbed in broad daylight, by businessmen who broke no laws, assisted by the West's best friends in the Kremlin – the young reformers'. Not surprisingly, the oligarchs claimed they were reviled in their own land because Russians did not understand entrepreneurialism and were not prepared to tolerate conspicuous personal wealth. In the West, they were labelled 'robber barons' to equate them with the Rockefellers, Vanderbilts and Carnegies of American fame.

They certainly found an ally in Lord Browne of Madingley, the former BP boss who had been recommended for a knighthood and then a peerage by Tony Blair. 'You know, people criticise the oligarchs but one has to remember they took gigantic risks,' he says in an interview at the energy consultants Riverstone in Mayfair. 'They bought all these shares, they may have been cheap but they had to get hold of huge amounts of money to do what they did and it could all have gone phut. Was anyone else prepared to risk those gigantic sums to buy those shares? I think not, so these men are huge risk-takers. They are people you would form a professional relationship with but not a personal one – I'm not sure they would want that either.'

Putin was now a member of Prime Minister Viktor Chernomyrdin's centrist party, Our Home is Russia (Nash Dom – Rossiya, NDR). In June 1995 a group of around 200 Chechens led by the maverick field commander Shamil Basayev took more than 1,500 people hostage in a hospital at Budyonnovsk in southern Russia. About 120 Russian civilians were killed before Chernomyrdin was able to broker a ceasefire with Basayev. The raid enforced a temporary halt in Russian military operations in Chechnya, allowing the Chechens time to prepare a national guerrilla campaign, in which they were successful.

Chernomyrdin was desperate for his party to do well against the Communists, led by Gennady Zyuganov, in the federal parliamentary elections.

In late 1995, despite having little experience as an election manager, Putin was put in charge of Our Home is Russia's campaign in St Petersburg. The party's candidates attracted just 10 per cent of the vote and much of the blame was heaped on the luckless campaign manager. Chernomyrdin was furious with him, but in reality there was little that Putin could have done in the prevailing economic climate to prevent the Communists sweeping to victory.

The result convinced most Russians that Boris Yeltsin could not win a second term in the 1996 presidential election. Opinion polls put him in seventh place, with Zyuganov easily the front-runner. Throughout autumn and early winter Yeltsin had either been hospitalised with cardiac trouble or recuperating at one of his dachas. Yeltsin suffered his most serious heart attack to date in late December 1995, a fact which was kept out of the media at the time. Rumours about his prodigious vodka consumption were legendary and he was widely believed to be incapable of fighting a vigorous campaign. Many observers suspected that some pretext would be found for cancelling the election because, in the event of a Communist victory, Yeltsin and his cronies would face investigation for corruption.

'There was an alcohol problem but I think that when my father did drink it was because of the enormous stress he was under,' his daughter Tatyana says today. She describes the caricatured image of Yeltsin as a tottering drunk as 'absolutely untrue. It's unfair, biased and unacceptable to look at Yeltsin's presidency and its many achievements exclusively through this very narrow prism. It should be assessed in its entirety. He was the leader of a great country who did much for his nation. No other country has undergone such tumultuous change in so short a time as Russia did under Yeltsin.'

Yeltsin made an amazing recovery when General Korzhakov was quoted as saying that Russian society was too volatile to permit an orderly poll, hinting that the election might be cancelled. Yeltsin swept back into the Kremlin in the New Year to deliver a stinging public rebuke to his drinking chum and to announce that the election would go ahead as planned.

Yeltsin blamed the hawkish Korzhakov for having influenced his decision to start the first Chechen War, which, along with unremitting economic malaise, was largely responsible for his miserable performance in the opinion polls. Fearful of losing his privileged position, the general switched tack and urged Yeltsin to sack the real architect of his problems, Anatoly Chubais, whose flawed privatisation schemes had enriched a tiny minority, while the vast majority of Russians yearned for the good old days of the Soviet Union, when they could at least afford to eat regularly.

Korzhakov was supported by a right-wing group, including the FSB director Mikhail Barsukov and industrialist Oleg Soskovets, in calling for Chubais' head. It didn't take Yeltsin long to appreciate the wisdom of their argument: Chubais was widely unpopular with the masses and his departure would deflect public attention from Yeltsin's own erratic performance. Yeltsin decided to run for election. On 17 January 1996 he launched his campaign with the shock announcement that he had dismissed Chubais and also several liberal members of his Cabinet. Adding insult to injury, he appointed Soskovets to run his re-election committee, with the two generals, Korzhakov and Barsukov, as his deputies.

Yeltsin's sudden lurch to the right to appease the hardliners in his camp was a blatant betrayal of the reform movement, a fact that was noted when the world's leading tycoons and politicians gathered at the World Economic Forum in the Swiss ski resort of Davos the following month. Western business chiefs swarmed around Gennady Zyuganov in the belief that he would become Russia's next president. Assuming the mantle of a Western-style social democrat, Zyuganov embarked on an implausible charm offensive. 'We want a mixed economy, a stable balance of public, private and collective ownership,' he said in William Safire's column in the *New York Times*. 'Communism means collegiality, sustainable development, spiritual values, major investment in the human being.'

After a session with Zyuganov, George Soros warned Boris Berezovsky that the game was up. 'My advice to you,' Soros told him over breakfast, 'is to take your family, sell what you still can, and get out of the country before it is too late.' Khodorkovsky overheard this conversation and admits it caused him a great deal of concern. To Berezovsky, however, Soros' warning was like an electric charge. He swallowed his pride and arranged a meeting with his mortal enemy, Vladimir 'Goose' Gusinsky, at the Fluela Hotel. Berezovsky came straight to the point: a resurgent Communist Party would overturn the reforms that had made them fabulously wealthy, cancel the second round of 'loans for shares' auctions and 'hang them both from lampposts'.

Gusinsky knew that even if Yeltsin was re-elected, he was in for a rough time. The President thought he was getting too big for his boots. Naina and Tatyana had complained about being been cut up by his motorcade on the highway from their home into Moscow. Moreover, he was supporting Yuri Luzhkov in his quest for the presidency, while NTV was the government's strongest critic over Chechnya. The final insult was that the channel had just launched a satirical puppet show called *Kukly,* which lampooned the President and the Family. Yeltsin ordered Korzhakov to 'deal with' Gusinsky.

Shortly afterwards, Gusinsky was harassed by a squad of masked men armed with sub-machine guns on his way into town. He managed to reach his office, but his bodyguards were beaten up and forced to lie face-down in the snow for hours. The episode so unnerved the oligarch that he sent his wife and child out of the country. Gusinsky had no doubt that Yeltsin's enforcer General Korzhakov was responsible for the campaign against him, which meant that it had been sanctioned by Yeltsin himself. Even so, the Communists would be worse than Yeltsin, so he shook hands on a deal with Berezovsky to back Yeltsin's re-election.

By the time Berezovsky met the President at the Kremlin in late February he was the leader of a pro-Yeltsin cabal comprising Gusinsky of the Most group, Mikhail Khodorkovsky of the Menatep group, Vladimir Potanin of Onexim Bank, Alexander Smolensky of Stolichny Bank, and Mikhail Fridman and his English-speaking partner Pyotr Aven of the Alfa group. Yeltsin's appearance came as a shock. His face was bloated and his big athlete's body sagged from alcohol abuse and heart disease. He looked like an ageing wrestler who had fought one bout too many, but his great Russian brain was still deceptively active.

Berezovsky explained that many members of the business community were trying to do a deal with the Communists, while the rest 'are packing their bags to flee abroad'. 'Give us an opportunity to help your campaign,' he pleaded. 'We have the media, money, people, contacts in the regions and the main thing: determination. We just need a word from you.'

Yeltsin wasn't fooled. He knew that the oligarchs stood to make billions in the second round of auctions under the 'loans for shares' scheme if he won the election and that they were therefore motivated only by greed and self-interest. 'Are you suggesting I fire Soskovets and put you in charge of my campaign?' he asked.

'No, of course not,' Berezovsky replied. 'Create another entity – say, an analytical group. Let it work alongside your staff. And we propose Anatoly Borisovich Chubais as its leader.'

Yeltsin's face reddened. 'Chubais?' he roared. 'Chubais is to blame for everything.' Then, according to Berezovsky's friend Alex Goldfarb, he thought it over for a few moments. 'Well, okay, since he's to blame, let him clean up the mess. All right, give it a try.'

Valentin Yumashev suggested it might be a good idea for Tatyana to act as a conduit between the campaign team and the president. Yeltsin readily agreed. So with Berezovsky as chief strategist, Chubais as quartermaster, and Tatyana as the go-between, 'Team Yeltsin' charged head-long into battle. The President was like a man reborn. He threw himself into the campaign, travelling widely, dispensing state funds, even dancing to rock bands.

By March 1996, the opinion polls showed a swing towards Yeltsin and by April the public seemed to accept that he was now a serious contender, even though he still faced an olympian struggle to beat Zyuganov. By May it seemed that many people were prepared to vote for him because the next presidential elections would be held no later than 2000 and he would not be eligible to stand for a third term. The oligarchs' electoral machinations were starting to return dividends. The defender of women's rights and ethnic minorities, Galina Starovoitova, prophesied that Russia's 'democratic house of cards' would collapse unless Boris Yeltsin, despite all his faults, was re-elected as president and led parliament's small group of reformers in continuing the democratic revolution. Yeltsin's successor, she warned, might be a 'potential dictator', or one of the oligarchs who had little interest in democracy.

Like Yeltsin, Anatoly Sobchak was also up for re-election on 16 June. The campaign would be another painful experience for Vladimir Putin, but one that would draw him inexorably closer to Yeltsin and to the Kremlin.

8

Slings and Arrows

PUTIN'S BAPTISM of fire in the trenches of civic government had put him in the media spotlight. For the first time, questions were being asked about his background and character: Was there more to this pragmatic official in whom Anatoly Sobchak had placed so much trust – or was he as colourless as he appeared? Putin was an intensely private, even secretive, man and he did not welcome this public scrutiny. It was just the start of a long and difficult relationship with the world's journalists and commentators.

The first issue to emerge in print was Putin's membership of the KGB. 'Russia observers East and West have pounded away at his KGB roots as the sole determining factor of his actions,' Gordon M. Hahn wrote in the *Russia Journal*. 'They never so much as hint at his other formative political experience: his work in semi-democratic and corrupt administrations in Leningrad/St Petersburg and Moscow.'

While this was undoubtedly so, it was Putin's KGB experiences that were the key to his personality in dealing with other people. After many years in the field, he had learned to control his feelings, an ability that sometimes gave the impression that he was emotionally cold when indeed he was a lot more interesting – and emotional – than he seemed. The most startling example of this trait was provided when the Putins' Caucasian sheepdog Malysh was hit by a car outside their state-owned dacha at Zelenogorsk. Lyudmila picked up the wounded animal and drove her to a veterinary clinic but the vet was unable to save the animal. Lyudmila phoned Putin's secretary Marina Yentaltseva and asked her to pass on the sad news to her husband.

Marina did as requested and was astonished at Putin's reaction. 'I looked at him and there was zero emotion on his face,' she says. 'I was so surprised that I said, "Did someone already tell you about it?" And he said calmly, "No, you're the first to tell me". In fact, he is a deeply emotional man, but when he has to, he can hide his feelings.' Another individual, who is close to him but begs anonymity for fear of incurring disfavour, says somewhat more expansively: 'You never get to know Vladimir just by looking at him or even by listening to him. Someone asked me [at the economic conference] in Davos: "Who is Mr Putin?" Well, the answer is hard to explain. Just as Winston Churchill said about Russia: "It's a riddle, wrapped in a mystery, inside an enigma; but perhaps there is a key. That key is Russian national interest". Well, that description could just as easily be applied to Vladimir. No one can ever be sure what is going on in his head, but you can be certain that what he is doing is good for his country.'

Quite apart from the high drama in which Putin was involved day-to-day at City Hall, the loss of his pet was just the start of several more serious incidents, which would have severely tested a weaker man. The first happened in October 1993, when CNN founder Ted Turner and his actress wife Jane Fonda visited St Petersburg to discuss the Goodwill Games; the international sporting event that Turner had launched in Moscow in 1986 to help take the chill out of the Cold War was due to be held in St Petersburg the following year. During their stay the American couple checked into the Astoria Hotel and Vladimir Putin was delegated by the mayor to accompany them to all of their meetings. It was a tight schedule and Putin, noted for his lateness, was struggling to meet it when he received a call from Marina telling him that Lyudmila had been in an accident.

'Is it serious?' he asked.

'No, apparently not,' his secretary replied. 'But the ambulance took her to the hospital just in case.'

'Let me try to get out of this meeting and go to the hospital.'

The Putins had spent the previous night with the children at the dacha at Zelenogorsk. In the morning Putin's chauffeured car had picked him up and driven him into the city to meet the Turners. The accident had happened later that day when Lyudmila, with seven-year-old Katya lying asleep in the back seat, was driving to pick up Masha from school in the Putins' Zhiguli.

She was going through a green light not far from Smolny when another driver swerved around a stationary car, jumped the red light and ploughed into the front of their vehicle at 80 kilometres an hour. 'I didn't even see it,' Lyudmila says. 'I had the green light and didn't even look to the right.'

It was fortunate that the driver crashed into the right front side of the car: if he had hit the front or back door, either Lyudmila or Katya would probably have been killed. As it was, Lyudmila was knocked out for half an hour. When she regained consciousness, her first thought was for her daughter. She gave a woman driver, who had stopped to help, the telephone number of Igor Sechin and asked that he pick up Katya. This woman called an ambulance and then rang Sechin's number. The ambulance took forty-five minutes to reach the scene of the accident. By the time it arrived, Lyudmila was in a state of shock and failed to tell the medics that she was qualified through her husband's position to be taken to the Military Medical Academy. Instead, she was driven to the vastly inferior 25 October Hospital, which was supposed to specialise in trauma cases. Her nightmare was just beginning. The state of the hospital shocked her. The casualty department was littered with bodies of the dead and the dying. 'I will remember it for the rest of my life,' she says.

It is quite likely that Lyudmila would have died if she had stayed there. The doctors examined her and noticed that her ear had been torn in the collision and that she had hurt her back but failed to notice that she had several cracked vertebrae and a fractured skull. Untreated, she would have contracted post-traumatic meningitis.

Making his apologies to the Turners, Putin dashed to the hospital. In the emergency room the chief physician assured him: 'Don't worry,

Taking a trip on the newly launched Sapsan high-speed train linking Moscow and St Petersburg, 19 December 2009.

she's not in any danger. We're just going to put a splint on her back, and everything will be fine.'

'Are you sure?'

'Absolutely,' he said.

Meanwhile, Igor Sechin had picked up Katya, who was bruised and seemed subdued, and taken her back to Smolny. Marina took her to see a local doctor who advised that she consult a paediatrician to determine whether she was concussed. At the Paediatric Institute, a neurologist said that Katya was in shock and advised peace and quiet.

When Marina and Katya returned to Smolny, Putin asked Marina to phone Yuri Leonidovich Shevchenko, a surgeon at the Military Medical Academy (and later Putin's Minister of Health) and inform him of Lyudmila's accident and present whereabouts. Shevchenko immediately sent one of his medical officers, Valery Yevgenevich Parfyonov, over to the 25 October Hospital. 'My ear was torn and they had decided to sew it up,' Lyudmila says. 'They had gine away, leaving me naked on the table in a freezing operating room, in a terrible state of semi-consciousness.' When Parfyonov arrived at the hospital, he was told, 'She doesn't need anything. We just did an operation. Everything's fine.' He decided to check on the patient for himself. Lyudmila awoke in the operating room 'to find an officer standing in front of me, holding my hand. He had a very warm palm. It warmed me up, and I knew that I had been saved'.

At the Military Medical Academy an X-ray revealed the serious nature of Lyudmila's injuries and she received the proper treatment. It was more than a month before she was able to leave hospital, and then she could only crawl around the apartment. Putin was furious about the treatment his wife had received at the first hospital but, pragmatic as ever, he wasn't too proud to ask for assistance. Shortly after she returned home, he telephoned Bernard Walter at the Dresdner Bank. The bank responded favourably. 'For humanitarian reasons', it paid for Lyudmila to be airlifted to a clinic in Bad Homburg, Germany, for specialist treatment, and covered at least part of the costs. Walter confirmed that the bank had paid for Lyudmila's medical treatment, which he called 'completely self-evident from a humane point of view'. Such assistance does not appear to have violated any Russian laws. Putin could not have afforded the treatment his wife needed, since salaries, even of high-ranking officials, were exceedingly low.

IN MID-APRIL 1996 Anatoly Sobchak asked Putin to supervise security arrangements for a visit by President Bill Clinton, who was stopping over in St Petersburg on his way to one of his regular meetings with Boris Yeltsin in Moscow. Air Force One touched down just after 10 p.m. and, despite the late hour, Anatoly Sobchak took him on a tour of the Tsar's Village at Pushkin, including Catherine the Great's palace. It was well past midnight before Clinton turned in at the Grand Europa Hotel.

In the morning the US President attended a memorial service at the Piskarevsky Memorial Cemetery, where nearly half a million victims of the Nazi siege were buried. He was then driven to the Hermitage to see Russia's art treasures. Clinton was due to meet a group of students at the museum, but Putin was taking no chances: much to the President's annoyance, he cancelled the meeting on security grounds.

Sirens blaring, Clinton's motorcade roared from the Hermitage to a restaurant where Clinton was due to dine with Sobchak and other dignitaries. On the way, Clinton wanted to pull over so he could shake hands with people lining the streets, but was told that the schedule didn't permit it, or that 'our Russian security friends' had vetoed it. Lunch was held in a windowless basement to minimise the chances of assassination. Strobe Talbott, Clinton's Russia expert who was travelling with him, says: 'The US consul-general in St. Petersburg, John Evans, saw considerable evidence that Putin was active behind the scenes, particularly in supervising the security for the visiting dignitary'. So much so that on the flight to Moscow Clinton moaned he'd been 'kept in a goddamn cocoon' throughout his stay in St. Petersburg.

Sobchak had advanced the date of the mayoral poll in St Petersburg by a month to 19 May in order to wrong-foot the opposition, hardly a democratic move. His challenger was one of his own deputies, Vladimir Yakovlev, and Putin warned the mayor that it would be a hard campaign. Perhaps influenced by Putin's earlier failure, Sobchak appointed his own wife Lyudmila as campaign manager, despite a warning from Putin that the campaign office might refuse to work with her.

Yakovlev's team fought a dirty campaign, orchestrated by Korzhakov and a cabal of Moscow power brokers, who viewed Sobchak as a possible future rival to Boris Yeltsin. Moreover, Naina Yeltsina, the president's wife, was godmother to one of Yakovlev's grandchildren. And yet Yeltsin, in the third volume of his memoirs, *Midnight Diaries*, expresses horror that Korzhakov and his fellow conspirators had supported 'the gubernatorial candidate Yakovlev' with substantial funds.

YAKOVLEV GOT HIS big television break when Oleg Poptsov sent journalist Andrey Karaulov to St Petersburg to make a short programme about him. Poptsov had been persuaded to do this by Korzhakov, and although Yakovlev put in a poor performance, the television exposure helped him to become known to a wider public.

Sobchak's opponents pointed to the failed stockholding in the city's gambling operations and accused him of corruption by allegedly colluding with the casino operators. Today Putin finds that allegation almost comical, although at the time he was so worried about the tone of the campaign that he slept with a gun beside his pillow. 'Everything we did was so absolutely transparent,' he says. 'You can only argue about whether our actions were correct from an economic point of view. Obviously, the scheme was ineffective and we didn't achieve what we had planned.'

The prevailing air of sleaze did not augur well for Sobchak. His slim chances of remaining leader of St Petersburg (the office was changing from Mayor to Governor) were made even slimmer when thousands of leaflets detailing his alleged misdeeds were dropped on the city from a plane. No one could prove who had organised the airdrop, but Putin pointed the finger at 'dark forces' in Moscow, with General Korzhakov and Oleg Soskovets the chief suspects. Yakovlev's platform was that Sobchak had patronised the arts with city money for his own self-aggrandisement and had spent much of his time getting involved in federal politics, instead of dealing with the serious day-to-day problems of ordinary St Petersburg citizens. Behind the window-dressing, he said, the city was actually going downhill.

At the last possible moment, Putin and the third mayoral deputy, Alexei Kudrin, were placed in charge of Sobchak's campaign. 'We tried to jump into the fray but it was hopeless,' he says. On television Putin described Yakovlev as 'a Judas' for standing against his former benefactor. 'The word seemed fit and I used it,' he adds. The opposition fired back with a broadside of allegations against Putin himself, which were so wide of the mark that he sued Alexander Belayev, chairman of the city legislature, for libel. Belayev admits he lifted allegations that Putin had bought houses abroad from published reports and had no concrete information of his own from any independent source.

Sobchak lost the election by a mere two per cent of the vote and Yakovlev moved into his office at Smolny. Putin turned down an offer to remain as first deputy mayor in the new administration. He came up with the quote of the campaign when he said: 'I would rather be hanged for loyalty than rewarded for treason' – words which truly summed up his ethic.

A few weeks before the presidential elections in June/July, Boris Yeltsin announced plans for a ceasefire in Chechnya, but the conflict had not been resolved and in reality he seemed powerless. He had suffered two more heart attacks the previous year and alternated between drinking bouts and recovering from one or other of a plethora of health problems. Oh, how Russians yearned for a younger, fitter president!

Yet, against the odds, Yeltsin performed an astonishing Lazarus act to inflict a sensational reversal on the Communists. After the first round on 16 June, he led the poll with 35 per cent of the vote to Zyuganov's 32, with General Alexander Lebed, a gravel-voiced former paratrooper, in third place on 15 per cent. Yeltsin had pulled off what William Safire described in the *New York Times* as 'a *shturmovshchina*', a work project rushed to produce early results at the cost of its quality.

Three days later Anatoly Chubais' closest lieutenant Arkady Evstafiev and the advertising mogul Sergei Lisovsky were both arrested by General Korzhakov's agents as they were leaving one of the Kremlin buildings carrying a box filled with $500,000 in cash. Lisovsky ran a talent agency, Media International, which was coordinating campaign performances for Yeltsin, and the money was clearly intended for that purpose, but Korzhakov was convinced that Chubais' people were simply embezzling the money.

Chubais was at the Logovaz Club with Boris Berezovsky and Goose Gusinsky. When he heard of the arrests, Berezovsky summoned Tatyana Dyachenko and Valentin Yumashev – now known jointly as 'Tanya-Valya' – the most effective team in dealing with the unpredictable President. They arrived at the club just after midnight. Shortly afterwards, Berezovsky's bodyguards reported that snipers had taken up positions on the rooftops, while other forces had surrounded the building. Berezovsky went into hysterics, but Chubais remained cool and collected. The presence of Tanya-Valya ensured that the clubhouse would not be attacked; but just in case, Chubais phoned Mikhail Barsukov, the FSB director, at his home and warned him: 'If a single hair falls from their heads, you are finished!'

Yeltsin was asleep when Tatyana phoned him. 'Papa, you have to watch the news,' she said, 'something important is happening.' By then, Evgeny Kiselev, the top announcer on Gusinsky's NTV network, was on his way to the newsroom and Berezovsky had called General Lebed, who agreed to make a statement on air. At 2 a.m. Kiselev informed startled viewers that a coup d'état was taking place in Moscow in an attempt to destabilise the government and induce a state of emergency. As proof he revealed that two of Yeltsin's campaign workers had been arrested by secret service agents. Then General Lebed came on the screen and declared that any attempted coup 'would be crushed mercilessly'. The report was taped and repeated 15 minutes later on Berezovsky's ORT network.

Yeltsin watched the programme with mounting fury and confusion. He was confused because he simply had no idea how to handle the situation; after all, the two adversaries (Chubais and Korzhakov) were supposed to be his men. Fury because this was dangerously close to the election. He is reputed to have made one phone call, presumably to Korzhakov, and then retired to his bed. At 4 a.m. Arkady Evstafiev and Sergei Lisovsky were released from custody. Later that morning, Chubais was summoned to the President's office. 'I will demand that he fire Korzhakov and Soskovets,' he told Berezovsky. 'Barsukov should go too,' Berezovsky advised, according to his confidant Alex Goldfarb. 'If one of them stays, sooner or later it will start all over again.' To ensure that Yeltsin did not change his mind, Berezovsky stationed a TV crew outside the Kremlin.

At 9 a.m. Yeltsin fired Korzhakov, Barsukov and Soskovets in a nationally televised broadcast. His decisive action did wonders for his standing in the polls. With his former rival General Lebed now enthusiastically endorsing his re-election, he emerged victorious[*] in the second round on 3 July, with an impressive 54 per cent of the vote, compared to Zyuganov's 40 per cent. Berezovsky's brilliant handling of

---

[*] Rumours circulating at the time suggested that Zyuganov had really won and Mikhail Poltoranin, the former deputy prime minister, said he believed that Zyuganov had given the election to Yeltsin.

'the coup that never was' placed him even closer to the centre of the Family.

Putin had worked on Yeltsin's campaign in St Petersburg, but he was marking time at Smolny while looking around for a full-time job when a third misfortune struck his family like a bolt from the blue. He had no income, but had managed to accumulate savings of $5,000, which he kept in a briefcase at the dacha he had been building for six years, mostly with his own hands, 100 kilometres outside St Petersburg. The Putins had lived there for about six weeks, sewing curtains, cleaning up the building debris and arranging the furniture, when in August 1996 they invited Marina and her husband and daughter to spend the day with them. The visitors arrived late and as evening approached Lyudmila, who had only just recovered from her physical injuries, suggested they stay the night.

Putin fired up the brand new *banya* on the first floor of the brick-and-wood building, and he and Marina's husband had a sauna and then went for a swim in a nearby river. They were relaxing in the lounge next to the sauna when they heard a crack and saw smoke and flames shoot out of the wooden *banya*. Putin says he shouted 'in my loudest and most commanding voice' for everybody to get out of the house. The sauna cabin was ablaze.

Katya was having a meal in the kitchen and, possibly conditioned by the car crash, dropped her spoon on the table and ran out of the house without a second thought. Putin dashed up to the second floor where he found Masha cowering in fear. He took the little girl by the hand and led her out on to the balcony. Then he tore the sheets off the bed, knotted them together, tied them to the balcony railing and told Masha to climb down, but she was paralysed with fear. Putin admits he threatened her. 'I'm going to pick you up and throw you off here like a puppy,' he said. 'Don't you understand that the house is about to burn down?' His words made no difference, so he picked up his daughter and dropped her down to Lyudmila and Marina, who caught her in their arms.

Putin suddenly remembered the cash in his briefcase. He dived back into the room and started searching for it. By this time smoke was

ON A VISIT to the Siberian republic of Tuva, Putin took off his valuable Patek Phillipe Perpetual Calendar watch and gave it to the small son of a local shepherd.

billowing up the stairs and blotting out the light. He groped around blindly with his hand, but couldn't locate the case. The heat became too intense to remain any longer, so he retreated on to the balcony and, as flames licked around him, clambered over the railing, grabbing the sheets as he descended. The future president was stark naked and as he tried to wrap a sheet around himself, it caught the wind like a sail. Neighbours who had gathered in the garden watched his descent with great interest.

The house was blazing fiercely when the fire brigade finally arrived. Their tender quickly ran out of water and although the dacha was situated beside a lake, their hose wasn't long enough to reach it. The dacha burned to the ground, destroying almost all of the Putins' possessions, including Masha and Katya's toys and Barbie dolls. Lyudmila was philosophical. Having been close to death three years earlier, she realised that houses, money and other material things were not what mattered. The only thing that Putin retrieved from the ashes was his little aluminium cross, which had been around his neck when he was baptised at the Cathedral of the Transfiguration, and which he had taken to Israel on a 1993 visit to have it blessed at the Holy Sepulchre.

Fire inspectors concluded that the builders hadn't installed the sauna stove correctly and that burning coals had fallen onto the wooden floor. As the builders were culpable, they completely rebuilt the dacha for the Putins – minus the sauna.

While the cottage was being restored the family lived in their apartment on Vasilievsky Island and Putin entered the nearby St Petersburg Mining Institute to complete his 218-page dissertation on 'The Strategic Planning of Regional Resources during the Formation of a Market Economy', in which he argued that the state should control the exploitation of raw materials irrespective of the deposits' ownership. But by the time the thesis was accepted on 27 June 1997, making him a Candidate of Economic Sciences, Putin was already working inside the Kremlin.

THE GEORGIAN TYCOON Badri Patarkatsishvili had moved to Moscow in 1993 to run Boris Berezovsky's lucrative Logovaz car dealership while hunting for even more profitable business. Patarkatsishvili subsequently claimed that it was he who found Putin a job on Yeltsin's staff through his friend Pavel Borodin, but this was not the case; indeed, by this point Putin had no need of any help from Patarkatsishvili, for Borodin was already an ally.

After Yakovlev's victory, Putin went off to Moscow. Yakovlev, knowing Putin's qualities as a businessman, had implored him to stay, but Putin rejected the offer. In the capital he met Nikolai Yegorov, head of the President's administration, who offered him a job as one of his deputies. Putin accepted but, before his appointment could be confirmed, Yegorov lost his job. His replacement, Anatoly Chubais, did not like the idea of a man with a KGB past appearing at his side, particularly one who had a reputation as a 'hitman' for Sobchak.

Next Putin met Pavel Borodin, Yeltsin's administration manager.

Realising what was going on and 'mindful of what a caring and hard-working person he had proved to be in St. Petersburg,' Borodin recalls, 'I said: "Vladimir Vladimirovich, how would you like to work for me as deputy for international economic relations?"' Although he needed a job, Putin's reply was cautiously non-committal: 'Well I'm not really the sort of man who would be any good at such work, I would prefer to work in the President's administration...'

'So I went to Boris Yeltsin,' explains Borodin, 'and I asked him: "Can you take this lad, who's a really great guy, into the administration?" At once Yeltsin replied: "Yes!" He rang the head of the Presidential office and arranged for an order to be drawn up. But the next day Yeltsin was ill and remained so for two weeks, while his head of administration Chubais came into the picture. Chubais was an important man to Yeltsin, having pushed through Potanin's infamous loans-for-shares scheme, which was to secure his re-election as president that year.

'Seeing the papers with Putin's name on them he simply tore them up before my eyes,' continues Borodin. 'Then I again asked Putin to become my deputy, and took the papers to Yeltsin myself for signature.' A deal was struck.

Initially Lyudmila Putin was reluctant to leave St Petersburg, but she was delighted when she saw the six-room state dacha in the Arkhangelsky district to the west of the capital which went with her husband's new job; in any case, she was to come to love 'noisy Moscow' and its crowded streets.

IN SEPTEMBER 1996 Yeltsin approved the second series of auctions for the 12 state-owned enterprises which had been offered to the oligarchs as collateral for their loans. The inherent crookedness of the scheme meant that the 'reformers', who had tried to build Western-style capitalism, had ended up selling the family silver to a small group of slick operators in return for peanuts.

Anatoly Chubais admits that his privatisation schemes were reckless. In four years, he flogged tens of thousands of enterprises to the oligarchs and their set, and shifted more than half of Russia's workforce into the private sector. 'Every enterprise ripped out of the state and transferred to the hands of a private owner was a way of destroying Communism in Russia,' he told David Hoffman. 'And at that stage, it didn't matter at all to whom these enterprises went, who was getting the property. It was absolutely unimportant whether that person was ready for it.'

Chubais and four close colleagues were thrown out of office in 1997 for accepting a total of $100,000 as publisher's advances – for a book that had not been written – from a firm controlled by Potanin's Onexim Bank group. The amount of money was minuscule by Russian standards, but by accepting it they had abandoned the moral high ground and looked not unlike the controversial characters they had enriched.

Khodorkovsky (in the view of many) rapidly came to represent the unacceptable face of capitalism. His arrogant methods in tightening his grip on Yukos became legendary among foreigners. Bob Dudley, a Mississippi-born oilman who later headed BP's abrasive partnership with Mikhail Fridman's TNK, found himself in a battle royal with Khodorkovsky after he gained control of Yukos.

Dudley first came to Moscow in 1994 as the executive in charge of developing the Amoco Corporation's upstream and downstream businesses. It wasn't long before he learned about gangster capitalism first-hand. Back in 1993 Amoco had won a tender to develop the massive Priobskoye field in Western Siberia in a 50/50 joint venture with Yukos. But after four years – by which time Amoco had invested $300 million in the desolate stretch of marsh and Arctic forest, which was about to produce its first oil – Yukos' new owner Khodorkovsky refused to recognise the partnership and asserted his right to develop the field independently.

Bob Dudley met with the young billionaire to clear things up, and produced Amoco's signed contract. Khodorkovsky smirked and shook his head. Amoco would have to renegotiate the deal with him, he said, and for a smaller percentage of the field. Negotiations broke down and Bob Dudley was pulled out of Russia. After a brief revival of the talks, Amoco officially abandoned Priobskoye in August 1998. As we shall see, Yukos' foreign shareholders were treated in an even more cavalier manner.

9

Rising Tsar

BY THE TIME Vladimir Putin started work in the presidential administration building at No. 4 Old Square in the autumn of 1996, Moscow's brave new world was being assailed by warring politicians, mafia-style gangsters, black marketeers and the new breed of super-rich tycoon, the oligarchs, who – as we have seen – had risen to the starry heights through *perestroika* and the mendicant state of Boris Yeltsin's presidency.

Putin was in charge of the legal division of the directorate of presidential affairs, whose task was to defend the Kremlin's ownership of important buildings against the sticky fingers of other ministries, and to manage Russia's huge portfolio of overseas properties, numbering some 715 sites in 78 countries. The directorate published no accounts and was not answerable to parliament, despite the fact that its assets were worth billions of dollars and its annual revenue from hotels, airlines and car fleets at this time amounted to $2.5 billion.

Putin's boss Pavel Borodin had been discovered by Yeltsin in the remote Siberian city of Yakutsk, where he was the mayor. Recognising a kindred spirit (and potential drinking partner), he brought him to Moscow in 1993. Dressed in well-cut suits, with cufflinks, watch and pen, and handing out engraved, gold-rimmed business cards, Borodin lived extremely well on his official salary of $1,000 a month plus perks. To keep in touch with his empire, there was a bank of nine telephones, including hotlines to the president, prime minister and the security services on a special desk in his office, with a further dozen phones in an anteroom.

The directorate was also involved in the renovation and restoration of a couple of Kremlin buildings, including the Great Kremlin Palace, a project that would take a hefty $488 million chunk out of the national budget and would subsequently link Borodin to allegations that the Kremlin's property empire was being used as a slush fund.

'Putin worked for me for nine months during which he travelled widely,' Borodin explains. 'He proved himself a really good worker. I am not saying this because of the lofty positions he went on to reach, but because I liked and admired him a lot then and still do. You can see how highly professional he is in the way he conducts international relations.'

Putin's rise to the top was defined as much by hard work as by opportunity. Popular legend has it that he was a nobody who emerged from the shadows to become prime minister; in fact, he was a well-travelled lawyer who spoke three languages and was used to dealing with politicians as a senior member of the *apparat* (the country's top bureaucracy). On 26 March 1997 he was promoted to Alexei Kudrin's old post as head of the main control directorate (GKU), with a brief to audit the state agencies where kickbacks of one kind or another were an accepted custom.

Putin's work inevitably brought him into contact with Boris Yeltsin and members of the Family. He barely needed his legal training to recognise the prevailing air of corruption that hung over the Kremlin, or to notice that among those who had the President's ear were Boris Berezovsky and his sidekick Roman Abramovich. Indeed, Berezovsky had replaced Alexander Korzhakov as Yeltsin's chief courtier. But the person whose judgment mattered most was undoubtedly his daughter Tatyana. 'A grimace of dislike on her face was enough to get someone fired,' Lilia Shevtsova writes in *Putin's Russia*, 'while an approving smile could speed someone else up the ladder of success.'

There were encouraging signs that the president might serve his full second term. His health had improved markedly following multiple bypass surgery at the Moscow Cardiological Centre the previous November to circumvent five clogged arteries supplying blood to his heart. During the seven-hour operation, he had transferred his formal powers to Prime Minister Chernomyrdin, including the black attaché case carrying codes to activate nuclear weapons. After coming out of the anaesthetic, he had quickly reclaimed them. Berezovsky and Abramovich knew that Yeltsin had to find a successor before he stepped down in 2000, someone who would be acceptable to Parliament, yet pose no threat to himself. It would be very much in their long-term interests if they could suggest the successful candidate.

In his new role at the GKU Putin set up an analytical group which uncovered misconduct by many state officials. Putin also prepared a report on the mismanagement of Borodin's directorate, which almost precipitated another heart attack when Yeltsin read it. His report was quietly shelved. Yeltsin did not like washing dirty linen in public.

With unconscious irony, Yeltsin later commented that Putin's reports while he was with the GKU were 'a model of clarity'. He was also impressed by his businesslike manner and 'lightning reactions' to interjections. 'Putin tried to exclude any sort of personal element from our contact,' he wrote in *Midnight Diaries* (which was compiled from notes made during his second term of office while suffering from insomnia). 'And precisely because of that, I wanted to talk to him more.'

Putin's art of detachment served him well in his work. At home, he was much more open about his feelings and he made no secret of his pride in his two beautiful daughters. His relationship with his wife was turbulent at times and Lyudmila wasn't afraid to speak out about their differences. In a rare move of independence she spent four days in Hamburg with Irene Pietsch, the friend she had met in 1995 when Vladimir was on an official visit to St Petersburg's sister city. Pietsch recalls that Lyudmila was angry with her husband for refusing her permission to use a credit card. 'That's silly. I will never be like Raisa Gorbacheva,' said the future First Lady.

The two women developed a close friendship and Lyudmila shared intimate secrets in a series of personal emails and letters – never suspecting that Pietsch would one day profit from their publication. According to Pietsch, Lyudmila said the reason Vladimir was the right man for her was because he didn't drink or beat her up. But it has been pointed out on Lyudmila's behalf that she was merely quoting a Russian saying that a good man doesn't do such things – not singling out her husband for such narrow attributes. Pietsch also made much of Lyudmila's apparent interest in astrology, saying that Putin bracketed it with occultism and paganism 'and shushed her whenever she started talking about the zodiac'. This gave a distorted view to the mild interest Mrs Putin – a strict Orthodox Christian – has in, say, reading her horoscope in the daily newspaper.

AGAIN ACCORDING TO Pietsch, Lyudmila admitted in her correspondence that she found some of her husband's habits annoying. 'He spends too much time with his friends in the evenings,' she is said to have written, 'and when he brings them home I have to serve them drinks with gherkins and fish.' Bizarrely, she also revealed that her husband 'always goes to Finland when he has something important to say – he doesn't think there is anywhere in Russia where you can speak without being overheard'.

On another occasion Pietsch says Lyudmila confided in her: 'It will happen that I try very hard and do something particularly well and Volodya praises me for it, but then I'm certain to be at fault some time later and my good deeds don't count any more and I can be rehabilitated only by working on my mistakes. That hurts me.'

Pietsch also claims that when she spent a week with the Putin family at their dacha at Arkhangelskoe in 1997 – during which time Lyudmila played the good wife, cooking home-made soup in the kitchen while Vladimir, clad in pants and a pullover, was a charming host – Lyudmila joked to her guest: 'Unfortunately, he's a vampire'.

Clearly never intending to be invited back into the Putin home, Pietsch publicly describes the Prime Minister's blue-green eyes as 'two hungry, lurking predators'. Although he probably loathed his indiscreet guest, Putin accepted Pietsch as his wife's friend and contented himself with a little leg-pulling, telling her with a straight face that she would deserve a monument if she could put up with his wife for three weeks.

Pietsch's disclosures brought unwanted media attention to Mrs Putin. But when he was subsequently asked by a journalist about his wife's indiscretions, he replied: 'The citizens of Russia elected me, not my wife, as the president. I am very grateful to her; she has a difficult cross to bear.'

BACK IN ST. PETERSBURG the campaign against Putin's friend and political mentor Anatoly Sobchak had intensified. 'At that time there was a conflict between two major groups in the Kremlin,' says Galina Starovoitova's aide Ruslan Linkov, a member of the local Democratic Russia party. 'Korzhakov and Soskovets were on one side, and Chubais was on the other. Both of them were fighting for access to Yeltsin, and St Petersburg appeared to be a part of the fight.'

Korzhakov might have been sacked as Yeltsin's security chief, but he continued to wield power in the Interior Ministry and through his friends in the FSB. He also held sway over the prosecutor-general, Yuri Skuratov, which allowed him to continue his vendetta against his political rival. 'They wanted to get a lot of *kompromat* [compromising material] on Sobchak,' Yeltsin writes in *Midnight Diaries,* 'to drag him into a serious corruption case.'

According to Yeltsin the two conspirators pursued Sobchak with further allegations of corruption, while Sobchak accused Korzhakov of fabricating evidence against him. In an interview with the *St Petersburg Times*, he said his phones were being tapped and that he was being tailed – a fact later confirmed by Yeltsin in his memoirs. Then, during an interrogation in November 1997, Sobchak was taken ill, apparently having suffered a heart attack. On 7 November he was smuggled out of the country in a private charter plane to Finland and from there to France, supposedly to seek medical treatment.

Until his death in 2007 Yeltsin maintained that Putin had facilitated the escape of his great friend and mentor, which cost some $10,000. 'When I learned what Putin had done, I felt great respect and gratitude towards him,' he wrote. Putin has always denied having anything to do with Sobchak's escape and claims the former mayor went through the

WHILE BEING shown around the Ussuri Game Reserve in Russia's Far East corner
by Moscow Zoo's chief vet, Mikhail Shenetsky, Putin went in search of Siberian
tigers, but his gun fired only tranquiliser darts.

normal customs and passport procedures at the border like any other
law-abiding citizen. 'They hounded the poor guy all over Europe,' he
says. 'I was absolutely convinced that he was a decent person – 100 per
cent decent – because I had dealt with him for many years. He is a decent
man with a flawless reputation.'

Putin stayed with the GKU for a little over a year and was relieved
when, on 25 May 1998, he received another promotion – this time to
First Deputy Chief of Presidential Staff, responsible for relations with
the regions. The move came just in time: while he recognised that his
work at the GKU was important, Putin found it uninteresting and had
toyed with the idea of resigning in order to open his own legal practice.
His new boss was Yelstin's favoured son, Valentin Yumashev, who was
chairman of the Presidential Executive Office.

In his new role Putin chaired a commission drafting treaties on the
division of responsibilities between central government and the 89
constituent parts of the federation. In conversations with regional

PUTIN conducted a judo session at the Top Athletic School during a visit to
St Petersburg in December 2010, and found time to sign an autograph for a
young admirer.

governors, he developed his idea of creating a 'new federalism' after
learning that the vertical chain of government had been destroyed during
the break-up of the old Soviet system and that it would need to be
restored in some new way if Russia was to be governed effectively.

Putin had been in that 'most interesting' job for just three months
when he received the biggest shock of his life. On 25 July 1998 he was
asked to meet the new prime minister, Sergei Kiriyenko, at the airport.
Kiriyenko, who had replaced Chernomyrdin in March, was returning from
a visit to see Yeltsin, who was holidaying in the Karelia region on the Gulf

of Finland. At the airport Kiriyenko, a self-assured 37-year-old, greeted him with the words 'Hi, Volodya! Congratulations!' Putin was taken aback. 'What for?' he asked. 'You have been appointed Director of the FSB.'

Putin had been given no hint that he was even being considered for this forbidding office. 'The President simply signed a decree,' he says. 'I can't say that I was overjoyed. I didn't want to step into the same river twice.' He was now 46 years old and had set his heart on a career in regional reform. He rang Lyudmila, who was on holiday at a resort on the Baltic Sea. Conscious that such calls were monitored or could be intercepted, he told her that he had 'returned to the place where I began'. Lyudmila thought he was saying he had been demoted to being Borodin's deputy once more, but when she finally got the point she was devastated. It meant re-entering 'the closed life' which they had abandoned in St Petersburg after returning from Dresden.

The first thing that had to go was her friendship with Irene Pietsch (an act which Pietsch repaid by betraying her confidences). According to Pietsch, Lyudmila complained in a final telephone call to her: 'It's terrible; we won't be allowed to contact each other again. This awful isolation – no more travelling wherever we want to go, no longer able to say whatever we want. I had only just begun to live.'

Yeltsin recalls in *Midnight Diaries* that he had offered Putin the rank of general, but Putin insisted he return to his old agency as a civilian, just as his hero Yuri Andropov had done when he took over the KGB in 1967. Yeltsin claims to have noticed Putin in 1997 and, once again, it was Putin's eyes that had made such an impression: 'Putin has very interesting eyes,' he says. 'They seem to say more than his words.' He goes on to praise Putin's intelligence and democratic instincts, his good ideas and impressive military bearing. Yeltsin 'had the feeling that this man, young by my standards, was absolutely ready for everything in life, and could respond to any challenge clearly and distinctly'.

More important than Yeltsin's feelings was the fact that Tatyana had been impressed by the cool way Putin got on with his work while offering no opinions about what was going on around him. The power of Tanya-Valya had become an established fact of life in the Kremlin, while their antics outside the red-brick walls were a national scandal. They drove around Moscow in armoured Mercedes, surrounded by bodyguards and fawned over by flunkeys. Yeltsin's loyal old guard were replaced by Tatyana's nominees; these guys took over government institutions and were handed huge chunks of state property. Anyone perceived to be an opponent could find themselves out in the cold.

The inner circle consisted of Valentin Yumashev, Alexander Voloshin, Boris Berezovsky and Roman Abramovich, with three politicians, Victor Aksenenko, Viktor Kalyuzhny, and Vladimir Rushailo in the outer circle. It was noticeable that Abramovich had become indispensable as the Family's treasurer. He had even displaced his mentor Berezovsky in Tatyana's affections. Berezovsky had political ambitions and saw himself as a kingmaker. He talked too much, whereas Abramovich said nothing.

Yeltsin's biggest headache was that the Russian economy had been hit by another financial tsunami following a sudden plunge in world oil prices to just $8.50 a barrel. The crisis had begun on 27 May 1998 – Black Tuesday – when share prices plummeted more than 14 per cent, bringing the stock market slide to 40 per cent since the start of the month. Interest rates, which had fallen from 42 per cent in January to 30 per cent, were suddenly raised to 150 per cent. The government owed more than $140 billion in hard currency and $60 billion in domestically traded rouble debts, short-term state bonds.

Yeltsin summoned Anatoly Chubais (who, in a typically eccentric move, he had sacked from the Cabinet just two months earlier) to the Kremlin and asked him to go, cap in hand, to Washington. Chubais returned with a promise of financial help from President Clinton 'to promote stability, structural reforms and growth in Russia'. No one, however, had any confidence in Kiriyenko's ability to manage the situation and it was the oligarchs who imposed Chubais – against Yeltsin's wishes – as the head of the government's team in crucial talks with the IMF. The $10 billion the international bankers were offering was not enough; Russia needed $35 billion.

On his next visit to the United States Chubais was successful in persuading the IMF to raise its loan to $22.6 billion over two years. Before the end of July a down-payment of $4.8 billion had secured matters until October at least – or so they thought. Unfortunately, foreign investors decided this was the moment to get out and they withdrew so much money that by the end of August the Russian banks were not so much squeezed as crushed.

There were too many variables in the Russian economy and one of the most unpredictable was the 65-year-old President's health. With striking miners camping out in the city and people going hungry, Moscow Mayor Luzhkov threw down the gauntlet with a statement that if Yeltsin 'cannot work and fulfil his duties, then it is necessary to find the will and courage to say so'. The attack was acutely wounding – Yeltsin had hand-picked Luzhkov for political advancement during *perestroika* and they had campaigned together as recently as 1996.

As he walked into the notorious grey-stone and yellow-brick Lubyanka building that housed the FSB headquarters, Putin says he felt as though he had been plugged into an electric socket. One of his main priorities would be to inflict a series of cost-cutting measures on the service, and that would mean making enemies. He reported to the outgoing director Nikolai Kovalev, who opened his safe with the words: 'Here's my secret notebook. And here's my ammunition'. Kovalev had been keen to root out corruption in banks and businesses, but had failed to see that such corruption percolated right to the top of the Kremlin. Putin's natural inclination might have been to carry on Kovalev's work, but he knew he had been given the job (and with it the President's ear) to stop the FSB from interfering in the lives of the Family. If the KGB had taught him nothing else, he had learned how to obey orders.

Putin quickly discovered that the agency might have changed its name, but it had retained its traditional paranoia in what he describes as 'a constant state of tension'. 'They were always checking up on you,' he says. 'It might not happen very often, but it wasn't very pleasant.' There were also petty restrictions, such as expecting FSB officers to take their meals in one of the Lyubanka's canteens because the common view was that 'only black marketeers and prostitutes dined in restaurants'.

Nor was he welcomed with open arms: Putin had demonstrated himself to be too close to Sobchak for the liking of many of his fellow officers, and had in fact turned his back on the KGB to take a job at City Hall, where he had declined an approach to spy on the mayor. Putin's solution to the problem was one that he would follow from now on: lacking support among the existing hierarchy, he brought in his own team from the security services in St Petersburg, notably his friends Victor Cherkasov, Sergei Ivanov and Nikolai Patrushev, all of whom he had known either from Leningrad State University or from his early days in the KGB. And as a mission statement, he restored a plaque to Yuri Andropov which had been removed from the entrance hall.

As the nation teetered on the edge of bankruptcy, Kiriyenko was forced to announce that the Government would allow the Russian currency to slide to 9.1 roubles to the dollar, a fall of more than 50 per cent, which drastically reduced imports and shattered public confidence. Yeltsin sacked Kiriyenko and his entire cabinet soon afterwards, but this did nothing to ease matters. Apparently Putin, defying the risk of associating with black marketeers and prostitutes, was overheard in an Italian restaurant blaming Alan Greenspan, chairman of the Federal Reserve, for Russia's plight. Hundreds of thousands were losing their jobs, people's savings were becoming worthless and the shops had little or nothing to sell.

Yeltsin wanted to replace Kiriyenko with his faithful old war horse Viktor Chernomyrdin – a man well-known for Yogi-Bear-like malapropisms, including 'the situation is utterly unprecedented—the same old story all over again!' and 'I'd better not talk, or else I'm going to say something...' – but his appointment was blocked by the Duma. Yevgeny Primakov, former head of the SVR (the foreign intelligence service), who had served as foreign minister since January 1996, took over the post in September as a compromise figure acceptable to the majority of deputies. Primakov had turned down Yeltsin's offer, but, as he later disclosed in his memoirs *Years in Big-Time Politics*, on leaving Yeltsin's office he had run into Tanya-Valya, who persuaded him to accept. 'For a moment, reason took a back seat,' he wrote, 'and feelings won out.' As we will see, Primakov was far too independent and inquisitive for his own good and in less than a year he would be deposed.

ON 20 NOVEMBER Putin heard that Galina Starovoitova had been assassinated in St. Petersburg. Dr Starovoitova and her aide Ruslan Linkov were attacked by two men on the staircase of her apartment building. The 52-year-old democrat was shot three times in the head and died on the spot. Linkov was also shot in the head but recovered. Dropping their guns on the stairs, the killers fled in a waiting car.

Dr Starovoitova was a controversial figure, who had made many enemies. On frequent visits to the West she warned that Russia's reformers were under attack by powerful groups 'striving to restore the old economic and political system', which sought to exploit nostalgia for Communist times. At one point, Yeltsin had made her his adviser on ethnic minorities. They had fallen out over Chechnya in 1994, but had later been reconciled.

The problem for her enemies was that Starovoitova – a doctor of psychology – could not be bought. She was planning to present to the Duma evidence of corruption by Communist members, and had just announced that she would run for the governorship against Yeltsin's old adversary Vladimir Zhirinovsky, the nationalist leader she accused of trying to build 'a criminal dictatorship', when she was killed. One of her favourite targets was the Russian army. 'Our military is not accountable to civil society and does not answer even to the President,' she chided. Yeltsin suggested she should run the defence ministry, but she joked that Russia was not ready for a defence minister in a skirt.

On hearing the news of her assassination, Yeltsin described his friend as 'my closest comrade-in-arms'. He sent his interior minister Sergei Stepashin, a veteran of Russia's security establishment, to St Petersburg to find her killers. The main suspects were thought to be hitmen hired by the GRU, the foreign military directorate of Russia's armed forces. The murder investigation took place under the personal direction of Stepashin (a former FSB boss and future Prime Minister). In June 2005 two hitmen, Yuri Kolchin and Vitali Akishin, were convicted of murder and sentenced to 20 and 23 years in prison, respectively. A few other suspects are still wanted in the investigation into Starovoitova's death, which re-opened in 2009.

Meanwhile, Putin had launched the eighth reorganisation of the FSB in as many years as part of an economy drive. He abolished two departments (economic counter-intelligence and defence of strategic sites) and dismissed about 40 lieutenant-generals and major-generals and about a third of the central staff, reducing it from 6,000 to 4,000. As the axe had fallen mainly on those approaching or beyond pensionable age, it was argued that the service had lost its most experienced officers, and indeed Putin's intention had been to weed out the ones with the strongest links to the old Soviet system.

This was a difficult time for him and his task was made no easier by the death of his adored mother Maria at the end of 1998 after a long fight with cancer. He took leave to be at her bedside for her final days. Though he closed her eyes on her deathbed, in typical Putin style he did not show much emotion. If he wept, he did it in private. Meanwhile, his efforts had not gone unnoticed at the Kremlin. Yeltsin said later he appreciated Putin's sense of decency, in ensuring that officers dismissed from the FSB had a 'soft landing', a new job or a generous pension. At the time, it is doubtful that Yeltsin was too well-informed about Putin's cost-cutting efforts or his humanitarianism, but he was about to get to know him very well. Very well indeed.

AT A CABINET MEETING on 28 January 1999 Primakov pledged war against the speculators and black marketeers who he believed were guilty of economic crimes against the state. Boris Berezovsky was top of his list. Soon afterwards prosecutors and a squad of armed men in black masks raided Berezovsky's companies in Moscow, the Sibneft headquarters and Aeroflot in search of incriminating documents. They left the Sibneft building with several boxes of materials. Berezovsky discovered to his fury that the Prime Minister had personally ordered the raids.

At the same time, Yuri Skuratov began investigating Pavel Borodin over allegations that he had taken massive bribes from a Swiss engineering company called Mabatex, which had carried out multi-million dollar restoration work in the Kremlin. Skuratov, the son of a police officer, had begun his career as a law professor in Yeltsin's home province. He had supported Yeltsin as the local Communist Party boss and later as a leader of democratic reform. In 1989, he joined the staff of the law department of the Communist Party's Central Committee in Moscow. By 1991 he was a member of Yeltsin's team as adviser to the KGB and later drafted the 1993 Constitution with Anatoly Sobchak, another of his targets.

When he was named Chief Prosecutor in October 1995, the opposition in the Duma welcomed him as someone who was politically neutral. He was provided with a dacha on the outskirts of Moscow by Borodin's property directorate and drove around in an armoured Mercedes. By 1999, however, the general public knew only too well that Skuratov, despite his bravado and broad powers, had failed to prosecute any major figures involved in corruption or solve any of the contract killings of politicians and other prominent citizens.

Skuratov claimed in an interview with the *New York Times* that he had broken with the Yeltsin regime during the 1996 elections, when he was investigating the case against Lisovsky and Yestafyev. He had quickly

Putin and Olympic medalist Svetlana Gladysheva visit a ski resort in Sochi.

learned that Kremlin denials were false, while top government aides pressed him to drop the case. Now he claimed to have documentary proof from the Mabetex offices at Lugano, Switzerland, that the company had provided credit cards to Yeltsin and his two daughters, Tatyana Dyachenko and Yelena Okulova. These documents also indicated that Mabetex had footed the bill for purchases made on those cards amounting to tens of thousands of dollars.

The case was just building up a head of steam when it emerged that Skuratov was open to blackmail. A man resembling him had been filmed cavorting with two prostitutes in a sauna while apparently high on stimulants. The film was first shown on RTR state television on 16 March. It caused a sensation, with stills taken from the video published in most Russian newspapers. Skuratov's identity was never proven, and he claimed it was a case of mistaken identity and his enemies in the Kremlin were out to destroy his reputation. Although nobody knew for sure who had made the film – nor indeed who it really featured – it bore all the hallmarks of an FSB honey-trap. Then Putin stepped forward to confirm that the moon-faced naked man in the film was indeed the Prosecutor General.

On the same day as the raids against Sibneft, legend has it that Yeltsin summoned Skuratov to his dacha in Gorky-9 where, to his surprise, he found Putin at the President's side. In front of Putin, Yeltsin 'suggested' Skuratov write his letter of resignation there and then. The prosecutor had little choice. Yeltsin laughed as he held out the document and shook Putin's hand to pile on the humiliation.

Putin's version of the story differs in important respects. He says there were four people at the meeting: Yeltsin, Skuratov, Primakov and himself. Yeltsin had put the videotape and copies of the photographs on the table and said, 'I don't think that you should work as prosecutor any longer.' Primakov agreed. 'Yes, Yuri Ilyich, I think that you had better write a letter of resignation.' Skuratov thought it over, then took out a piece of paper and wrote out his resignation.

But Skuratov did not give up. His most powerful ally was Yeltsin's rival, Yuri Luzhkov. As a regional leader he was a member of the Federation Council, the upper house of the Russian Parliament, responsible for overseeing the prosecutor's operations. The council voted to support Skuratov, who then withdrew his resignation and released details of his half-finished investigation into the Kremlin restoration contracts. Luzhkov fanned the flames as part of his own aggressive political agenda and demanded that the prosecutor be allowed to complete his work.

On 24 March Yevgeny Primakov was flying to Washington for an official visit when he heard that NATO had started to bomb Yugoslavia. Primakov ordered the plane to turn around over the Atlantic and return to Moscow. This decision was dubbed 'Primakov's loop' by the Russian media and it was wildly popular with the public. In fact, Primakov had become too popular, too ambitious and too dangerous for his own good. Such was the paranoia in the Kremlin that Yeltsin believed the Prime Minister was plotting with one of his closest aides, General Nikolai Bordyuzhey, to overthrow him.

Bordyuzhey's rise had been meteoric and his fall was equally spectacular. The former KGB officer had been chief of the Federal Border Service when on 14 September 1998 he was appointed head of the all-powerful Security Council. Four months later, he also became Yeltsin's chief of staff, making him one of the most powerful men in Russia. Bordyuzhey lost both posts in quick succession. On 19 March the bearded economist Alexander Voloshin, one of Berezovsky's former business partners and a man singularly suited to this Byzantine world, replaced him at the Kremlin, and a few days later Putin took over the chair of the Security Council.

Nevertheless, Primakov continued to turn the screw on Berezovsky. On 5 April a warrant for his arrest was issued by the deputy prosecutor Nikolai Volkov, accusing him of misusing Aeroflot's revenue. Berezovsky had never owned any Aeroflot shares, but he had access to millions of dollars in hard currency from the airline's foreign ticket sales. Berezovsky was in Paris at the time and got the warrant quashed with a phone call to his allies in the Kremlin. 'Primakov intended to put me in prison,' Berezovsky says. 'It was my wife's birthday [and] quite unexpectedly, Putin came to the party. He came and said, "I don't care in the least what

Primakov will think of me. I feel that this is right at this moment".'

Putin either knew or guessed that he was on safe ground. On 12 May Yeltsin sacked Primakov. Three days later the Duma attempted to impeach the President, but its efforts ended in humiliating defeat when the Kremlin, or its corporate allies, allegedly paid $30,000 for each of the votes to support him. The strain was too much for Yeltsin's fragile health. He was too sick to see Jose Maria Aznar, Spain's prime minister, providing Luzhkov with fresh ammunition to question his fitness for office. Russia, he declared, was not being run by Yeltsin but by a 'regime' in the Kremlin that included Berezovsky, his confederate Alexander Voloshin and Tanya-Valya.

Yeltsin, however, recovered sufficiently to nominate Sergei Stepashin (who had previously been his interior minister) as Prime Minister. There was no further opposition from the Duma and the appointment was confirmed by 301 votes to 55. The new premier promised to crack down on gangster capitalism, impose higher taxes on alcohol and fuel, and introduce a more efficient system of tax collection. With Chubais' support (backed by the Interior Ministry's 180,000 troops), he pledged to enact the laws demanded by the IMF as the price for its loan of $4.8 billion that would save Russia from defaulting on its foreign debts.

Mikhail Khodorkovsky, however, took the opportunity to default on a $236 million debt to a consortium of western banks and to shake off a number of minority investors in order to gain total control of Yukos. 'If a man is not an oligarch,' he told one journalist, 'there is something wrong with him. Everyone had the same starting conditions; everyone could have done it. If a man didn't do it, it means there's something wrong with him.' In early 1998, he had purchased another oil company, Tomskneft, and started to extract oil from its rich fields instead of developing Yukos' own deposits. One of Tomskneft's investors was Kenneth Dart, an American who owned 13 per cent of the stock. He used his vote to block Khodorkovsky's plans to consolidate the company into Yukos in the hope of being bought out with a significant profit. Khodorkovsky, however, reacted by diluting the value of Dart's shares through a series of slick financial moves until they were virtually worthless. Dart was heir to the Styrofoam coffee cup fortune and had plenty of money behind him. He mounted an expensive public relations campaign to portray the Russian as a thief in the world's media. The matter was settled by a secret deal, in which Khodorkovsky acquired Dart's shares, but it did nothing to restore his reputation.

Meanwhile, Putin had quietly been making his mark. On 11 June he attended a tense meeting with an American delegation to discuss the growing crisis in Kosovo. He impressed Strobe Talbott, the US Deputy Secretary of State 'by his ability to convey self-control and confidence in a low-key, soft-spoken manner'. According to Talbott, Putin 'radiated executive competence, an ability to get things done without fuss or friction (which had been his reputation in St Petersburg when I'd first heard of him.)' Talbott went on to say that there was nothing bombastic about Putin: 'None of the mixture of bullying, pleading and guilt-tripping that I associated with the Russian hortatory style'. He thought Putin was 'just about the coolest Russian I'd ever seen. He listened with an attentiveness that seemed at least as calculating as it was courteous.'

Putin let Talbott know that he had done his homework by referring to the Russian poets that Talbott had studied at Yale and Oxford: Vladimir Mayakovsky and Fyodor Tyutchev – whose philosophy is reflected in such lines as 'One can't grasp Russia with one's mind/ No measurements its bounds perceive/. A special fate for her's designed/ In Russia one must just believe.' The American found the experience quite unnerving.

In late July the prime minister of Israel, Ehud Barak, flew to Moscow for talks with Yeltsin about the Middle East. He returned home with the news that Stepashin would be replaced within a matter of days. Yeltsin subsequently admitted that his loyal lapdog had had no chance of succeeding him. 'Even as I nominated Stepashin,' he writes in *Midnight Diaries*, 'I knew that I would fire him.' So who was next in line for the ill-fated premiership? 'The replacement that was mentioned to me,' the Israeli prime minister said in a phone call to Bill Clinton, 'was some guy whose name is Putin.'

10

Premier Putin

IN LATE JULY 1999 Boris Yeltsin summoned Sergei Stepashin to his dacha in Gorky-9 and sacked him. There in the corner of the room to witness the deed was the ubiquitous head of the Security Council (and still director of the FSB), Vladimir Putin. Putin was not comfortable about being asked to witness Stepashin's dismissal and subsequently gave him a job as head of the Audit Chamber, placing him in the frontline of the war against the very oligarchs Yeltsin sought to protect.

Having sacked his fourth prime minister in less than a year and a half, Yeltsin had found a man he could trust, both to run the government and to ensure his own continued freedom and prosperity. He had arrived at Vladimir Putin by a none-too-subtle process of elimination – in the final analysis, Putin was the only one who measured up to his exacting specifications.

'He invited me to his office and said that he was thinking about offering me the post of prime minister, but that he had to talk to Stepashin first,' Putin says. '[Stepashin] knows I had nothing to do with his dismissal. Still, it was terribly awkward when I was telephoned on the eve of the event and asked to come to visit Yeltsin in The Hills the next morning. You can imagine the state I was in. It was all very unpleasant.'

As his health (and temper) vacillated during the late 1990s, Yeltsin had insisted that his aides find 'a person who would continue democratic reforms in the country, who would not turn back to the totalitarian system, and who would ensure Russia's movement forward, to a civilised community'. He made no mention of the allegation that his successor would have to grant him immunity from prosecution once he had left the Kremlin.

According to Lilia Shevtsova, 'the political class was preoccupied with when Yeltsin would step down and who would rule Russia after him. How did Tsar Boris look today, was he compos mentis or not? Everything else was secondary.' The only certainty about the President, whether he was in his office at the Kremlin, his sick-bed or the solarium at his dacha, was that he would change his mind (or Tatyana would change it for him). Yeltsin changed his mind like other men change their socks, so his quest for a successor had been an abject failure. Many were called but none chosen.

Indeed, nomination as Yeltsin's successor was like drinking from a poisoned chalice. 'If Yeltsin declares someone his successor,' Gennady Seleznev, speaker of the Duma, moaned, 'it's the kiss of death for his political future. This has already happened many times.'

One of Yeltsin's less endearing tactics was to prod a pretender to gauge his attitude towards the succession. Any willingness to assume the highest office in the land was deemed unacceptably ambitious. Having been permitted to hold the sacred 'black box', Prime Minister Chernomyrdin came to regard himself as the heir apparent and had been dumped for that very reason.

The next three prime ministers – Sergei Kiriyenko (March-August 1998), Yevgeny Primakov (September 1998-May 1999) and Sergei Stepashin (May-August 1999) – had all failed the 'Tanya test' or been discarded for other reasons. 'Tanya, by her humble presence and occasional bit of advice, really did help me,' he writes in *Midnight Diaries*, although according to Lilia Shevtsova, this 'sweet young woman' was at that time the virtual ruler of the country.

Casting his net wider, Yeltsin had considered a mixed bag, including Sergei Shakhrai, Vladimir Shumeiko, Oleg Soskovets, Alexander Lebed, Boris Nemtsov, Nikolai Bordyuzhey and Nikolai Aksenenko. For a while he flirted with the idea of Nemtsov, governor of Nizhny Novgorod, a young, flamboyant liberal who would become one of the leaders of the Union of Right Forces (SPS), but that infatuation fizzled out after Nemtsov failed to gain any measurable public support. After that he closely observed Bordyuzhey, but – as we have seen – he also came to grief for being too pally with the unfortunate Primakov.

His next choice was to shock everyone. Vladimir Putin was a man who had never stood for election to any office and showed no political ambition. In fact it was Boris Berezovsky, whom he had met in St. Petersburg, who first recommended Putin to Yeltsin. According to Berezovsky's own account, the President duly dispatched the oligarch to France, where Putin was on holiday with his family, to determine whether he would take the job. Berezovsky says the two men spent a day discussing the prospect in Putin's rented condominium before Vladimir finally turned to Boris and said, 'Okay, let's try it. But you understand that Boris Nikolaevich has to ask me himself.' Berezovsky says he nodded affirmatively: 'Volodya, of course. I came here to make sure there would be no misunderstanding when he starts talking with you.' Putin, he says, replied: 'No problem, let's do it'.

Around this time Putin had been flying to St Petersburg every weekend to see his father who was desperately ill. Vladimir Spiridonovich, a hero of the Siege of Leningrad, died on 2 August at the age of 88. Putin was grieving for the loss of his father when Yeltsin summoned him to the Kremlin and informed him that he had decided to appoint him prime minister. He also intimated that this was just a step up the ladder to 'the very highest post'. Putin wore his most impenetrable mask throughout the interview, but his mind must have been racing. His first thought was that he would be plunged into the vortex of Russian politics at the forthcoming parliamentary elections. Thinking of his bitter experiences of electioneering for Chernomyrdin's NDR party back in 1995 and Sobchak in 1996, he expressed his intense dislike of election campaigns. 'I don't know how to run them,' he told Yeltsin, 'and I don't like them.'

Yeltsin waved this objection aside; it was a mere technicality. The conversation ended with Putin saying 'I will work wherever you assign

DURING the Christmas service at the Church of St Procopius the Righteous in
Veliky Ustyug, northern European Russia, 7 January 2008.

me.' Yeltsin took that as a sign of acceptance and introduced Putin to the country on 9 August, referring to him as 'a prime minister with a future' and as 'someone who can consolidate society, based on the widest possible political spectrum, and ensure the continuation of reforms in Russia'. Putin's take on his appointment was characteristically pragmatic. 'I thought, "Well, I'll work for a year and that's fine. If I can help save Russia from collapse, then I'll have something to be proud of." It was a stage in my life. And then I'll move on to the next thing.'

Yeltsin claimed that Putin had risen steadily in his estimation since he had appointed him head of the FSB in July 1998. 'The more I knew Putin, the more convinced I was that he combined both an enormous dedication to democracy and market reforms and an unwavering patriotism,' he writes in *Midnight Diaries*. '[He] did not allow himself to be manipulated in political games. He would not do anything that conflicted with his understanding of honour. He was always ready to part with his high post if his sense of integrity required it.'

Putin dismisses such rhetoric. 'I did not have a particularly close relationship with Boris Nikolayevich, just a good working relationship,' he says. 'Only when he began to discuss the question of his resignation with me did I sense a certain warmth in him.' On 16 August the Duma ratified Putin's appointment by 233-84, with 17 abstentions. Many of the deputies assumed he would vanish like those before him. He was too shy, too inexperienced, too unremarkable, too unknown, to run a government that was rated among the most obstreperous in the world. None seemed to realise that this time Yeltsin had actually anointed his true heir.

Nothing was a greater challenge to Putin than being underestimated by supposedly superior men. The belief that his character could somehow be divined by looking into his eyes was as flawed as the assumption that he must have an inferiority complex because of his humble origins and relatively short stature. In fact, these were the very assets that had driven him since childhood to out-do his competitors, no matter what the personal cost.

'How strange,' Lyudmila ruminated. 'I'm married to a man who yesterday was really just an unknown official in St Petersburg, and now he's the prime minister.' The seemingly nondescript chap she met on a blind date outside a Leningrad theatre and who had, on that occasion, so little to say for himself, was to run the government that ruled the biggest country on earth. How would he cope? Indeed, the new prime minister would need to draw on his inner strength more than ever before to survive the tumultuous months ahead.

THE PUTINS MOVED to a bigger dacha outside Moscow. For security reasons Masha and Katya were taken out of the Deutsche Schule Moskau, Moscow's German School, and taught privately at home. It was a sensible move. There could be no greater kidnap target for the Chechen warlords than Putin's daughters. The children also found that their father's new status made life difficult at school. 'People began to treat us with a lot more respect, it was really noticeable,' Masha says. 'Some of them would flatter us or try to get in our good books. And that really bothers me.'

Having lived according to a strict regime for years, Putin found it easy to stay in shape. Their new dacha came equipped with a 12-metre pool in which he would swim after his daily workout. He also took care with his diet: breakfast consisted of fruit and *kefir*, a type of yogurt; he skipped lunch but ate a meal in the evening. Sometimes he watched cartoons with his children, but couldn't make time to see their latest favourite film, *The Matrix*, although promised to do so as soon as things quietened down.

Later that month Putin began his first day in the office as Prime Minister. As his motorcade of armed security men swept into the Kremlin's 80-acre site in central Moscow, he had time to consider his programme for the day ahead. By the time his limousine had pulled up at the entrance to Administration Building No. 1, he had decided on the first name on his list of people to call. Jacket off, he wandered through the elegant suite of rooms, reflecting on his good fortune. The financial crisis of the previous year had ended; oil, gas and steel prices were rising and international borrowing rates were low.

Some of the members of his first cabinet had been selected for him by the presidential administration, which with enough practise had become adept at the game of musical chairs. The first Deputy Prime Minister would be Victor Aksenenko, a rascal who openly pursued his own business interests and those of the Family; while two of the ministries – energy and interior – would go to Family favourites Viktor Kalyuzhny and Vladimir Rushailo, respectively.

In a bizarre move, Putin then summoned none other than market trader-turned-billionaire tycoon, Roman Abramovich, and asked him to interview candidates for the remaining cabinet positions. The quiet tycoon seemed an unusual choice for this latest mission. But so it was, while the new Prime Minister proceeded with other matters, senior politicians stood in line outside a room on the floor above. One by one the men were trooped in for a short meeting with Abramovich, who nodded and listened while vetting each of the candidate's suitability to run important state departments.

Alexei Venediktov, a political commentator and editor-in-chief of Echo of Moscow radio station, spotted the queue. He told me: 'I talked to some of the candidates that I knew and I asked them what they were doing there, and they said "We're having an interview". I then asked them who they were having an interview with and they said that, as well as other people, they were having an interview with Roman Abramovich. "What does he look like?" I asked. And when they described him to me I realised he was the young man [I had previously seen] in one of the Kremlin corridors.'

The fact that one of Moscow's best-informed pundits (later to become one of Abramovich's closest friends) had not recognised a billionaire with the ear of the new Prime Minister may seem surprising, but at the time no photograph of Abramovich had ever appeared in print. Indeed, when news of the oligarch's power and influence first spread, newspaper editors were obliged to use artists' impressions of him until one publication ran a competition and a reader came up with a fuzzy picture of the publicity-shy oligarch.

It was equally puzzling that a man who had achieved billionaire status through the 'loans for shares' scheme under Yeltsin should have the ear of the new reformer. But Putin knew exactly what he was doing. Abramovich was the weak link in the oligarchs' chain of command. The richest men in Russia had also become the most powerful and in order to break their stranglehold on the Kremlin, Putin had to get among them: Divide and rule. In the short time he had known Abramovich, Putin had surmised that, unlike the others, this man posed no threat to the administration, since he had no interest in politics; his interest lay only in making money.

Berezovsky was shocked when he learned of the task Putin had allocated to his former pupil. 'I didn't know anything about this,' he said at his fortress of an office in Mayfair. The shock must have been all the greater considering that Berezovsky had approached Putin on his appointment to tell him who *he* wanted in the Cabinet. But at that stage he still regarded Putin as malleable. Separating Abramovich from the other oligarchs in the line of fire was part of the game Putin would play. His first priority, however, was the burning issue of Chechnya.

IN EARLY AUGUST 1999 Islamic militants had invaded Dagestan from Chechnya. Sergei Stepashin had worked out a credible plan to deal with the rebels and all Putin had to do initially was to follow it. The military move conceived by Stepashin involved dividing Chechnya by cutting off the separatists' bastions in the mountainous south from the pro-Moscow north. The ex-premier reasoned that this would allow Russian forces to stop the warlords from seizing hostages and either holding them to ransom or murdering them. Yeltsin's personal envoy, Major-General Gennady Shpigun, along with an Interior Ministry general, had been kidnapped at Grozny airport that spring and brutally slain. Captured Russian soldiers had been forced into slavery and others, including six foreign Red Cross workers and four Western telecom engineers, had been decapitated.

Putin concluded that the action proposed by Stepashin was not strong enough to deal with the threat. The hostage-taking and the killings were sapping Russia's prestige as a strong nation; the invasion of

Dagestan went even further: it pointed to the very break-up of the Russian Federation. Putin had to be seen to be stronger than the enemy. Shamil Basayev, who had led the invasion, made no secret of his ambition to form a trans-Caucasian Islamic republic. His ruthlessness had been proven four years earlier, when 150 people died in the Budyonnovsk hospital siege. As well as Basayev, there was a Saudi known as Khattab (real name Samir Saleh Abdullah Al-Suwailem) – a known cohort of Osama bin Laden – who had turned his attention to the Caucasus in 1995 after fighting in Afghanistan. Funded by bin Laden, Khattab set up headquarters in a border village for his 1,500-strong guerrilla army and shared Basayev's dream of an Islamic state.

Putin made it clear that this was no time for half-measures. His only reservation was that the world – and perhaps his own people – would consider the action he contemplated too heavy-handed. Heavy-handed or not, his judgment proved to be accurate: thanks to the course he followed, the war in Chechnya eventually ended and terrorist attacks became fewer.

In his memoirs Yeltsin suggests that Putin – who was to succeed him as President – had the necessary characteristics to face such challenging times: 'Putin is ready for anything that life might dish out to him... He will answer everyone in the accustomed Russian way – with a wave of his hand.' He added: 'With steel teeth behind his smile'. Putin could cope with any task. Yet Yeltsin's own hand in the Chechnya issue is dubious. When he signed the often overlooked Khasavyurt agreement with the Chechens, Yeltsin agreed that Chechnya could leave Russia at any time. There can be little doubt that if Yeltsin had remained in power the break-up of Russia would have been assured. He had already destroyed the Soviet Union, Russia was next in line.

ALTHOUGH THE bombing of apartment blocks in poor areas of Moscow, Volgodonsk and Buinaksk – which killed 300 civilians – was seen by some as just too convenient for Putin, it gave good reason for retaliation. Chechen rebels were blamed for the bombings. An FSB defector, Lieutenant-Colonel Alexander Litvinenko, and his mentor,

RALLY DRIVER Mika Hakkinen, Russian president Vladimir Putin and world pole
vault record-holder Yelena Isimbayeva attend the 9th annual Laureus World Sports
Awards ceremony in the concert hall of the Mariinsky Opera and Ballet Theater,
18 February 2008.

Boris Berezovsky, later came up with a speculation (matching popular
9/11 conspiracy theories) that the Kremlin contrived the bombings in
order to win support for an all-out war in Chechnya. Few believed that
Putin was capable of sanctioning the slaughter of Russians just to win a
propaganda battle. Nevertheless, a strange incident demonstrated that
the FSB – now commanded by his old friend and colleague from St
Petersburg, Nicolai Patrushev – played superbly into the hands of the
conspiracy theorists.

A particularly interesting event took place in Ryazan, not far from
Moscow, which was widely – and freely – described in Russian
newspapers. *Novaya Gazeta* returned to this extraordinary story in several
editions. Police – in a high state of readiness for further bombings – were

summoned to a block of flats on Novosyolov Street, Ryazan, where they found two men and a woman unloading bags into the basement of a building. The police inspector who was first on the scene had sufficient knowledge of bombs to recognise that the sugar sacks, along with an electronic device and a clock with wires attached, were components of a bomb. He called the bomb squad, who defused the device, establishing as they did so that it used hexogen – just like those which had killed 300 people in the earlier atrocities. The following day explosives engineers took a sample from the suspicious-looking sacks for testing.

Thanks to the speed of the caretaker who alerted police, the 'bombers' were caught red-handed. They tried flashing identity cards which showed that all three were members of the FSB, but the cards cut no ice with police, who took them into custody. However, when Patrushev intervened the following day, the trio were released without charge. Patrushev's explanation was that the detonator and explosives had been planted by his agents as part of a training exercise to see if everyone was on their toes. Adding to the mystery, inspectors who carried out tests on the substances 'planted' said that they failed to explode.

SOME SAY THAT the bomb casualties already suffered were enough to give Putin public support for his military operation in Chechnya. Most Russians supported Putin when he sent in more than 80,000 troops to flatten Grozny, killing thousands of civilians in the process and making nearly half a million homeless. It was a brutal war that the West condemned, but Putin replied he was only doing what NATO had done in its air campaign in Kosovo, which had gone on for 70 days, and his supporters would later point to the invasion of Iraq, which cost more than 100,000 civilian lives.

The campaign was as effective as it was brutal, and Putin emerged the hero of the hour to his people. The Chechen onslaught had put him on course to win another victory – that December's battle for the Duma, which had long been dominated by the Communists.

Putin would have preferred to be seen as non-political, above the fray – and his popularity was rising steadily, but Yeltsin needed to be propped up and his own prospects might be damaged by a coalition of the Communists and the Fatherland-All Russia Party. This party had been formed by an alliance between Yuri Luzhkov's Fatherland movement, established in December 1998 in order to campaign against the oligarchs, and the All Russia bloc, formed in April 1999 by a cabal of regional leaders, including Putin's enemy Vladimir Yakovlev, the governor of St Petersburg. At the head of the new Fatherland-All Russia Party was Putin's old nemesis Primakov, who made no secret of his presidential ambitions.

Yeltsin and the oligarchs could not risk a powerful anti-Yeltsin coalition taking control of the Duma, so Berezovsky created the Unity Party with the cooperation of 39 regional leaders. His main official post had been running the Commonwealth of Independent States (CIS), a pale shadow of the Soviet Union, and he had somehow found time to get himself elected to the Duma as deputy for the impoverished southern republic of Karachaevo-Cherkessia. Roman Abramovich was chosen by Berezovsky as paymaster and the driving force behind the new party. Leaving his energy empire for others to run, he began wooing more and more regional governors, enlisting their help in promoting Unity nationwide. This was particularly important because one of Putin's principal opponents in a forthcoming presidential race was Luzhkov, who held enormous sway in Moscow as well as in other regions of the Federation.

While Abramovich worked on Unity, Berezovsky set about a campaign to destroy the chances of Luzhkov and Primakov and their Fatherland-All Russia Party. The most potent instrument at his disposal was the scurrilous news show host Sergei Dorenko, widely billed 'the TV presenter politicians love to hate'. Berezovsky had met Dorenko following the car-bombing in which he was injured and his driver decapitated. He had flown to Switzerland for treatment for burns. From his hospital bed on his first night, he watched Dorenko's show and heard the satirist make typically insensitive remarks about the attempt on his life. 'Another moneybags was hit by a bomb today – too bad,' was the thrust of Dorenko's message. Instead of taking offence, Berezovsky decided he had discovered a potential star for his own network and told his secretary to track down Dorenko and arrange a meeting on his return to Moscow. When the presenter refused to see him, Berezovsky stalked him until he accepted an invitation to lunch, at which Berezovsky talked him into signing a contract with ORT.

Berezovsky – through the acid wit of Dorenko – began a merciless campaign to humiliate Putin's rivals. Over a series of 15 shows, the mayor of Moscow was ridiculed remorselessly on primetime television. In the beginning the taunts were cruel, but not very serious. When Luzhkov's ally Primakov had a hip operation, for example, Dorenko mocked it by showing gory details of surgeons operating on hips and thighs. Primakov was caricatured as a sick old man. And when Luzhkov took the credit for the rebuilding of a hospital destroyed by Chechens, Dorenko baited him: 'Why don't you just thank the donor?'

The Berezovsky-Dorenko smear campaign continued unabated for weeks and greatly amused Putin, who watched every show. It was hinted that Luzhkov was involved in 'mysterious money transfers' from Moscow to foreign banks. He was made to appear ridiculous with the back-to-back showing of video clips of him filmed two years apart, first praising Yeltsin during the 1996 presidential campaign and then attacking him for being too sick to fulfil his role. Even Putin was shocked when it was alleged that the mayor was to blame for the murder of businessman Paul Tatum, who was shot dead in the midst of a dispute over the ownership of a Moscow hotel – a crime for which no one had ever been charged.

Goaded beyond endurance, Luzhkov sued for libel and won $4,500 in damages, but the whole affair distracted him from matters of far greater importance. His dream of becoming president was dashed as his standing in the polls was eradicated. Meanwhile, the only real thorn in Putin's side was Gusinsky's NTV channel, which subjected him to a series of comparatively harmless personal attacks.

In September Putin travelled to Auckland, New Zealand, for a meeting of the Asia-Pacific Economic Co-operation (APEC) countries. 'My political prospects were still unclear,' he says. 'I did not know myself what lay ahead.' Among the delegates was Bill Clinton, who met the new Russian prime minister for the first time in that capacity on 9 September. 'Putin presented a stark contrast to Yeltsin,' he says in his memoirs, *My Life.* 'Yeltsin was large and stocky; Putin was compact and extremely fit from years of martial arts practice. Yeltsin was voluble; the former KGB agent was measured and precise.'

Clinton came away from the meeting believing Yeltsin had picked a successor who had the skill and capacity to better manage Russia's turbulent political and economic life.

At one of the APEC dinners, Clinton showed his appreciation by making a simple gesture to the Russian. 'He came round this table at which all the APEC leaders were seated and whispered in my ear, "Volodya, I propose that you and I leave together".' Putin says: 'This came as a complete surprise to me. We both got up and our colleagues all stepped back to form a sort of corridor and we walked along this corridor together to the applause of those present. I will never forget this and I am very grateful to him.'

Meanwhile, Putin's support had rocketed from a mere two per cent in August 1999 to 15 per cent by the end of September, rising to 25 per cent in late October and 40 per cent by late November. His sense of humour on the campaign trail came as something of a surprise from someone so apparently strait-laced. When Putin visited Primorsky Region as Prime Minister in the autumn of 1999, the governor Yevgeny Nazdratenko heaped such lavish compliments on him that Putin replied: 'Yevgeny Ivanovich, you praised me so much, I began to think that I must have died'.

11

Yeltsin's Bombshell

IT WAS COMMON KNOWLEDGE among Vladimir Putin's friends that he had familiarised himself with the history of Napoleon Bonaparte, the 'Little General' who had imposed order on France after the chaos and bloodshed of the French Revolution. Anatoly Sobchak certainly knew this. 'Putin has the same principles and goals that Napoleon had in his time,' he said in an interview in 2000. 'Restoration of state authority.' Sobchak was confident that, once in power, his one-time pupil would restore that authority to Russia, although he could never have anticipated how difficult the task was to prove and how painfully slow its progress would be.

Sobchak had spent a year and a half in voluntary exile in France before returning to Russia in July 1999, a month before Putin was appointed Prime Minister. More than 100 journalists thronged St Petersburg airport to meet his plane. Exuberant as ever, Sobchak said he would never go away again. 'You don't need to rush,' he said, 'because I have returned forever. I have arrived in my city, and I am happy to be home.'

When his protégé was installed as prime minister, Sobchak believed himself immune from prosecution. By late 1999 all criminal charges against him had been dropped and the former law professor was poised to return to national politics.

Unity became a credible force within a matter of weeks and helped to consolidate Putin's position, but he held back from personally endorsing the party. It was an untried enterprise and if it failed in the parliamentary elections he would be severely handicapped in the upcoming presidential race. His advisers were stunned when, during a television interview, he suddenly committed himself. Asked which party he would vote for, he replied: 'There is only one party that clearly and definitely supports our cause, and that's Unity'. He had considered Abramovich's advice that Unity was a winner and acted on it. In the event, he made the right choice: on 19 December 1999, Unity won 23 per cent of the vote. It polled only around 10 per cent in Moscow, where Luzhkov dominated the electorate (and was re-elected mayor), but it was a different story in the regions, owing to Abramovich's intervention with the governors. Sobchak and his wife Lyudmila, however, both lost their bids to be elected.

If Primakov and Luzhkov thought they had time to recover before the presidential election, which was expected to take place the following summer, they were about to be wrong-footed in a most spectacular way. Twelve days after the Duma elections, Yeltsin did the unthinkable: he resigned his presidency on primetime television during his annual New Year address. The wily old fox had taped his address as usual on 28 December but, after signing off with New Year greetings to his people, he told the producer that he was not happy because he sounded hoarse. He said he would tape it again shortly before its transmission on New Year's Eve. He knew all along what he intended to do – use his most high-profile television slot of the year to announce that he was going and that he would be installing Putin as acting president in his place. Yeltsin had wanted to keep the move secret – from all but Putin himself – until the last moment; and he had succeeded.

Yeltsin had sounded Putin out two weeks earlier in a meeting at his dacha. Putin had wondered aloud if he were fit for it and has since maintained that he told Yeltsin he did not feel ready. After reassuring him, Yeltsin got down to the business of setting out what he expected for himself. He was to be immune from prosecution and investigation for life. It was the same kind of deal that the disgraced Richard Nixon allegedly cut with Gerald Ford when he handed over the presidency of

PUTIN and First Deputy Prime Minister Dmitry Medvedev, the President-elect, attending a gala concert on Vasilyevsky Slope, near Red Square, in honor of the presidential election, 2 March 2008.

the United States. Yeltsin's demands did not end there. His immediate family and closest aides were to be granted the same immunity, a number of them were to keep their jobs and he was to keep various trappings of office, including the presidential dacha in Gorky, where he had spent most of the past year. Furthermore, he and his family were to be guaranteed security (a promise that would cost the Russian people $1.4 million a year up to his death and still costs around $1 million to protect those still remaining). Oh, and on top of that, he was to receive a substantial pension from the nation, despite the assured private generosity of the billionaire oligarchs he had helped create.

Putin would not have had it any other way. Having watched Yeltsin fire at will anyone who showed aspirations to replace him, he was in no mood to risk confrontation. Having agreed to all of Yeltsin's demands, he went home to discuss the news with his wife.

The news was received in the Putin household with mixed reactions. One Kremlin wife told me that when Vladimir relayed to Lyudmila that Yeltsin had asked him to take over the leadership of the country, she replied: 'And what did you tell him?' to which he flippantly retorted: "Oh, if I must". However, that story is probably apocryphal. Better to trust the words of Lyudmila herself, who says she was shocked when she learned what was about to happen early in the afternoon of New Year's Eve: 'A friend called [me] and asked "Have you heard?" I replied "What's up?" And that's how I learned it – from her. Then I cried all day because I realised that my personal life was over.'

And the Putin daughters? Katya says: 'I was shocked to learn that dad had become Acting President. When mother told me I thought she was pulling my leg, but then I realised she wouldn't joke like that. At midnight we turned the TV on and watched people congratulating dad. I liked it. He was so serious... or calm. As he always is. Dad is dad.'

Masha adds: 'On the one hand I didn't want him to become President, but on the other hand I did. We also listened to Boris [Yeltsin] that day.' And then, in an effort to describe the emotion that welled up inside her, the younger Putin daughter said: 'It was as if I had a sore throat, but not like when you're sick. He touched my soul'.

Lyudmila offered no objection to her husband's new status once he confirmed the news. Indeed, a part of her was becoming pleasantly accustomed to the trappings of his ever-higher office. 'I have never tried, or even had to try, to economise on our children's education or holidays,' she was to say in a later interview with *Pravda*. Such benefits made up for the difficulties of being married to such a single-minded man. His faults included his black humour and his sense of irony: 'I like simple and kind humour,' she continued. She went on to say that whether he admitted it or not, Vladimir did have his sentimental side: 'On one birthday he gave me a gold cross and chain. When I woke up it was lying on the bedside table. It turned out he had bought it two months earlier in Jerusalem. His self-control and patience always amaze me. When I buy presents I have to give them straight away.'

Unbeknown to anyone else, Yeltsin was paying a sentimental

farewell to his Kremlin office when Putin turned up the day after the first New Year address had been taped. Putin assured him that Alexander Voloshin would be kept on as chief of staff and presented the President with a letter giving the required assurances. Yeltsin had suggested, and Putin had agreed, that he would remain Prime Minister as well as Acting President until an election was held the following March.

The tape of the New Year's Eve resignation speech – delivered under armed guard to the Ostankino tower – was in fact transmitted in Moscow at noon in order for it to be seen at midnight in the far eastern territories. A number of ministers and VIPs were summoned to Yeltsin's office to hear the news and to salute Yeltsin's heir before the broadcast went out. They included the leader of the Russian Orthodox Church, Patriarch Alexei, who bowed deeply to the new President-elect, a move that was promptly reciprocated.

Putin issued what was called his 'Millennium Statement', written with the assistance of German Gref, an economist friend from his St Petersburg days, in which he guaranteed freedom of speech and freedom of the press and promised to 'crush corruption'. His election cry was rather like Blair's on arriving at 10 Downing Street: 'Education, education, education', only in Putin's case it was 'Prosperity, prosperity, prosperity'. He knew that after decades of deprivation his people were not searching for idealism; what they wanted was food in their bellies, new clothes on their backs and some money left over to spend on life's little luxuries.

Then, just before Yeltsin left the building for the last time as President, he handed Putin the nuclear 'black box'. 'Putin treated it,' says an onlooker, 'like your Queen would treat the crown jewels.' He had been relatively free of expression throughout the morning's momentous events, 'but the bomb case seemed to stir something in him. It must have made him feel very powerful indeed.' It was not the only emotion Putin showed in those hours: according to another witness, a tear rolled down his cheek when he watched Yeltsin's resignation speech and heard his predecessor talk about the 'new, intelligent, strong and energetic' people who were taking over. His parting words to Putin were: 'Protect Russia'.

BORIS YELTSIN assured the Russian people that their Homeland was in safe hands
when he announced on New Year's Eve 1999 that Vladimir Putin was to succeed
him.

HAVING DIGESTED the night's news about their new commander-in-chief, Russian soldiers based in the embattled Chechnyan town of Gudermes – less than 20 miles from war-torn Grozny – could hardly contain their surprise when a heavily-armed convoy swept into their camp in the early hours of New Year's Day and out stepped the acting President. He had been there before – as Prime Minister – the previous month. This trip was to keep a promise he had made to a soldier on that occasion that he would return for the New Year celebrations, and Vladimir Putin always keeps his promises. What's more, he had persuaded (though it was not easy, he admitted later) his wife, who was now Russia's First Lady, to accompany him on this potentially dangerous mission.

As proof that he had indeed been there, the soldiers were given photographs of him presenting each of them with a hunting knife. Putin had planned the highly surprising visit as soon as he was certain that Yeltsin would be gone before the Millennium began. Although it proved to be the first of many photo opportunities he would take ahead of the March elections, he argued with his press secretary about using such stories for campaign purposes. Nevertheless, he preferred to be seen 'in action' to campaigning conventionally. Not for him the humbling process of presenting policies and having them challenged on the stump. Via television and newspapers, Putin would be seen carrying out the activities of an already-elected President, chairing meetings of ministers in the Kremlin, presenting honours and – rather like the Queen – visiting schools, factories and hospitals where all he had to do was smile and make gracious remarks. To keep the drumbeat of war alive, he also arranged to be flown to a military base in Chechnya in a jet fighter.

Putin soon made it known that he intended to stifle the power of any oligarch who opposed him, emphasising at every opportunity that the interests of the state must come before those of the individual. His targets were Mikhail Khodorkovsky, now the unchallenged head of Yukos, and Vladimir Gusinsky, who had unwisely allowed NTV to attack him. Although he had promised Boris Yeltsin that he would look after his relatives and cronies, one of Putin's first actions, once the former President had gone, was to ask his daughter Tatyana Dyachenko to vacate her suite at the Kremlin. The rule of Tanya-Valya had definitely ended, although he had promoted Mikhail Kasyanov.

Putin's promise to 'crush corruption' was obviously aimed at the oligarchs, yet he stayed close to Abramovich, who had gained more than most from Russia's asset sales – including a large chunk of the country's aluminium industry. And when controversial reports from Chechnya by Radio Liberty's Andrei Babitsky offended the Kremlin, Russian forces were ordered to arrest him and hand him over to the Chechens in exchange for three Russian soldiers. Babitsky had outraged public opinion when he declared on one occasion: 'The Chechens cut soldiers' throats not because they are sadists inclined to treat them with brutality, but in order to make the war more convex, visible, vivid; to reach the public and to explain that a war is actually going on, scary and cruel.'

At the time Nataliya Gevorkyan, one of the three authors of *First Person,* was enjoying a few weeks' access to Putin for the book she was writing, and decided to confront him about the Babitsky issue. 'I said to him directly: "The guy has children and a wife. You've got to put a stop to this thing". And he said: "Soon a car will deliver a videotape showing your friend is alive and well". I said "Hello! You are supposed to have handed him over to the bandits? So this information comes directly from them then?" He didn't answer and I ran out of the room to call Andrei's colleague, so she would tell his wife he was still alive".'

Two hours later the colleague at Radio Liberty called Gevorkyan back: 'You are not going to believe this,' she said. 'A car showed up at the bureau. They said they had a videotape of Andrei and we bought it off them for $200.' The tape showed that Babitsky was alive and he was released a few days later.

Soon after, Gevorkyan moved to Paris. Like many who have crossed Putin, she now lives abroad in self-imposed exile.

Whether it was pressure from Gevorkyan or protests from around the world which obliged Putin to 'take care of the matter', Babitsky was released by his captors after a full month in captivity, but the journalist claimed that Russian soldiers had initially held him in a notorious detention camp and beaten him badly for daring to report his observations on their behaviour.

Putin compared campaigning for election with 'television advertising for Tampax or Snickers'. His preferred method was to manipulate the media. Gusinsky's paper *Sevodnya* came under pressure for 'rocking the boat of public accord and calm in our country' when it criticised him for posing for a photograph stroking his pet poodle before the 2000 presidential race had officially started. He also wrote letters to *Izvestiya* on a variety of subjects and passed on chunks of his hurriedly written 'autobiography' *First Person*, for publication in *Kommersant Daily*.

One of his most successful gambits was to take part in a radio phone-in during which dozens of people were allowed to speak to him on a number of carefully selected topics. What he would not do was submit himself to questioning by the Russian media, and the one interview he agreed to was with Sir David Frost for British television. This surprised some in his team, since he had been fully briefed about how Frost had reduced Richard Nixon to tears in a series of TV interviews. He was determined the interview should happen, despite warnings from his advisors that the Englishman would persist with a line of questioning if any answer seemed to be evasive.

The episode did not pass without incident. However, during the interview, Frost asked him about Russia joining NATO. Clearly put on the spot, Putin replied, 'Why not?' After all, he already believed that Russia was part of the West. He hoped his answer might merely suggest something that was a distant possibility, but to Russian hard-liners the very thought of NATO telling it what to do in Chechnya was outrageous. A defence minister was rushed in to say that while it was hypothetically possible, NATO would first have to change its ways and allow Russia to veto any decisions it made, virtually ruling out any prospect of such an alliance. Chastened by his Frostbite experience, Putin himself said a few days later that Russia had no need to join NATO; it was capable of securing its own defence. And in any event, the organisation would have to mend its ways after backing the ethnic Albanians in former Yugoslavia, and what most Russians regarded as its 'onslaught' in Kosovo.

Ahead of the election Putin reshuffled his key team and replaced a number of those left over from the Yeltsin era with even more of his St Petersburg people – the *Siloviki*. Particularly significant were the appointments of Nikolai Patrushev – the man entrusted with his FSB job – as deputy prime minister, German Gref as deputy privatisation minister and the lawyer Dmitri Medvedev as campaign manager. It was vital to Putin that he surround himself with people he could trust. Lord (Chris) Patten, who had dealings with him in his capacity as European commissioner for external relations, says in his book *Not Quite the Diplomat* that Putin blatantly lied to him and others at a lunch in Helsinki during the EU-Russia Summit in 1999. Standing in for the indisposed President Yeltsin, Putin had been asked during the lunch about news agency reports that very day of explosions and great loss of life at a market in Grozny.

Putin said he knew nothing about it but would check it out. Patten continues: 'He came back to us to say that it was what counterterrorist experts call "an own goal". The Chechen rebels had run a weapons bazaar and some of their own explosives had detonated... He looked us in the eye and repeated the story. It was odd... Normally mendacity comes in better disguise. The damage had, of course, been done by Russian forces, which were soon to reduce Grozny to a ruin similar to Beirut or Kabul.'

Patten said he found it hard to believe that there was a weapons market in the centre of the town, but in condemning Putin's account he failed to make it clear whether he had ever been there himself and knew it from personal experience. Russian journalists also wanted to know if Patten had any view on people being sold to slavery on an adjacent market.

ON 20 FEBRUARY 2000 Anatoly Sobchak died at the age of 62 in Kaliningrad, where he was helping to organise the forthcoming presidential election campaign. Yury Shevchenko, a doctor friend of the Putin family – who would later be appointed Federal Minister of Health – announced that Sobchak had died of a heart attack, supposedly his fourth. But when Polina Ivanushkina, a 19-year-old reporter for a Moscow weekly, interviewed the pathologist who had examined Sobchak's body, she says he told her that Sobchak had never had a heart attack, much less died of one. He concluded Sobchak's death had resulted from cardiac arrest caused by the consumption of certain kinds of medication – possibly Viagra – and alcohol. The controversy-loving Valeria Novodvorskaya, leader of the Democratic Union party, ignored the pathologist's hair-splitting theory but added to the mystery when she made an official statement claiming that not only Sobchak, but also two of his aides, had heart attacks simultaneously, suggesting that all three had been poisoned. Then Sergei Stepashin and Anatoly Chubais further muddied the waters by going on Russian television to accuse Yuri Skuratov of damaging Sobchak's health with unfounded allegations of corruption.

It was reported that several hours before his death Sobchak met with the Governor of the region, Leonid Gorbenko. Gorbenko was renowned for his fondness for booze and, by his own admission, had taken a bottle of alcohol with him to the meeting. Sobchak had only a couple of glasses and the Governor says he drank the rest himself.

Months later several people close to Sobchak's widow, Lyudmila Narusova, came out of the woodwork to claim she believed her husband was murdered 'in order to cut off the channel of free and fair information from Putin'. Putin himself made it known he did not believe it and when later asked about it , Narusova – who was appointed a senator under the new regime – said she was tired of the gossip and had no wish to discuss the matter further.

Putin had Sobchak's body flown back to St Petersburg for burial in the Tikhvin Cemetery at the Alexander Nevsky Monastery. The time of the funeral was changed at the last moment because there was speculation that Putin himself might be the target of an assassin. In a rare show of emotion, Putin wept at the graveside. He had loved Sobchak and loathed Vladimir Yakovlev for ousting his mentor, and more recently for supporting the Fatherland-All Russia party in its bid to hound him out of office. Yakovlev was not present at the funeral: Sobchak's widow made it clear he would not be welcome. For his part, Yakovlev knew that his days as governor were numbered.

Nowadays Putin finds time to take phone calls from Sobchak's daughter, Ksenia, the hostess of a lurid Russian television programme. A brazen self-publicist, Ksenia – billed as Russia's answer to Paris Hilton – made much of the fact that she was the then-president's goddaughter. She tried to get into politics by launching a youth movement called *Vse Svobodny*, which translates as 'All Are Free', having starred in movies entitled, respectively, *Babes* and *Thieves and Hookers*. Needless to say, few took her seriously.

Lyudmila Narusova chooses her words carefully in summing up her husband's stalwart collaborator: 'We knew Putin as competent,' she says. 'He was chosen for his professional qualities.'

12

Blair Flies East

LESS THAN THREE months after being made Acting President – and, more significantly, just a fortnight before the election which would confirm his appointment as head of state – Putin pulled off a masterstroke in international diplomacy. He picked up the telephone in his Kremlin office and called Tony Blair in London: 'Come to Russia so we can get to know each other. Bring your wife; it will be a social occasion'.

Blair's antennae twitched. How should he respond? Putin was ostensibly inviting Tony and Cherie to St Petersburg to join him and Lyudmila at a gala performance of Sergei Prokofiev's opera *War and Peace* at the Mariinsky Theatre, where his close friend Valery Gergiev was artistic director. It was an offer they could hardly turn down, even though it was transparently obvious that the new Russian leader was really fixing an unofficial summit meeting with the British Prime Minister. The role had fallen to Blair because President Clinton was in his last year of office, there would soon be a new leader in the Oval Office and, anyway, Putin had already made his acquaintance.

As one of several candidates in the forthcoming election, Putin was in no position to issue a formal invitation for Blair to meet him in Moscow. Had he done so, Blair would have been obliged also to meet with the other candidates, and that would have meant spending time with – God forbid! – the Communist Party's Gennady Zyuganov. There was also considerable suspicion in the United Kingdom about this former KGB man taking the helm of the old enemy, who was already facing huge human rights issues over his aggressive stance on the conflict in Chechnya. But – reassured by his spin doctors that meeting the man who seemed certain to become the next democratically-elected President of Russia before the month was out could be presented as a positive move – he rang Putin back to say he and Cherie would be delighted to join him at the opera. He made one concession to those of his cabinet who opposed the plan – yes, he *would* raise the issue of human rights in Chechnya.

The Blairs set off for St Petersburg on Friday 10 March 2000. During the flight Blair and his press secretary Alastair Campbell spent time 'schmoozing with the hacks', in Campbell's evocative phrase. The plane landed late at night and John Stoddart, the photographer hired to accompany the Blairs, travelled into St Petersburg with them in a green minibus. Both Blairs appeared nervous: 'She was heavily pregnant with her fourth baby, but Tony was the one who seemed to need mothering,' says Stoddart. 'She kept talking about the shirts she had packed for him and he said: "I hope you've packed the pink one, I like the pink one".'

Putin had already paved the way for a smooth discussion with Blair. He had indicated that he was prepared to bypass problems which divided not just Russia and the UK but also Russia and Europe – in particular, the disagreements over Chechnya – 'Russia's legal sore spot', as he knew one senior British minister had described it. He would not insist on raising such contentious details as British monetary interests in Chechnya, an issue which would later be the topic of a major discussion with Colonel-General Leonid Ivashov, the President of the Academy of Geopolitical Sciences.

Furthermore, Putin was also prepared to bury the hatchet over the thorny issue of Russia forging closer co-operation with NATO, which had been on hold because of Russia's disapproval of NATO's role in Kosovo. Going against advice from both his defence and foreign ministries, Putin had decided to resurrect plans for the opening of a NATO military liaison mission in Moscow, as well as a staff information office. His defence minister had particularly advised against him having anything to do with the organisation's secretary-general, Lord (George) Robertson, unless the latter made a formal apology for its action in the Balkans.

Realising that Robertson was never going to do that, Putin had nevertheless invited him to Moscow. 'He just cut through the crap,' is how one senior NATO staff officer puts it. 'He asked George to visit unconditionally. He was putting his stamp on things. George was certainly taken aback, but he was flattered and of course he accepted.' Putin never had any intention of Russia joining NATO. He was later to say (in a December 2007 interview with *Time* magazine) 'I would not say that NATO is the stinking corpse of the Cold War. But it is certainly something that is a holdover from the past. There is no point in pretending otherwise: first NATO was created and then, in response, the Warsaw Pact was created. It was two military and political blocs opposing each other. How, for example, can NATO fight terrorism? Did NATO prevent the September 11 terrorist attack on the United States that killed thousands? Where was NATO to respond to this danger, to eliminate it, to protect America from it?' He added that Russia would not join a military-political bloc 'in order to limit its sovereignty, because participation in a bloc is, of course, a restriction of sovereignty'.

But this was no time to express such views and he merely nodded each time Robertson pressed the matter. Meeting the secretary-general was simply a diplomatic task the new leader had to perform, and he carried it out superbly, as Robertson reported back to a doubtful Blair.

With the main stumbling block cleared, an agenda was drawn up for the Putin-Blair meeting, which had little to do with a night at the opera. The subjects to be discussed included organised crime, the forthcoming G8 summit, closer economic ties between the two nations, the Balkans and – as a concession to the British Prime Minister – Chechnya.

On Sunday morning, Tony Blair was in good spirits when he headed off in an official Zil limousine to meet Putin at Peter the Great's magnificent Summer Palace at Peterhof. The British ambassador, Sir Roderic Lyne, had advised him to be 'friendly without being overly-

IT'S NOT only world leaders who get invited to the President's country residence. Here Putin entertains a group of Russian youth activists.

chummy, in case he turned out to be in disfavour or in six months time, in real trouble'. Putin welcomed Blair effusively and took him on a long tour of the palace which ended up in a grand, rather dark room where the meeting would take place.

Blair was somewhat taken aback to discover that the two leaders would be sitting on raised thrones, with their respective officials fanning away from them. He was used to conducting such meetings on a relatively informal basis in a study at 10 Downing Street with everyone crammed into armchairs and sofas that had seen better days. He was clearly thrown to be faced with Russian bureaucrats watching their trainee President like hawks, ready to report back to their respective bosses on his performance.

Despite the acting President's attempt to avoid contentious issues, Chechnya inevitably became the hot topic. Blair set out British concerns in the plausible tones of a barrister addressing a jury and Putin responded that at least his views were more balanced than those of the French. 'You got the strong impression that he'd not just spent the entire previous night mugging up on his brief, but he'd learned it all by heart,' says a senior British diplomat who was present throughout the meeting. 'You got the impression a gramophone record had been switched on. This was still the early days of the [second] Chechen War, but the moment Tony raised it, Putin delivered a very long response – it probably took about 10 minutes, but it seemed to go on much longer – a completely prepared, uninterrupted and well-rehearsed line that left little room for animated discussion.' Putin had simply prepared himself well for the meeting, so well that it was difficult for Blair to participate in the discussion on an equal footing; it was apparent Blair had limited detailed knowledge of the situation in Chechnya and knew only the general outlines. Then Putin launched into his tirade. The thrust of his argument was that the war had a criminal basis: the criminals maintained that their motivation was religious but, in fact, they were aggressive extremists constituting a real threat to Russia. That threat emanated from terrorists; criminal elements were threatening to break up the Federation. Russians had found themselves fighting Arabs, the Taliban and Muslims from Pakistan, Putin argued, but their real opponents were criminals who only pretended that their motivation was religious.

Blair was caught off-guard. The promise of a debate on human rights in Chechnya and the destruction of Grozny had been swept aside. Instead he was shown some privately made videos of Chechens torturing Russian soldiers and officers, decapitating them and shooting them in the presence of Shamil Basayev. There were 17 episodes in all, a scary digest of the recent raid around Dagestan. Blair learnt later from his intelligence sources that the films were genuine. Both men were fired up by their Chechen discussion and, as Alastair Campbell recorded in his diary: 'it was a relief when they got on to the domestic front, economic reform, developing a market economy'.

After the meeting the two leaders gave a press conference in a grand, mirrored ballroom. The lecterns had obviously been placed some distance apart in order to mitigate the fact that Putin was a half a foot shorter than the British PM. There were a number of questions from newsmen on the subject of investment. Putin had obviously anticipated them and read out a long prepared statement. 'It was terribly old-speak,' the British diplomat recalls, 'and I remember standing there listening to it and thinking: "This man is marketing himself as somebody who is here to reform and modernise the Russian economy". Mind you, he'd already made a number of speeches to that effect including his Millennium Statement. That was a very important manifesto – the only one he put out prior to the election on 26 March. I suspect some old-timer in the Ministry of Foreign Trade who'd been there since the early days of the Soviet Union must have had an input into his speech because it assumed that investment was something done by governments and talked about Britain's great shipbuilding industry which we hadn't had for 40 years. You came away from that thinking that this was a guy who was not yet up to speed on market economies.'

When they retired to lunch, an atmosphere of gloom pervaded the room. Blair's hopes of making Putin his new best friend had been quashed, while Putin realised that his own what-I-say-goes message was not sinking in. The Russians were happy that their man had not stepped out of line, but the small British team seemed disconsolate. It had been, they reflected, a stilted two-hour meeting followed by a mediocre press conference. The vibes improved, however, as the lunch progressed and the presence of Cherie and Lyudmila helped to lighten the mood. The women were then taken on a short sightseeing tour prior to their husbands' second round of talks, which were convened in another equally grand room in the Hermitage.

Diplomat Sir Roderic Lyne had the idea that all of the officials should leave the two leaders to get on with it for the afternoon, with just their interpreters present. He put it to Blair, who readily agreed, but the Russians were having none of it, especially those from the Defence Ministry, who seemed not to trust their President any more than he appeared to like them. 'Bear in mind that the men from the Russian Foreign Ministry and the KGB have never got on and the thought that a former KGB officer – not even a very senior one – was about to become their elected president appalled them,' the senior British diplomat says. 'So the Russians insisted on marching back into the room with Mr Putin and Mr Blair, who duly reascended their thrones for the required photo call with all of us gathered around. Once that was over one of our number said to Tony – on cue, mind – "Would you rather this next conversation was just between the two of you?" He replied: "Yes, I think that would be a good idea". So we all got up and walked out of the room. The Russians had no alternative but to leave as well. They were furious, but I think that the Acting President was as amused as he was pleased. He obviously knew the whole thing had been stage-managed.'

Blair later told his team that not only had the one-to-one session gone infinitely better than the first one, but that he and Putin had actually developed something of a rapport, which was exactly what the President's old guard had feared. They had nothing to fear: Putin was not about to become a member of the Blair fan club. Nevertheless, they seemed on excellent terms as they sat side-by-side in their box at the Mariinsky Theatre that night, even if the opera was not to pop-loving Blair's taste. Cherie Blair recalled the evening with a shudder, complaining later that 'the opera seemed endless'. She added: 'As I was then six months pregnant with Leo, the trip wasn't easy. Although the hotel was like an oven, outside it was bitterly cold.'

Determined that his visitors should not go home without a lighter moment to remember from their trip, Putin took the couple to a restaurant and, during the meal, asked the Prime Minister if he knew there were bears on the street in that part of the world. 'Tony looked at him with that sort of vacant look he can put on when he doesn't know what to say and shrugged his shoulders,' says someone who witnessed the event. 'With that Putin grabbed him by the arm and took him to the window where – lo and behold – there was a huge bear on the pavement outside. Of course the bear had a chain around one ankle and there was a trainer not far away holding the other end. But Putin was emphasising a point he had made throughout the visit: he might be a novice but he was capable of pulling the wool over the eyes of a major player on the world stage. It ought to have taught Blair a lesson...'

On the flight back to London Blair gave an upbeat account of his meetings to the attendant press corps, making it clear that if nothing else he, Cherie and the Putins were now good friends. On the business front, Blair said he had found Putin to be 'highly intelligent with a focused view of what he wants to achieve in Russia… Given what Russia has been through and given the economic task of reconstruction, it's not surprising he believes in a Russia which is ordered and strong, but also democratic and liberal.' He gave no hint of how difficult he had found it to engage with Putin on matters that he had said were important before leaving home. When reporters tried to draw him on how tough *he* had been when it came to Chechnya, he said there had been human rights abuses on both sides.

Privately Blair had to concede that he was not dealing with a Boris Yeltsin figure, but a new, strong Russian leader who would expect him to be better prepared for any future meetings, especially when Chechnya was on the agenda.

IN THE RUN-UP to the presidential election Putin inevitably found himself faced with skeletons from his past. Marina Salye, the liberal politician who had called on Mayor Sobchak to dismiss him following alleged misappropriation of funds, campaigned against Yeltsin's appointed successor, drawing attention to the results of her St Petersburg investigation. In somewhat dramatic interviews which, she said, turned her into a 'world media star', Salye claimed 'they're going to kill me' before retiring to a remote house in the country. Few took her claims seriously, and even she was forced to deny one report that Putin had sent her a telegram on New Year's Day 2001 which read 'Here is wishing you good health… and the opportunity to use it'! Salye compounded her fears by reminding interviewers that St Petersburg's other leading liberal politician, Galina Starovoitova, was murdered just yards from her front door on November 20 1998.

PUTIN'S SELECTION as President on 26 March 2000 was more a coronation than an election. His 53 per cent of the poll in the first ballot assured him of a comfortable ride to the Kremlin. Apart from voting at his local polling station, an obligatory task, he showed little interest in the detail of the event, taking time out to ski in the hours leading up to the declaration of the results.

The Communists' leader Gennady Zyuganov came second with 29 per cent, and the egotistical liberal Grigory Yavlinsky third with six per cent. At 47, Putin became Russia's youngest president since Stalin when he was inaugurated in the Great Kremlin Palace on Sunday 7 May. Two former presidents, Yeltsin and Gorbachev, stood with the country's leading politicians, foreign ambassadors, judges, religious leaders and members of Putin's family to watch their new leader take the long walk along the red carpet that led him through the magnificent 19th century building. As 30 cannons fired a presidential salute and a troop of the Kremlin guard marched past to the accompaniment of a military band, the boy from Baskov Lane was sworn in as Russia's second elected president.

The reporters from *Time* magazine were unfairly merciless in their appraisal: 'He is so colourless, so ordinary a man you could not pick him out of a crowd,' they wrote. 'Prying eyes would slide right by the slight, spare figure with the bland, expressionless face.' And once again it was his eyes that caught their attention. 'Look at his eyes,' they wrote. 'Blue as steel. Cold as the Siberian ice. They bore into you, but you cannot penetrate them. Sometimes they're a mirror, reflecting what you want to see. Sometimes they're a mask, disguising real intentions. Those eyes are Putin's strongest feature – not counting his unflinching will.'

Later Putin and Lyudmila attended a service of blessing conducted by Patriach Alexei II in the Kremlin's onion-domed Annunciation Cathedral. He was visibly more relaxed treading in the footsteps of the Tsars than he had been standing where Stalin had once stood.

'I did everything I could,' Yeltsin had said in ending his resignation speech. 'A new generation is coming that will do it more and do it better.'

13

Putin's Revenge

COMFORTABLY SETTLED in the presidential office for the next four years at least, Putin realised that he now had a multitude of problems to deal with. Some were serious, others merely irksome. The latter category included members of his wife's family who sought to jump on the bandwagon – particularly a cousin who openly sought to exploit the relationship and had to be 'dumped', which caused Lyudmila some distress and created domestic friction when Putin least needed it.

'This is the point at which he discovered he had two kinds of friends,' says a helpful VVP Man. 'There were those who wanted to use him – they didn't last long – and those of us who genuinely wanted to help.' And that's when a group of unappointed Putin supporters was formed; an all-male circle Putin believed he could trust to watch his back as much as to offer guidance on the road ahead.

'At our very first meeting, we congratulated him and asked him how it felt to be President,' continues the VVP Man. 'His reply was: "Well, it beats selling bananas". Chechnya was his first priority. It was all about pain, corruption, assassinations, corrupt prime ministers and ministers. And then of course there was [Ahmed] Zakayev, the Chechen warlord who was one of Boris Berezovsky's cohorts... the man who managed to win the support of the British actress Vanessa Redgrave, even though he had been linked to the murders of hundreds of people in 1995/6.'

On a swelteringly hot day in July 2000, the President-elect

summoned all 30 oligarchs – both major and minor players – to a meeting at the Kremlin. All but one, that is. A little bewildered about the purpose of the meeting, they were for the first time required to leave their air-conditioned limousines at the Spassky Gate and go on foot to the grandest of the Kremlin's gilded halls to face their President. All wore sunglasses, adding to the impression of a Mafia gathering ordered by Don Corleone, yet this was a meeting of ultra-rich men summoned by the undisputed leader of the Russian Federation.

They were punctual; Putin, as was his custom, was not. He had even been late for his reception in London by the Queen, so he was not averse to keeping these men waiting. Indeed, it gave them time to speculate on the possible reasons for the summons. They had been seated around the highly polished boardroom-style table for more than half an hour when the President finally made his entrance.

Cool and calm, he looked down the table and began to speak. 'You built the state yourselves to a great degree through the political and semi-political structures under your control,' he began. 'So there is no point in blaming the reflection in the mirror.' Confused, the wealthiest men in Russia looked at each other. Was he blaming them? For what? The explanation was swift to follow: Putin's message was that their days of meddling in politics were over. They could keep their lot on three conditions: they must pay their taxes, they must enter into no more sweetheart deals with corrupt ministers or officials, and they must not interfere in politics. The oligarchs were left in no doubt that if they broke these new rules they would be in trouble.

This, then, was a *diktat* they would ignore at their peril. Furthermore, they were aware that the tide of public opinion was turning against them. The average Russian had a pretty good idea of how their vast wealth was acquired. Mikhail Fridman later recalled: 'We had to admit we were not popular. One of our number suggested we hire an image consultancy company. I said we had to go further than that. Ordinary people who could not afford to visit their families in Russia saw us going to St Tropez and [for tax purposes] calling it a business trip. We had to be seen as personally irreproachable.'

This is ironic, for it was Fridman who, when he received his summons to the Kremlin summit, had telephoned a fellow oligarch to say that big business had become far too important for the President to fall out with those who controlled it. The now-humbled Fridman was the one who had suggested the oligarchs hire a powerful PR firm, more to damage the President's image than to improve their own.

Putin was in no doubt that his 'guests' that morning had more than vast riches with which to wage war on him; several of them had used parts of their fortunes to buy virtual control of the Russian media with its entrée into the hearts and minds of its people. But the new President had a trump card: he controlled the jails and, by way of a warning shot, had already had one of those present, Vladimir Gusinsky, arrested and briefly imprisoned the previous month on charges of embezzling tens of millions of dollars from Gazprom, which he did not intend to return. The charges were only dropped when the tycoon agreed to sign his powerful Media Most conglomerate (which included NTV, the *Segodnya* newspaper and *Itogi* magazine) over to the government-dominated Gazprom energy conglomerate – leaving him with just a small stake in the popular *Echo of Moscow* radio station, which is still broadcasting today – in return for a one-off payment of $300 million. Gusinsky had arrived at Putin's doom-laden conference still complaining that, as the agreement was reached while he was in jail, it was made under duress and therefore not legally binding; the oligarchs were not used to giving back what they had taken from the state.

As they left the Kremlin building that fateful day, the oligarchs broke off into groups. Some were protesting, a few were planning rebellions – rebellions that would see one of their number jailed for longer than Putin could expect to be in power and others dispatched to uneasy exiles. Without exception, however, they all had one question on their lips: where was Roman Abramovich?

ONCE A PENNILESS ORPHAN, Abramovich, still three months short of his 34th birthday, had not only joined the ranks of Russia's oligarchs, but become one of the most successful of all; yet when

PUTIN TRAVELLED to the Vatican City for this meeting with Pope Benedict XVI
in the library of the Apostolic Palace, the Pope's official residence.

Vladimir Putin called them together on that summer day in 2000, Abramovich was conspicuous by his absence. Like the others, Boris Berezovsky had not dared to refuse the presidential summons. As he looked around the table, he could see that every seat had been filled, confirming that Abramovich's presence was surplus to the President's requirements.

Had he already satisfied Putin that he would abide by the three conditions imposed that day? Or was the man from the KGB demonstrating a divide-and-rule tactic by demonstrating that one of their number had already changed sides? The answer was yes to both questions. The President and the entrepreneur – an unlikely twosome – had already forged a pragmatic relationship; it was an uneasy alliance with one of those responsible for bringing the country to its knees by participating in Boris Yeltsin's fire sale of Russia's natural assets.

Although a man of seemingly unbending principle, Putin was also a realist. He knew better than most that Yeltsin had had little choice when, four years earlier, he bought his victory in the 1996 presidential election by scraping together the funds to pay pensions and public sector wages, saving his homeland from a return to Communism in the process; even if it had meant selling off Russia's family silver for a fraction of its worth to a group of men who, in some cases, would become multi-billionaires from their acquisitions. Clawing back the national treasure could wait until another day.

ABRAMOVICH HAD FIRST encountered Putin at the Kremlin, when he was required to dance attendance as the business face of government. At that time Berezovsky had been happy to see his apprentice accepted into Yeltsin's inner court; he had failed to realise that the blossoming relationship between him, Abramovich and Putin would lead to his own expulsion from the Kremlin. After all, when Yeltsin decided to appoint Putin prime minister, hadn't he sent Berezovsky to sound him out?

Berezovsky and his fellow oligarchs expected the new man at the head of government to be their man, that Putin would be malleable. From the moment he was installed in office, however, the new leader wasted no time in demonstrating the fallacy of that belief and pointedly ignored Berezovsky's attempts to impose himself on his premiership. Berezovsky's Achilles' heel was that he could never bring himself to compromise. 'He must always win and be seen to win,' says Robert Cottrell. 'But in politics and high finance the inability to give ground is dangerous.'

In his first State of the Nation address, Putin warned: 'We are facing the serious threat of turning into a decaying nation.' He was referring to the grim demographic prospects Russia faced: after the Soviet Union collapsed the population shrank by five million overnight. His experts told him they expected the population to shrink by more than 30 per cent to just over 100 million before the new century was half over. Such a low population for a country as vast as Russia presents a potentially catastrophic situation, especially considering the far greater numbers who live in neighbouring China and Japan and threaten to encroach on Russia's sovereign territory.

When Putin took office as President, Russia's annual death rate exceeded the birth rate by 70 per cent and two thirds of the population lived below the poverty line. The consumption of drugs, alcohol and tobacco all contributed to the highest mortality rate in Europe and the lowest birth rate.

German Gref, the young liberal reformer, was appointed trade minister by Putin and put in charge of the Centre for Strategic Studies, which produced a 10-year development strategy paper. Gref and Putin knew each other well from their St Petersburg days. Putin's choice of men he had long trusted strengthened his position and such was his level of influence that they in turn changed to adapt themselves to his behaviour: not just Gref but Kudrin, Chubais and even Vitaly Ignatenko, the long-standing director of the ITAR-TASS news agency. Reports to the President from his kitchen cabinet were not kind about Gref, however. 'We recommended the incentive scheme for parents,' said my VVP man. 'We re-introduced the old scheme whereby parents get more, or better, accommodation in return for producing more children, plus there's a monetary incentive. Gref lives in a dream world. He wanted to encourage people to go and settle in the outback, where no one wants to live. The parts of Russia he was talking about are virtually uninhabitable, plus they have no infrastructure. There are no roads to these places, no airports and no likelihood of getting them in the foreseeable future. It was a potty plan.'

One month later, five months after Putin was elected President, Berezovsky saw his chance to strike back. Just before 11.30 a.m. on Saturday 12 August, the *Kursk*, a state-of-the-art, guided missile submarine, sank in the Arctic Barents Sea. The length of two jumbo jets laid end-to-end, the *Kursk* had once been the pride of Russia's Northern Fleet and, having been designed to defend its waters against aircraft carriers and their battle groups, it was not merely a submarine, but a symbol of state power. It had gone down with all hands after two explosions, the result of unsuccessful tests on torpedos. The mighty vessel's loss was to shake the fledgling presidency.

At the very moment the accident occurred, Putin's motorcade was sweeping out of the Kremlin, escorting Vladimir and Lyudmila on the first leg of their journey to the Black Sea resort of Sochi, where he was to spend his summer holidays. He was not informed of the sinking of the *Kursk* until early the following morning, and at that stage the fate of its 118 crew was undetermined. A more experienced head of state might have realised he was being let down gently when the elderly defence minister, Marshal Igor Sergeyev, called him at 7 a.m. to tell him that the ship 'was not communicating'. The naval authorities had delayed giving him the news in the hope that the problem would be resolved. Sergeyev reassured him that everything was under control and there was no reason to interrupt his holiday. The torpedos the submarine was testing had been brought out from stores somewhere in Dagestan. A similar problem had led to the destruction of a British submarine 50 years earlier, but the reports of that incident had been classified.

As a result of the procrastination, while the cream of the Russian navy was suffocating to death at the bottom of the sea, Putin, still unaware of the extent of the tragedy, spent the day jet-skiing, sunbathing and writing a birthday card to a 70-year-old actress he admired. The families of the *Kursk's* crew, meanwhile, tried in vain to get more information about their loved ones, while the navy refused all offers of help from the West to mount a rescue operation.

It took a telephone call from President Clinton that lasted more than half an hour to make Putin realise that the crew's predicament had become an international preoccupation. Clinton argued that unless Putin accepted help with the rescue he would appear no more human than his Soviet predecessors. But Putin had to balance Clinton's argument with strong objections from his own top brass, who believed the West was out to steal their military secrets. He eventually sided with Clinton (who had, after all, made such a fuss of him as Russia's new Prime Minister when they first met in Auckland) but when a British mini-sub was offered by Tony Blair in response to the emergency, Putin's admirals defied him, refusing at first to give permission for it to be used because of the highly secret status of the vessel. They remained convinced they could handle

PRIME MINISTER abandoned his limousine and cycled to President Medvedev's
Gorky residence on a fine summer day in 2011.

the situation, but while they prevaricated the crew perished and the media laid the tragedy at Putin's door.

With all hope lost, the naval authorities continued to stonewall and it was not until *Komsomolskaya Pravda*, owned by oligarch Vladimir Potanin and normally a pro-Kremlin newspaper, paid a $600 bribe to an officer of the Northern Fleet to obtain a full list of the crew that relatives learned which of their men were aboard the vessel lying at the bottom of the sea. There followed extraordinary scenes. The Deputy Prime Minister, Ilya Klebanov, and Admiral Vladimir Kuroyed flew to the port of Vidyayevo to meet relatives. In the confusion, reports appeared that most of the relatives had been fed copious quantities of tranquilisers in a bid to control mass hysteria, but these turned out to be untrue. One woman, Nadezhda Tylik, whose son was among the dead sailors, was said to have been stabbed with a needle containing sedatives when she shouted at Klebanov and had to be carried from the meeting room, but she said later that it was 'a lie'. She had been given an injection on her doctor's recommendation and at the request of her husband and after 'five minutes and a drink of hot tea' returned to the meeting room.

A NATIONAL TRAGEDY had been turned into an international scandal. It was not until the early hours of Saturday 19 August, a full week after the *Kursk* sank, that Putin slipped back into Moscow to be briefed on the reasons for the tragedy. That night it was officially confirmed that all the crew were dead. The whole country was in deep mourning and Putin was facing one of the most severe trials of his life. Facing up to it boldly, and in full realisation of how great a tragedy had befallen his country, he set off for Vidyayevo on August 22 to meet the families of the victims – fully aware of the harsh reception they had already given to Klebanov.

Newly tanned from his holiday and dressed in a black suit and shirt buttoned to the neck but with no tie, he appeared at the Officers' Club to face a hostile audience of 600, who grilled and barracked him for six agonising hours. Never before had a Russian leader had to endure such a hostile reception. Doing his best to change his normally dour expression, he told the assembly that the tragedy had 'hurt his heart' and promised to side with them in their struggle to obtain answers as to why it had been allowed to happen, but all this did little to placate the grief-stricken relatives, who wanted to know why he had lost so much crucial time before accepting the help of international rescuers. Why had he continued sunbathing on the beach instead of going to sea to direct operations personally?

On his return to Moscow, Putin made it known that after being told of the accident, he had wanted to interrupt his holiday and fly at once to the scene: 'But I refrained, and I think I acted correctly. The arrival in the disaster area of non-specialists and high-ranking officials does not help, but more often hinders. Everyone should be at his post.' This was his response to media criticism of 'inaction' at a time when Clinton had interrupted his vacation to meet with firefighters battling blazes in the western United States, and Chancellor Schroeder had interrupted his holiday to attend memorial services for the Germans who had perished in the Paris Concorde crash.

SOME OF THE SAILORS' relatives were placated by his offer to compensate widows with up to 10 years' salary, though many thought they were being bought off and, unusually perhaps, were not afraid to say so.

Asked at one point why the navy's rescue equipment was so inferior to that of the nations which had come to help, Putin lost his cool and, in a rarely raised voice, said: 'I'm willing to take responsibility for my 100 days in power, but when it comes to the last 15 years I'm ready to sit on the bench with you and put the questions to them'.

Such was the strength of the *Kursk's* loved ones' anger that Putin was advised – advice he took – to cancel plans for a ceremony on the site of the sinking, during which he was to have lowered a wreath into the sea. He later explained that widows and mothers each received a package worth more than $30,000 plus a home in a city of their choice – a fortune to the families of sailors who, at the end of Yeltsin's era, earned less than $50 a month (even the boat's commander only received $2,400 a year).

$130 million was subsequently paid to raise the 18,000-tonne wreck and give the dead a decent burial; four new naval rescue centres were also created. Cynics were to call it the most expensive face-saving operation in Russian history.

This tragic episode cost Putin dearly in terms of popularity: he slipped by a full eight per cent in the polls. The international press was united in attacking him and his government for their apparent disregard. In London, the *Daily Telegraph* described him as callous and irresponsible. But nowhere were the attacks on him more savage than in Moscow, led by Berezovsky's ORT, NTV and Echo of Moscow radio – still owned by Gusinsky. Indeed, Berezovsky had just resigned as a member of the Duma, announcing that he was launching a 'constructive opposition' to Putin. All three media organisations alleged that the Kremlin had 'tried to control coverage of the president's meeting with angry relatives of the dead'.

This was exactly the kind of behaviour that Putin had warned the oligarchs he was no longer prepared to tolerate, and he was to respond with extraordinary cunning and ruthlessness. First, Berezovsky received an angry telephone call from the President complaining about ORT's reference to Chernobyl. As a result the two men agreed to meet but, when Berezovsky went to the Kremlin he was greeted not by Putin, but by Chief of Staff Alexander Voloshin. 'Either you give up ORT within two weeks or you will follow Gusinsky,' said Voloshin. Berezovsky snapped: 'You are forgetting something, I am not Gusinsky'. And with that he demanded a face-to-face meeting with the President.

Putin felt he could not ignore the demand and the meeting took place at 3 p.m. the following day. After a fruitless argument about ORT's coverage of the tragedy, Putin produced a file and began to read from it. The gist of his lecture was that ORT was a corrupt organisation run by one man who took all the money – Boris Berezovsky. Putin had dredged up a report compiled by Berezovsky's old enemy Yevgeny Primakov, who had ordered the raid on his business premises.

According to Berezovsky, when he asked Putin why he was bringing up this old complaint, Putin replied: 'Because I want to run ORT. I am going to run it personally.' Berezovsky says he replied: 'Listen Vlad, this is, at the very least, ridiculous. And secondly it's... Do you understand what you are saying? Effectively, you want to control all the mass media in Russia yourself.' At this Putin got up and walked out. Berezovsky returned to his office and wrote him a letter in which he effectively excommunicated himself from the Kremlin. It was their last communication.

The President dealt with Gusinsky in a more subtle way, according to the broadcaster Alexei Venediktov. With the help of his loyal ally Abramovich, Putin set out to bankrupt his empire. Putin's aim was indeed to starve all four of Media Most's leading outlets of their life-blood: advertising. It was a strategy that proved spectacularly effective: a more compliant team replaced the management of the television station, the newspaper became unprofitable and was taken over, and the editor-in-chief of *Itogi* was sacked, his successor transforming the title into a harmless glossy. In Venediktov's words, the group was 'completely destroyed', although his radio station survived and prospered as a commercial operation.

Abramovich was to buy the privatised half of ORT from Berezovsky and, by agreement with Putin, if not exactly on the President's instructions, promptly turn it over to the state. As this backstage manoeuvring was going on, Putin went public with his attack on the oligarchs. Towards the end of a broadcast to the nation, during which he appeared to have had something of a personality transplant in admitting 'a complete sense of responsibility and guilt for this [the *Kursk*] tragedy', he launched into a vitriolic assault on the media in general and the oligarchs in particular, declaring: 'They want to influence the masses and show the army and the political leadership of the country that we need them, that they have us hooked, that we should be afraid of them, that we should listen to them and let them plunder the country, the army, the fleet. That is their real aim. Unfortunately, we cannot order them to stop, although that would be the right thing to do.'

He included scathing references to those who had long advocated the destruction of the army and the navy and then given a million dollars to the *Kursk* victims' families – a reference to a fund launched by Berezovsky's *Kommersant*. 'They would have been better to sell their villas on the Mediterranean coasts of France and Spain,' he added, striking a particularly populist note. 'Only then could they explain why the property was registered under false names and behind illegal firms. And we could probably ask the question: where did the money come from in the first place?' The message was not lost on Berezovsky, who had a sumptuous villa at Cap d'Antibes, or Vladimir Gusinsky, who had a similarly well-appointed villa at Soto Grande in southern Spain.

THE GLOVES WERE OFF. Rubbished by the mass media at his time of greatest need, the President made it clear he was declaring all-out war on the oligarchs who owned them. Despite being one of those who had masterminded Putin's election victory, Berezovsky found himself under investigation by government prosecutors and the tax police. Could it be that, for them at least, Putin's Russia was turning into a much more dangerous place than Yeltsin's? Berezovsky and Gusinsky had no intention of sticking around to find out. By that winter both had fled the country for good, the former to France and later Great Britain, and the latter to Spain and then Greece, before finally settling in Israel.

By selling his shares in ORT to Abramovich, Berezovsky had made his protégé Putin's tool. Khodorkovsky was richer, but he lacked Abramovich's grasp of the realities of life. As Berezovsky and Gusinsky went into exile, Abramovich was doing what he had been told to do – campaigning for the governorship of Chukotka. And he was already distancing himself from his troubled partner, stating: 'We were close friends once, but Berezovsky didn't help me, he helped himself'.

Meanwhile, the *Kursk* tragedy gave Mikhail Gorbachev an opportunity to get his own back on Putin for supporting General Kryuchkov (if only by omission of any criticism) in the attempted coup back in 1991, and having declared since that Gorbachev had brought about the collapse of the once mighty USSR. 'It seems to me that Putin didn't get the facts at the start of the crisis,' Gorbachev stated in an interview with the BBC. 'The problem was he needed to intervene and instead of doing that he stalled for time. That was clearly an error of judgment. There was a succession of events. Putin made a mistake when he saw that something serious had happened – he stayed put and took no action. Only later did he go to the scene of the accident, he met sailors' relatives, he tried to make amends. But he'd already made a grave miscalculation. It's been a lesson to him.'

And in a harsh reminder of more difficult times, Gorbachev put the boot in by saying that the false and contradictory information given out by Putin's navy spokesman reminded him of the cover-ups of Soviet days – the days Putin had blamed him for ending. 'I've been through all that. Why do you think I pushed through the policy of *glasnost* and gave people some freedom? I used to say we couldn't have no-go areas for the public. That's what bureaucracy thrives on – lack of information.'

But that was the business of the past. Putin had been in the post of President for only a few months and was just beginning to clean out the Augean stables that Yeltsin had left behind. And in this respect, as he said himself, he could not be responsible for what had gone on in the 15 years prior to his election.

IN OTHER MATTERS Putin was putting to use a skill that he had acquired in his experience with Tony Blair. The Russian President mounted a charm offensive on the German Chancellor, Gerhard Schroeder. The two bonded closely and that can be partly credited to Putin's knowledge of Germany and his fluency in its language, an unexpected bonus from his university studies and his time in Dresden. Indeed, Schroeder seemed to overlook the fact that he had been there as a Russian intelligence officer. Putin had more difficulty, however, when it came to the French. President Jacques Chirac did not want to know about cordial talks. Of all the ill-feeling in Europe about Chechnya, it was strongest in France. The French press covered the terrible war in greater depth and at greater length than anywhere else, and the French intelligentsia were constantly reminding their foreign minister that neither he nor Chirac should have anything to do with 'the warmonger at the Kremlin'. When they did eventually meet amidst the splendour of

HE MAY be as fit as they are, but even Vladimir Putin could not bend this frying pan when he called on Russian athletes at their endurance sports club in 2011.

Chirac's Paris headquarters, their friendship initially seemed to owe more to a love of magnificent mirrored ballrooms than a mutual understanding of democratic freedom. However, French newspapers changed their tune when they saw that Chirac was falling under the spell of the young Russian President – due in no small measure to the influence he was having over Hélène Carrère d'Encausse, a Russian-speaking member of the French Academy, who had Chirac's ear.

Putin toured extensively in his first year in office, repairing relationships that had lacked attention during the Yeltsin years. Showering goodwill as far and wide as he could, he visited India, China and Vietnam, but attached relatively little importance to a brief stay in America, where he was deliberately low-key, since he was biding his time until he could deal with the outgoing President's successor. He did, however, spend an hour talking to Larry King on his CNN programme and that produced some dialogue clearly intended for White House ears.

In the interview the pair talked at length about the sinking of the Kursk, although King could not have been expecting much when Putin's answer to his first question on the subject – 'What happened with the submarine?' – was met with the curt reply, 'It sank', leaving American viewers with the distinct impression that they were listening to the most cynical leader in the western world. Putin clearly realised that at this point he was expected to produce the usual sighs and expressions of mortification in order to endear himself to his audience. When King posed the difficult question of why he had not sought help from other countries right away, Putin fudged his response with technical information about the operation his own navy had mounted. But the American TV impresario persisted: in retrospect, was there nothing Putin would have done differently?

'No,' he responded flatly. The only thing he could have done differently as Head of State was to suspend the meetings he was conducting at his holiday base and return to Moscow. But that would have been a PR exercise, he quipped, since he had contact with the military (in this case the navy) wherever he happened to be.

He could, he supposed, have gone to the site of the tragedy. King disagreed: 'I don't think security would have let you do that'. Here the Russian leader became noticeably riled: 'It wasn't because of security [that I didn't go], I would not ask permission from security. Security serves me, I don't serve them... I am Commander-in-Chief...' No, he reasoned, politicians should not be engaged in scoring points at a time when every moment counted for the would-be rescuers. He had turned the argument against him upside-down.

After that, the interview touched briefly on the imprisonment in

Russia of the American businessman Edmund Pope on spying charges, but here again Putin put the interviewer in his place, pointing out that in a democratic state only the courts could decide a case. Then he said something surprising: 'Even if the court confirms that Mr Pope has caused harm by his activities, I don't think that intelligence can be that harmful'. Here was an *ex-KGB* man saying that the art of spying was past its sell-by date. When King persisted: 'You were high up in the KGB – is spying among friendly nations still warranted?' Putin demurred, replying that information-gathering via clandestine means could help 'settle international problems'. Had he enjoyed his time in the KGB? King asked? 'It was an interesting job. It allowed me to increase my vision, to get certain skills, skills of dealing with people, with information. It taught me to choose what the priority is and what is less important.'

After one of the frequent commercial breaks – for this was live TV – King finally got round to asking an important question: Why was Putin trying to stop the United States from building an anti-missile system which would protect the country from nuclear attack? Putin replied: 'When our countries agreed on limiting ABM systems, that was not an accident. When we deploy ABM systems in our own territory we put together certain facilities that are hard to penetrate. If we... try to cover the entire territory this is mission impossible. But let's imagine it could be possible. That could create on one side an impression, an illusion [that that side] could deal a blow, decide on an attack, without fear [of reprisal]. That would disrupt the balance of strategic interest, of forces, which in my mind is very dangerous. When discussing this matter with our American colleagues, I'm always tempted to remind them of how the nuclear arms race began. I always recall the fact that nuclear arms were created in the United States.

'Subsequently, of course, some of the scientists who invented those arms transferred the secrets to the Soviet Union. "Why did they do that?" I always ask my American colleagues... [The scientists] were smarter than you and I. Voluntarily they transferred those secrets to the Soviet Union because they wanted to restore balance. And thanks to that balance mankind has survived without major conflict – large-scale wars – since

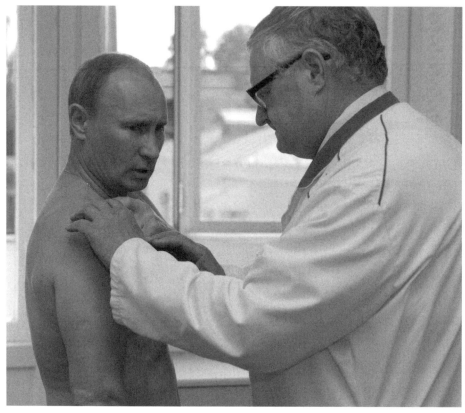

WHEN he injured his shoulder on a tatami mat during a morning workout in August 2011, Putin went to the Smolensk Clinical Hospital for treatment by the celebrated traumatologist Viktor Petrachenkov.

1945. If we disrupt that balance, then we'll put the whole world in great danger, which doesn't serve the interests of either country... That's why we seek to retain the balance, why we object to the deployment of the national ABM system.'

It was an answer that would not have been lost on Bill Clinton (whom Putin had farewelled at a Kremlin dinner with a jazz concert featuring Clinton's favourite living tenor saxophonist, Igor Butman).

After yet another break King raised the question of the hounding of media moguls Boris Berezovsky and Vladimir Gusinsky, asking his now-confident interviewee: 'Are you looking to stop opposition?'

'Opposition?' Putin began his reply. 'On whose side? On the side of those who are interested in hanging on to their power which, I believe, is very detrimental and dangerous to Russia today... The cases you have mentioned have nothing to do with the freedom of the press. In the first case, we are talking about [an organisation called] Media Most, of which Mr Gusinsky is the 70 per cent owner.' The company, Putin said, owed creditors more than $1 billion and that was why Gusinsky was in trouble. In the case of Berezovsky, Putin said that Russia's leading television channel was owned 49 per cent by him and 51 per cent by the government, which in turn gave the government – by the terms of the channel's charter – the right to decide on policy. Taxation policy was the same for commercial media enterprises as it was for government ones, so any talk of denial of freedom of expression was purely a matter of profit for the former owners.

NEXT KING TURNED to a matter of greater international interest: 'Now, let us discuss Chechnya. Is this solvable? Will the troops stay? I know that you had great support when you started. The Russian people are now having their questions. What's the situation today?'

    This question did not go down well. Putin's appointment as Prime Minister had coincided with the invasion of Dagestan by the Chechnya-based Islamic International Brigade (IIB), an Islamist militia. He had been prepared for it: the Security Council had briefed him the previous month about the likelihood of an invasion from the breakaway republic. It was a growing problem that had to be resolved without delay. The Chechens had been brutal and he knew he had to respond in kind. Captured Russian soldiers were being treated as slaves and foreign hostages held for ransoms of up to $1 million each – a bill which Berezovsky had footed personally on more than one occasion.

    And as far as Russia's President was concerned, it was not just his government that did not want the Islamic militants to take control of this corner of their territory: the people of Dagestan didn't want it either. A large proportion of the ethnically mixed population found the prospect of coming under Islamic rule horrifying and this, Putin had reasoned at the time, would soften the blow to the international community when he launched his attack. He had expected America to support his actions when it was learned that the Chechens had received around £15 million to finance their battle.

He could not have been more wrong. In fact, the operation in Chechnya shocked the world, with international reports condemning Russia's ruthless tactics. Many failed to add that during the conflict the 400,000-strong Russian population was wiped out. Huge numbers of civilians were brutally murdered, others kicked out of the country once their property had been 'confiscated'. And now here was an American interviewer asking the President to justify his actions.

Speaking via a translator, Putin began his reply: 'Today the situation is fundamentally different. If I may, I will probably give you a history of the situation, how it started, all those most recent events.'

Alas, he had to give way to a commercial break before completing his lesson: 'I will allow myself to remind you of the very start of those most recent events last year. Since 1996, Russia completely and fully fled Chechnya. Russia did not recognise the independence of Chechnya, but de facto they got full state independence.

'All the structures of governance of Russia were dismantled — the police, the military, public prosecutors' offices, courts — all the offices of administration were destroyed and a President was elected who by law did not comply with the procedures of the Russian Federation.

'What happened afterwards? You all know. They didn't get any independence and de facto the territory was occupied by foreign mercenaries and religious fundamentalist [fanatics] from Afghanistan and other circles in the Arab East. This is a fact of life. They started firing squads working on the thoroughfares, beheading people, mass capture, hostage-taking in the adjacent territories of the Russian Federation and inside Chechnya. Over this period they took hostage over 200,000 people. That was a market of slave-driving in the contemporary world in Chechnya.

'And Russia, finding itself in a similar situation like America found itself in the wake of the Vietnam War, did not respond to it at the time, and naturally that promoted, in a way, those international terrorists who swept – who had their cradle now in this area, their nest was set up there, and it resulted in the direct attack on Afghanistan, on Dagestan last year, armed-land direct attack, coupled with destruction of a shelter, property and death of people. And Russia had to react to protect its people and its territory.'

At this point King interjected: 'And is still reacting…'

Putin's assertive response surprised the interviewer: 'No, the quality of this reaction has changed. When our armed forces entered Chechnya, our armed forces were met with a surprisingly good reception by the local populace. Over the years of Chechnya regime, we probably didn't pay attention to certain new phenomena. It turned out the foreign mercenaries who captured, in fact, certain spheres of authority in the territory of Chechnya, they didn't have unified governance, it was broken, with certain chieftains, those military commanders governing certain segments of society.

'So it turned out that they also threw from outside into Chechnya a new ideological platform, religious platform for conception in Chechnya, coming from Middle East, and they tried to impose on the local population the Sunni trend of Islam. And our people in the Caucasus are mainly Shi'ites, therefore that caused a certain revolt on the part of the population there with respect to those mercenaries, and that caused tension between the two.

'So when the federal forces stopped resistance of the organised troops there, subsequently increasingly actively, the political process was started with the local population, and today there are no large-scale military operations in progress, none.'

So King asked: 'No more suicide bombings? No? Do the Russian people support you?' Putin had clearly prepared his prompt reply: 'Yes, absolutely so, they do support me. But this phase is over, like I said, and now we've started to look for a political solution and, at the time of the Chechnya, now the former clergy, mufti, the clergy head was put – it started after 1996 first and the other thing, just two or three days ago, as the whole territory of Chechnya we held elections for the deputy of

Chechnya to the parliament of Russia both the results and the figure of the population surprised me, over 69 percent of local population actively participated in this election campaign and elected their deputy to the Russian parliament'.

Putin arrived in Okinawa for the G8 conference. By this time, a number of the world's leaders had already met Russia's second president-elect and, although some were irked by the fact that he had visited North Korea on the way to the summit, on the day in question he managed to charm them all and emerged, as it were, smelling of roses. Putin had, in diplomatic terms, scored his first major international victory since talking Tony Blair into an unofficial pre-election summit (that night at the opera).

There was a rude awakening for him around the corner, however. When George Bush finally succeeded Clinton, the message from Washington to Moscow was decidedly cool; in effect it was: "Don't call us, we'll call you". This particularly galled Foreign Minister Igor Ivanov who was desperate (not least for the sake of his own career) to get to Washington and talk to Secretary of State Colin Powell, in order to prepare for early summit talks between the two presidents. Again and again Ivanov was told 'Russia, yeah, remind us again where you are in the GDP league tables? Okay, we'll get to you in due course'. The new masters of the White House clearly considered that the world had now become unipolar, and this seriously offended Moscow.

AFTER IVANOV WAS finally allowed into Washington, it was agreed that the two Presidents would meet in Ljubljana, Slovenia, in June 2001, during Bush's first visit to Europe since his election. 'The Americans picked it as a neutral spot. Nobody had ever heard of the place and 'Bush could only remember that the country had a name beginning with "S" and ending in "A",' opines a Kremlin insider who attended the talks.

Nevertheless, what initially had all the makings of a disastrous encounter turned into a love-in as Putin applied his superb grasp of psychology (from his old judo days) to the sceptical Bush, who had arrived from a very sceptical Washington briefing on the talks. Bush had

BAFFI GETS special attention: Putin with his Karakachan shepherd. A present from the people of Bulgaria, the dog joined Connie, a black labrador, at the Putins' home at Novo-Orgaryovo. Putin let a 5-year-old Moscow boy choose the name Baffi.

clearly agreed with his Republican colleagues that there was no future in continuing Clinton's cosy relationship with Eastern Europe but, to the astonishment of diplomats the world over, he emerged after just two hours of talking to Vladimir Putin clearly having been successfully romanced by the man they had warned him about. Conjuring up a phrase

Jimmy Carter would have been proud of, he was to declare: 'I looked the man in the eye and got a sense of his soul'. (When he was asked some time later if he had seen Bush's soul, Putin simply replied: 'Well, he impressed me as a reliable person').

Just what, his aides asked, had Putin done to create this Damascene conversion in America's leader? The simple truth is he that had taken a leaf out of Tony Blair's book, suggesting they leave their retinue of officials behind and go for a stroll in the gardens of the 16th-century castle to which their meeting had been assigned. Once outside, Putin – 'Call me Volodya, George' – unbuttoned his shirt, showed the American president the humble aluminium cross he wore around his neck and told him how he had been christened with it and how it had 'miraculously' survived the fire that could have cost him his life. Not a man to talk much about his Christian faith and values, Putin was well aware of Bush's deeply religious beliefs. According to Peggy Noonan in her book *When Character was King,* Bush told her that Putin was saying he believed in a higher power: 'I think you judge a person on something other than politics. I think it's important for me and you to look for the depth of a person's soul and character.' He told Putin: 'I was touched by the fact your mother gave you a cross'. And in response Putin apparently explained he had taken to wearing the cross, which he had had blessed in Jerusalem and later feared he had lost in that house fire: 'Putin said to me, "The thing I was most worried about was I'd lost the cross that my mother had given me".' Bush says Putin told him he instructed a workman to look for the cross, but the workman opened his fist and there it was: 'It was as if something meant for me to have the cross,' Putin told him.

THE RUSSIAN HAD played an ace and it won him an on-the-spot invitation to go and stay with George and Laura on their ranch in Texas: 'I wouldn't have asked him there if I didn't trust him,' Bush said later.

The friendship propelled Chirac into action. Never one to allow America to make all the running, the French President cornered Putin into forming the so-called Trilateral Alliance with himself and Schroeder.

It wasn't all about Iraq, Chirac insisted. But of course it was and for a while it strained the lovey-dovey relationship between Russia and America, although Bush never went so far as to say: 'And you can forget about hoe-downs in Texas'.

Putin got his own back some time later when Chirac visited St Petersburg as the President's guest. Putin insisted on inviting the French leader to a concert, knowing full well how much Chirac hated such events. Back through diplomatic channels came the message: 'No concerts, the President doesn't do concerts'. But the host was insistent and a clearly irritable Chirac went along. He duly sulked his way through most of the first half – and then fell asleep before finally leaving.

ONE OF PUTIN'S first deeds as Acting President had been to remove Pavel Borodin from the Kremlin by making him secretary of the Russia-Belarus union. There had long been more than a whiff of impending scandal around Borodin, and in any other circumstances Putin would have dumped him; but it has never been his style to discard people who have helped him along the way and, but for Borodin, he might never even have got to see the inside of the Kremlin.

The Borodin scandal of 1999, however, was not over yet. He may have thought he had put it to bed by discrediting Prosecutor Skuratov, but it was to come back and haunt him after he sent Borodin to America to attend Bush's presidential inauguration as his representative in January 2001. Borodin was astonished to find himself placed under arrest as he passed through John F. Kennedy airport in New York and subsequently extradited to Switzerland on a warrant issued through Interpol by one Bernard Bertossa, Geneva's chief prosecutor. The allegation was that Borodin had demanded – and received – $25 million in kickbacks on contracts worth $492 million, which he had awarded to a Swiss-based company, Mercata Trading and Engineering. This was the company he had engaged to refurbish the Kremlin when he was head of Yeltsin's General Affairs Department. Allegations published at the time stated that Borodin and Yeltsin's daughter Tatyana had transferred millions of dollars to their own accounts from Mabetex, a sister company of Mercata, which was in itself nothing more than a shell company, owned by a Russian businessman called Viktor Stolpovskikh. The Yeltsins were said to have millions of dollars frozen in Swiss accounts.

Borodin's arrest was seen in Moscow as a deliberate act engineered by the new Bush administration to provoke the Kremlin. Many observers say it was Bush v. Putin. Borodin was Secretary of the Russian-Belarus Union and Bill Clinton had already made clear his fury at Belarus for having the temerity to resist the neo-liberal policies he would have had the country abide by: its government had refused to sign up to the 'civil society' groups run by former Secretary of State Madeleine Albright.

Borodin had received his invitation on 13 January – just a week before the grand event was due to take place in Washington. The invitation came from an official member of the inauguration team – one Vincent Zenga, a wealthy lawyer from West Palm Beach, Florida, who had contributed sizeable sums to the Bush campaign.

Having not been abroad for a whole year, Borodin applied to the American embassy in Moscow for a visa to be stamped in his diplomatic passport, but the embassy decided to forward his request to the State Department in Washington seeking 'guidance'. Not having time to hang around, he boarded a New York-bound Delta flight on 17 January, travelling on his personal passport in which he had a visa allowing him into the U.S. for 'business or pleasure'.

The Swiss authorities had issued the international warrant for his arrest on 10 January and when the warrant was executed Borodin pleaded diplomatic immunity, but was reminded that he was not travelling on a diplomatic passport.

While he languished in a prison cell, Borodin says he received 'more than one' call from President Putin. Frenzied moves behind the scenes led to a diplomatic approach to the American authorities. It was proposed that Borodin should stay under house arrest at the home of the Russian consul-general in New York while the Russian ambassador to the United States, Yuri V. Ushakov, offered his personal guarantee that Borodin would turn up for his court appearances.

In a move that Putin is said to have taken as a personal slight to his representatives in the US, Federal Judge Viktor V. Pohorelsky turned down the request and, after a brief appearance in a Brooklyn courtroom, Borodin was ordered back to prison for a week without bail. His cries for recognition of his diplomatic status, his boasts that he was important enough in Russia to have been in charge of a $410 billion budget, as well as his insistence that he was a personal friend of Bill Clinton and had been on his way to Bush's inauguration, where he was an invited guest, all fell on deaf ears. To the US authorities, Borodin was just a middle-ranking Siberian official who had become a Yeltsin crony and was wanted in another country for questioning about a multi-million dollar fraud.

Meanwhile, a red-faced Vincent Zenga was telling the world's media that his invitation to Borodin – an offer which stated he would be provided with 'a car plus driver, a hotel room, and tickets to a candlelight dinner to be graced by the new President (but bring your own tuxedo and it's ball gowns for the ladies)' – had been a mistake, despite the fact that it bore his signature. Zenga said he had 'no idea' how the invitation luring Borodin to American soil had been passed on by someone in the Moscow office of his company, StarCapital. Republican officials, however, did not find his argument convincing and told Zenga that he and his guests were no longer welcome at the inauguration festivities, and subsequently returned the $100,000 donation the lawyer had made to the organising committee.

Borodin spent almost three months in a US federal jail before being handed over to the Swiss authorities, who detained him in Zurich for another week before freeing him on $2.9 million bail and allowing him to return to Moscow. In Geneva, public prosecutor Bernard Bertossa vowed never to drop the money-laundering case against him, saying: 'Justice in Moscow is today turning a blind eye... If the Russian people accept that their bureaucrats allow persons to run around free [and] put what comes into their hands into their own pockets, what can I do?' No further attempt was made to prove the crimes Borodin had been accused of, and he has since been able to travel unchallenged freely around the world.

Putin's loyalty to friends in trouble has long been a subject for raised

PUTIN surprised the audience at a charity concert in the St Petersburg Ice Palace just before Christmas 2010, when he took to the stage and accompanied himself at the piano while singing the old Fats Domino hit, *Blueberry Hill.*

eyebrows in political circles. It does not often sit comfortably with what many regard as his personal integrity, but as he has said himself: 'I have a lot of friends [who have] never betrayed me and I haven't betrayed them either. In my view that is what counts most. I don't even know why you would betray your friends.' Pavel Borodin is clearly a grateful, as well as loyal, friend. Camaraderie, rather than cronyism, is known to be a characteristic of Putin's. He does not believe in letting his friends down, but subscribes to the notion of friendship best summed up by Gogol, one of his favourite writers, in *Taras Bulba:* 'A Cossack has never abandoned or sold his comrade'.

14

Blood on His Doorstep

LYUDMILA PUTINA was at home watching television when she received a telephone call from her husband on 23 October 2002. It was, she recalls, shortly after 9 p.m. and she was surprised that he would call her at this hour. He rarely reached his office before noon but worked late, often until well past midnight, and this would have been his most intensive work period. He was not a phone-homer at the best of times, but at this hour? There had to be something wrong.

Putin was calling his wife to let her know he was unlikely to get home at all that night; something had come up. He would explain later. Lyudmila did not have to wait until later; she saw it on the news. A Moscow theatre was under siege, inside it as many as a thousand people were being held hostage by heavily armed terrorists. This was the sort of event to bring out the best in her husband. No shaking hands with people he was obliged to meet but had no wish to; no soothing the brows of ministers who found themselves out of their depth; just action, action, action. Decisions would have to be taken, decisions that could cost lives. Lyudmila knew that Vladimir would be in his element.

Putin approved each and every detail of the plan with the coolness that had become his trademark. Even when he was warned that every one of the 41 offenders – including the young women among their number – would be shot in the head, whether or not rendered unconscious by the gas, he showed no emotion.

There would be many deaths in the Dubrovska theatre, which stood less than three miles from where he was sitting in his Kremlin office, but that was unavoidable. This damaging siege had to be brought to a swift conclusion and his *Spetsnaz* (commandos) were just the men to carry out the grim task.

This was the dirty side of his job, but he would not shirk it. He could not expect – and would not have wanted – to spend his entire time in office uttering platitudes and shaking hands with visiting dignitaries. And, after all, had he not himself threatened to shoot dead those Germans who stormed his KGB offices in Dresden when the Berlin Wall came down?

Dr Leonid Roshal, whom the bandits permitted to enter the theatre centre, noted that ropes and cables were hanging from the windows in preparation for a possible escape. He also noted trip wires, grenades, Kalashnikovs and packets of marijuana lying about on the floor in addition to the 'cable-way' window escape route.

The bandits made only one demand: the telephone was not to be cut off. If it was, then the first corpses would come flying out of the window.

Putin had been working at the desk in his Kremlin office, studying documents prepared ahead of his visit to Germany for talks with Chancellor Schroeder, when first reports of the theatre siege reached him.

ONE OF THE PEOPLE in the theatre's auditorium at the time of the attack was a Russian police general on whose head the Chechens had put a price. The audience also included tourists from Britain, America, Germany, Australia, Canada, Switzerland and the Netherlands; they were all there to enjoy the performance of a romantic musical *Nord-Ost*. The Chechens had not come for music and love, they had brought two 45 kg bombs with them, one of which they set up in the centre of row 15. They attached other explosive devices to pillars supporting the balcony.

DURING THE ENTIRE 57 hours that the siege was to last, no one was allowed to go out to the toilets. The orchestra pit became a huge stinking lavatory. There was no food (no toilet paper, either), just a few cold drinks.

The actions of the terrorists were led by Movsar Barayev, the 24-year-old nephew of Arbi Barayev, a notorious terrorist, who had made a fortune from kidnappings, in which he demanded a million dollars for the release of each of his hostages. Three months after Arbi Barayev had been killed, Movsar became head of a unit in the so-called Islamic Special Purpose Regiment (ISPR), and began planning the theatre attack, aided by Shamil Basayev.

The 41 terrorists had joined up, one at a time, at an unoccupied, unnumbered and rather sinister Moscow mansion on the corner of Vspolny and Granatny streets. From there they had set off for the theatre in a truck. Soon after they began the siege, young Barayev sent the media a video recording of a somewhat incoherent appeal: 'Each people has the right to its own destiny. Russia has deprived the Chechens of this right, and today we want to take back the rights which Allah gave to us as he gave them to all other peoples…'

According to one of Putin's assistants, who dashed into the President's office after the video had been delivered, he was calmly reading Barayev's declaration, which went on: 'Allah gave us the right to freedom, the right to determine our own fate. The Russian occupiers have drowned our country in the blood of our children and we yearn for a just solution. No one knows that the innocent are perishing in Chechnya: sheikhs, women, children, defenceless people. Therefore we have chosen this method, for the sake of the freedom of the Chechen people. It doesn't matter where we die, so we have decided to die in Moscow.'

A number of people managed to escape from the building before the terrorists occupied it completely. Twenty-six-year-old Olga Romanova, in a fit of rage, slipped through the police encirclement outside the building and ran back inside, where she began arguing with the kidnappers, shouting to those taken prisoner that they should not be afraid of them. Barayev's men took her out of the hall and shot her dead in the foyer. This left the hostages in no doubt that their captors meant deadly business.

YOUNG hockey players practicing for the Golden Puck tournament final found an
unexpected player in their midst – Vladimir Putin.

THROUGHOUT THE CRISIS, Putin remained at his desk, surviving
on sandwiches and soup and never once allowing his emotions to show
through, although deep down he was seething with anger at those
politicians who had used the situation to their own advantage, taking the
opportunity, as Putin saw it, to 'promote themselves on blood'. This was
no time for political spin; and at some point, Putin knew, the theatre
would have to be stormed.

MEANWHILE, A NUMBER of extraordinary events took place. Risking his life, the *Sunday Times* correspondent Mark Francetti entered the occupied building and conducted a 20-minute interview with Barayev; the journalist reported that while some of the terrorists rested, others stayed close by the detonators. 'If the Russians try to take us by storm, the whole place will be blown sky high!' was the clear message. Their aim was not to live through it, but to force Russian troops to end the war at the cost of their own lives. There would be no mercy for anyone.

Another man, who succeeded in getting into the building to plead for the release of his captive son, was taken aside and shot dead as cold-bloodedly as the drunken teenage girl had been.

PUTIN ANNOUNCED that he was willing to make contact with the terrorists on condition they lay down their arms. He also promised to spare their lives if they released the hostages (there is no death penalty in Russia). At the same time he worked speedily through an attack plan produced by the *Spetsnaz*. An attack using gas, they said, was the only way; if stun-grenades were used, the terrorists would have time to detonate their bombs.

Using monitoring devices fitted into the external walls of the building's cellars and roof, the *Spetsnaz* kept track of the terrorist's positions. The information gained was scrupulously transmitted to the attack team. Just before 5 a.m. on the Saturday they moved into their starting positions under cover of darkness. Putin personally gave the signal for the operation to begin.

And then it did begin. Gas was silently pumped into the building through a recently installed ventilation system. There was no warning. The gas acted so quickly that many of the unsuspecting inside lost consciousness after taking just a few breaths of it.

One of the hostages, Anna Andrianova, a *Moskovskaya Pravda* correspondent, managed to place a call to the Moscow Echo radio station, and her desperate plea was heard on the air that morning: 'I have the impression that our forces have begun their operation. Lads, don't leave us in the lurch, give us a chance, if you possibly can, we beg you...'

AND THEN THE *Spetsnaz* appeared. They stormed the building through the drains, through the roof – from every possible entrance. Their first task was to shoot all the terrorists 'within one minute' (Putin himself had specified the time frame) in a bid to ensure that none of them would have time to detonate their explosives.

By the grace of God, not one of the terrorists charged with exploding the bombs was in the hall when the operation began. Barayev and two of his closest aides had gone to their operations room to watch television coverage of their siege; Barayev, clutching a half-empty bottle of cognac, received a bullet in the temple; several of the female suicide bombers were shot as they ran up steps, trying to reach the balcony. The shooting lasted precisely one minute, just as Putin had decreed it should.

All the terrorists were killed. One, using a rope escape, tried to jump out into the street, but was shot by a female FSB officer. Not one of the hostages died at the hands of the *Spetsnaz*. The effects of the gas, however, caused the deaths of 129 people, many of whom perished because of poor medical assistance. Some choked on their own tongues, some were asphyxiated, and others simply never regained consciousness. Many more victims might have survived had the capital's authorities made better preparation for their rescue. Only 80 ambulances had been assigned to take potentially hundreds of people to hospital. In the confusion the bodies of those who had died were laid out on the road alongside the sick and dying, unprotected from the falling snow. It is a mercy that 85 per cent of the hostages were saved.

Putin was seen on television, visiting a hospital and wearing a white medical coat, talking sympathetically to survivors. What the TV cameras had missed, though, was the President working ceaselessly at his Kremlin desk throughout the crisis. He had not paused, even to sleep.

SOME DAYS AFTER the Dubrovka affair, a number of groups of terrorists were wiped out simultaneously in battles close to Grozny. Putin declared that the measures taken 'were commensurate with the threat'. In response, Aslan Maskhadov, the leader of the separatists, made what he described as 'an unconditional offer' for peace negotiations. Putin did not dignify this with a reply, and the Ministry of Internal Affairs declared that such a call for Russia to enter into negotiations was like asking Europe to begin a dialogue with Osama bin Laden.

In a television address on the morning of 26 October Putin justified the use of 'special means', declaring that it had 'succeeded in doing the almost impossible – saving the lives of hundreds of people'; fundamentally it proved, he added, that 'Russia can never be brought to its knees'. In the wake of the infamous Moscow theatre siege, Putin thanked the *Spetsnaz* forces and the citizens of Russia for their 'bravery', as well as the world community for its support in the struggle against 'the common enemy'. He asked forgiveness for not being able to save more hostages and declared the following Monday a day of mourning for the fallen; furthermore, he pledged to continue the fight against international terrorism. Three days later Putin made another statement: 'Russia will respond with measures appropriate to the threat to the Russian Federation: wherever terrorists, crime organisers and their ideological and financial mentors are to be found. I stress, *wherever* they are to be found.'

FRANCE HAD BEEN most vocal in its condemnation of the Russian retaliation in Chechnya. In America, George Bush's protests were somewhat muted after Putin conveyed to him Russian intelligence that Osama bin Laden's al-Qaeda was behind the Chechen uprising and that Movsar Barayev had close links with the master terrorist responsible for the 9/11 attack on New York's Twin Towers. A hero to his own followers, Barayev had been responsible for a number of notorious kidnappings, including the capture of four British Telecom workers whom his late uncle, Arbi Barayev, beheaded when al-Qaeda offered $20 million more than the ransom put up by BT and Granger Telecom, providing they were killed instead of released. When Bush called Putin to assure him Americans stood in solidarity with the people of Russia, the Republican leader also promised to consider adding the Chechen separatists to Washington's list of terrorists, an action which was subsequently implemented.

ONE WEEK AFTER the deadly siege, the Danish government annoyed the Kremlin by allowing the Chechen separatist Ahmed Zakayev to stage his World Chechen Congress in Copenhagen. Accusing Zakayev of involvement in the Dubrovka siege the Russians said he was at the Congress as the envoy of Aslan Maskhadov, whom they described as Chechnya's 'rebel leader', and for good measure reminded the world that Zakayev was wanted in Russia on a warrant filed with Interpol for charges which included 'more than 300 murders between 1995 and 1997'.

Zakayev, an actor and former Chechen minister, had been staying in London for most of the year as the guest of actress and human rights campaigner Vanessa Redgrave, following a car accident in which he was injured during the siege of Grozny.

The Russians regarded Zakayev as Terrorist Public Enemy No. 1, so the Danes detained him despite his protests that neither he nor any of the Chechen leaders had had anything to do with the bloodbath at the Dubrovka. After a month in prison, he was released when the Danes decided that the Russians had insufficient evidence to justify his extradition.

Upon his release, Zakayev flew to Britain, where he was promptly arrested again on the same Interpol warrant at Heathrow Airport and held until Redgrave and Boris Berezovsky – who made no secret of his sympathy for the rebels – posted more than £60,000 bail for him. Describing Zakayev as a man of peace, Redgrave told CNN she was sure that he would die if Britain granted the Russian request for his extradition, which the Danes had boldly refused: 'If he was sent back he would be tortured, he would be killed in some jail,' she said, adding: 'He's not a rebel, he's an elected leader. He was elected in elections in January 1997, which were supervised and endorsed by the OSCE [Organisation for Security and Cooperation in Europe] and later endorsed by President Yeltsin.'

While all this was going on, Putin took measures to curtail the negative publicity some aspects of the *Nord-Ost* operation were getting at home. The lower house of the Duma approved tight restrictions on future press coverage of terrorism-related incidents, at the same time rejecting a proposal by the liberal Union of Right Forces party that an independent investigation be held into Putin's handling of the siege.

And just in case they failed to get the message, Chechens living in Moscow were subjected to increased police harassment. In a clear move to protect Maskhadov's political credentials, Shamil Basayev posted a statement on his website claiming responsibility for the siege, resigning all official positions within the self-proclaimed Chechen government and apologising to his so-called President for not informing him of the planned raid. The moves were dismissed in Moscow as mere political manoeuvring and Putin's spokesman said they had recordings of wire-tapped phone conversations which proved that Maskhadov knew of the plans in advance. Meanwhile, conspiracy theories abounded.

Anti-Putin writer Anna Politkovskaya interviewed Khanpasha Terkibayev, a Chechen political intermediary, and concluded that Terkibayev must have been among the hostage-takers, because he seemed 'evasive' when she tackled him about allegations that he was an *agent provocateur*. Such – unproven – allegations led some theorists to believe that terrorists had been allowed into Moscow with their substantial arsenal of weapons by the FSB, who had even suggested the theatre as a possible target. They surmised that such a highly provocative act would give Putin the freedom to step up his war in Chechnya. They also suggested that there had been more than 41 terrorists that night, and that as many as 10 might have been allowed to escape; those who could not move were shot rather than be allowed to 'talk'. Khanpasha Terkibayev later died in a car crash.

Putin flew into a rage when Vanessa Redgrave – seen by some as an anti-Semite supporter of the Palestine Liberation Organisation and of the Guantanamo Bay detainees – went into graphic detail about the fate she believed her friend Zakayev would suffer if he were returned to Moscow. In an article for *The Guardian* she wrote: 'There is widespread and increasing use of torture in Russia. This grows alongside the mounting brutality of the Russian government's war against the Chechen people.

'Suspects in pre-trial detention all over Russia are subject to *slonik* –

a gas mask, or sometimes a plastic bag, is placed over the suspect's head, the air supply is cut off and sometimes tear gas is pumped into the mask or bag. The victim loses consciousness or vomits. Many other forms of torture are used to extract confessions, which under Russian law can be signed without the presence of a lawyer and are accepted by the courts,' she claimed.

Her words did not go to waste. The following year Zakayev, who had specialised in Shakespearean roles during his acting career, was granted political asylum in the UK – just as Berezovsky had been – and promptly styled himself Prime Minister of the Chechen Government in Exile.

Putin was appalled that such a thing could be allowed to happen in a country with which he had established a healthy and friendly working relationship. In March 2006 Redgrave inadvertently played into the Russian leader's hands when she remarked in an interview with US broadcast journalist Amy Goodman: 'I don't know of a single government that actually abides by international human rights law, not one, including my own. In fact, they violate these laws in the most despicable and obscene way, I would say.'

15

Love Me Do

FROM THE MOMENT Paul McCartney set foot in Russia in May 2003 to perform sell-out concerts in Moscow and St Petersburg, it was obvious there was going to be a clash of egos between him and the President. Mark Haefeli, the celebrated American video director who filmed Macca's Red Square concert, told me that, on arrival in St Petersburg, McCartney received an invitation from Putin, a renowned Beatles fan, to join him at the Summer Palace. 'But Paul said no,' says Mark. 'It didn't suit his schedule. The concerts were very important to him and he needed all the time he had for rehearsals and sound checks. Anyway, he doesn't get involved in politics.

'When we subsequently arrived in Moscow there was a certain amount of to-ing and fro-ing between the Kremlin and Paul's management – principally about who should go to whom [I had the same problem when I brought the Beatles and Elvis Presley together in 1965], but on the morning of the Red Square concert an emissary arrived from the Kremlin with a formal invitation for Paul and Heather [his then wife, Heather Mills-McCartney] to take tea with the President there that afternoon, so that was it; Paul decided there was no way out.'

Haefeli accompanied the couple to Red Square, but found himself being shown around to the tradesman's entrance, only to meet up with the McCartneys again in a waiting room, where they were surprised to find a large contingent of the Russian press present; Putin was not about

WHEN Paul McCartney arrived in Moscow with his then-wife Heather Mills, the
President invited them to take tea at the Kremlin and then took them for a walk in
the grounds.

to pass up such a golden photo opportunity.

After a short wait, double doors sprang open and Putin made a grand
entrance. 'They were all smiles and lots of pictures were taken,' says
Haefeli. 'Putin said what a breath of fresh air the Beatles had been for
him and people all over the world in the Sixties – the funny thing is, the
entire time he was speaking to Paul in front of the press he spoke in
Russian and his words were translated into English.'

Once the press had been dismissed, however, and the trio retired to a more private room, Putin continued the conversation in good English. It was at that point that Heather made her blunder. Bored with all this talk of the Beatles (before her time) she switched the subject to landmines and the atmosphere changed dramatically. Putin couldn't believe what he was hearing as the musician's wife demanded his attention for the charity she had set up in the wake of the late Princess Diana's own campaign. What little colour Putin had in his face was drained as she lectured him – the president of the largest country in the world, that is, a man who had a reputation for doing the haranguing – about the perils of landmines and what he should do about them. Putin was clearly not used to being talked to in this way, particularly by a woman. He took her remarks as a reflection of alleged human rights abuses in Chechnya – a topic guaranteed to incur his wrath. Probed by a French journalist at a press conference in Brussels the previous November about the use of such weapons, he had given this sarcastic reply: 'If you seriously want to become a radical Islamist and undergo circumcision, I invite you to come to Moscow. We are a multi-denominational country, we also have specialists on this matter and I will advise them to perform the operation in such a way that nothing would grow out of you again'.

He could not suggest to Ms Mills that she underwent such an operation, but he knew exactly how to get rid of his now troublesome guests and suggested they all take a walk and get some 'fresh air'. To the delight of sightseers, the trio of internationally famous faces were to be seen striding around the Kremlin's precincts with the President in the lead, the McCartneys doing their best to keep up and the bodyguards ensuring that none of the surprised onlookers were ever in touching distance. Then, quite suddenly, Putin turned to the McCartneys, shook their hands, said goodbye and marched off with his guards, leaving Paul at the mercy of the autograph hunters.

The capacity crowd who turned out in Red Square to hear Paul belt out *Back in the USSR* and other numbers that night included former president Mikhail Gorbachev and a dancing defence minister, Sergei Ivanov. For a time it looked as though Putin was going to snub the event but then, at just the right moment, the gates swung open and the

President strode out with his guards. The tricky issue of landmines and meddling wives or whatever wasn't going to deter Putin from seeing a living legend perform in the shadow of the Kremlin walls.

A leading psychiatrist, who has extensive experience in dealing with Russian clients, has this to say: 'I find it very interesting that Putin would have gone to the trouble of issuing a second invitation to McCartney after being snubbed the first time around. After all, this was one of the most powerful men in the world dealing with a pop star, but chasing him like a fan. Putin has gone out of his way to say that his favourite Beatles recording is of McCartney's composition *Yesterday*. It shows a measure of immaturity that one would not normally expect from Putin, but that's interesting too, because it proves that he can easily conceal aspects of his true self. I don't believe the altercation with McCartney's wife has anything to do with personal ego: Putin would not have thought that he personally was being insulted but that his government, his country [was the target] when this woman tried to educate him about something as basic as landmines. He is a man of great pride and he has passed that on to millions of Russians who had lost so much hope in the Yeltsin years.'

It's an indisputable fact that, in private, Putin is inclined to outbursts where his ideals are concerned. When an outsider dares challenge the way things are going in Russia, he subscribes to the statement of the Soviet intelligence agent Gevork Vartanyan – the man who saved the lives of Stalin, Churchill and Roosevelt at the Teheran Conference in 1943 – 'A traitor deserves either a bullet or a rope around his neck'. He even made it clear to George Bush that he should not lecture him about democracy in front of reporters at a joint press conference in St Petersburg in July 2006. Well aware of how badly relations between their two countries had deteriorated since Washington began criticising his iron grip on Russia's media and politics, Putin delivered a barbed retort when Bush implied that he would like to see in Russia the kind of democracy America was struggling to set up in Iraq. Putin's response – hardly veiled – was: 'I'll be honest with you: we, of course, would certainly not want to have a democracy like in Iraq. Nobody knows better than us how we can strengthen our own nation. But we know for sure that we cannot strengthen without developing democratic institutions. And this is the path that we'll certainly take.'

Like the former Mrs McCartney, Bush had learned the hard way not to try to educate Vladimir Putin.

PRIOR TO PUTIN'S first visit to London as President an extraordinary note arrived on Tony Blair's desk. The highly confidential missive, delivered to 10 Downing Street by an emissary (according to a Blair adviser), alerted the Prime Minister to the fact that the Russian leader should not be expected to reach any decisions during their talks – and why. It had been sent from Moscow, apparently with Putin's knowledge, and Blair was not the only leader to receive it.

Blair's man says that ahead of the meeting he offered the puzzled Prime Minister this assessment of the way Russia was being run: 'The situation in the Kremlin is that things haven't actually changed under Putin as much as people think they have. It's still a very Byzantine system

EVEN on a rare day off at his country home Putin gets calls from the office. This time the Prime Minister's caller was President Medvedev.

and you don't know who exactly has the power. I have a feeling that if you went to see the boss in any department you would open the door and there would be Putin. He has a very big job in balancing the different centres of power and in that respect he is extremely clever.'

Medievalist Steven Runciman wrote of the relations between Medieval Europe and the Byzantine Empire: 'Ever since our rough crusading forefathers first saw Constantinople and met, to their contemptuous disgust, a society where everyone read and wrote, ate food with forks and preferred diplomacy to war, it has been fashionable to pass the Byzantines by with scorn and to use their name as synonymous with decadence.' In many ways, Russia has proven itself to be a willing inheritor of Byzantine culture, adopting her religion, theology and some social structures.

One of Russia's most renowned philosophers, Konstantin Leontyev, was an apologist of Byzantism and advocated closer cultural ties between Russia and the East in order to counterbalance 'revolutionary influences from the West'. He advocated Russia's cultural and territorial expansion eastward to India, Tibet and China. Russia's double-headed eagle that looks both East and West was, after all, adopted from the Byzantines.

Lord Browne, who has met Putin everywhere from Chequers with Tony Blair in 2001 to the President's dacha – 'quite gilded, very Russian, lots of furniture which looks antique or appears to be' – in 2005, has a clear picture of Putin as the nation's saviour. 'It's so clear when you meet him – your intuition says: "This is a very strong person I am with". Not physically, I mean, he doesn't look huge, but you know from his presence and the way he talks that he doesn't ever doubt himself. I wonder how far he will go, with the means he has, to get what he wants. If you can define that, you can define his character: how far will he go? I think there are limits.

'And the extraordinary thing is how popular he is. I knew from the first time I went there when he was in power that he had become a national hero. He has the respect of his nation for his tireless work to fix their problems. There was a saying there that if the trains went wrong in Sakhalin, Mr Putin would be there to fix them.'

16

Get Khodorkovsky

THE MEN FROM the Prosecutor's Office and the Ministry of Internal Affairs had planned it all with military precision. When the Tupolev 154 private jet landed at five o'clock on the morning of 25 October 2003, the pilot failed to spot two minivans with smoked glass windows waiting in the darkness at the end of the runway. This was, after all, merely a re-fuelling stop, and at that hour of the morning there were few people around the airport at Novosibirsk, deep inside central Siberia. Not until he had shut down the engines did the vehicles begin their short but high-speed dash towards the aircraft. The first those on board knew of the arrival of the vans' occupants was a loud bang reverberating through the cabin as the Tupolev's door was blown off its hinges. As smoke billowed around the cabin more than a dozen men in combat fatigues clambered on board, screaming at everyone on the plane to put their hands on their heads. The men from the FSB had arrived to arrest Mikhail Khodorkovsky. Putin's threatened war against the oligarchs had stepped up several gears at once.

AS KHODORKOVSKY was bundled down the steps of the aircraft in handcuffs – his own security men were rendered helpless by the speed of the operation – he demanded to know the reason for his arrest. His offence, he was told, was failing to turn up at short notice as a witness in a criminal trial. He knew, of course, that this was a ruse, though he could

NOT at the round table: Once Russia's richest man, Mikhail Khodorkovsky is now in prison on charges of fraud and tax evasion. Putin had warned him not to use his £15 billion fortune to meddle in politics.

not have known the detailed planning that had gone into it. Even while Putin was denying personal involvement, Roman Tsepov, former head of the private security firm which had guarded Sobchak, and who was present at Khodorkovsky's arrest said: 'It wasn't Volodya, it was us. It was a job that had to be done for him'. Tsepov died some time later in a St Petersburg clinic in highly questionable circumstances.

It was not as simple as that, however. Although Tsepov's men may have executed the plan it was – according to Khodorkovsky's own superb intelligence sources – a man closer to Putin than any other who gave it the green light: Igor Sechin, the Grey Cardinal, the man who once sat in the corner of Putin's office in St Petersburg and who had been rewarded with the job of heading Rosneft, the state oil company that subsequently acquired the huge assets of Khodorkovsky's own oil company, Yukos.

With minimum delay, Khodorkovsky was flown back to Moscow under armed guard and deposited in a grim detention centre called the Sailor's Silence (*Matrosskaya Tishina*), where he was locked in a cell with five other prisoners. Incarcerated so close to the president he had dared to provoke, the wealthiest man in the country was to breakfast each day on thin fish soup and tea, and dine on a buckwheat muffin spread with margarine. Much worse lay ahead.

The incarceration of Putin's most powerful opponent sent shock waves through the oligarch community. Roman Abramovich, who had bought Chelsea Football Club four months earlier, was in London for the team's match against Manchester City when he heard the news. Like everyone else, Putin was well aware that the two oil barons – Khodorkovsky of Yukos and Abramovich of Sibneft – had just agreed to merge their companies. Although Abramovich was fairly sure he was safe, Putin jailing his new business partner was just too close for comfort. One of his first actions was to place a call to Moscow, to his friend Alexei Venediktov, the maverick political commentator. He knew that Venediktov had his ears closely pressed to the Kremlin walls and had warned Khodorkovsky the previous June that he was going to be arrested sooner or later. At the time both oligarchs had laughed off the suggestion, but now Abramovich was anxious to find out if his best (probably his one and only) Russian media contact knew any more. He told Venediktov he would return to Moscow the following day and was anxious to meet with him. Venediktov was not so keen. He did not relish the prospect of journeying out of the city to Abramovich's dacha, but the oligarch was insistent. He would be in Russia for only one day and it was very important that they talk, and in secret.

The radio journalist relented, and when he did arrive at the oligarch's house he found it filled with flowers: it was Abramovich's 37th birthday. When a man as rich and powerful as Abramovich celebrates his birthday, the floral tributes can be prodigious, but Venediktov was unimpressed. He suggested to his friend that he take the flowers and sell them on the street to put some food on the table for the poor.

After that inauspicious start, they got down to discussing the arrest. Seated at a table in his favourite Georgian restaurant, Venediktov told me soon afterwards: 'Abramovich appeared stunned, nonplussed by the news. He had been sure of Khodorkovsky's immunity. That was one of his few miscalculations. He had summoned me because he wanted to make it clear to me [and probably to Venediktov's army of *Moscow Echo* radio listeners] that it was not him who had put Khodorkovsky in prison. I didn't quite believe him and I told him so. He said, "Is there no way I can convince you?" I said he could try. He could convey his thoughts but my mind was my own and I would decide for myself.'

While Abramovich wanted everybody to know that he had nothing to do with having Khodorkovsky put behind bars, he was willing to spend only 24 hours in Moscow to clarify the matter.

The inference has been from certain critics that Putin, with his deputy Sechin's encouragement had inspired his enemy's arrest and the dismantling of Yukos, officially described as 'the forced sale of assets'. The original explanation given to Khodorkovsky for his arrest came unstuck when the Prosecutor General's office announced that he was being charged with massive tax evasion, fraud and theft amounting to $1 billion in total. It was widely rumoured that Khodorkovsky had been planning to buy the support of a considerable number of members of the Duma in advance of the elections scheduled for 7 December. The – unsubstantiated – theory goes that Putin had hoped that, like Berezovsky and Gusinsky, Khodorkovsky would flee the country if the frighteners were put on his closest executives; thus his right hand man, Platon Lebedev, had been picked up and accused of a $280-million fraud relating to the privatisation of a fertiliser company almost a decade earlier. Two other Yukos managers had been charged with tax evasion and murder. By refusing to be goaded by Putin in this way, Khodorkovsky was either demonstrating huge bravery or a colossal error of judgment.

The persecution continued. Not only were the offices of Yukos raided, but also those of the Yabloko party, for which four Yukos executives were standing as candidates for the Duma. The move ensured that the party failed to get the five per cent of the vote necessary to qualify for seats.

The President didn't get it all his own way. The stabilisation of the Russian economy – the central plank of his policy – took a hefty blow as foreign investors rushed to get their money out. The stock market lost a tenth of its value in a single day. But if Putin had gambled on winning over the man in the street then he was definitely on to a winner. His personal popularity rose by two percent in the wake of his attack on the Yukos empire and the company's shares leapt 4.1 per cent when, on 3 November, Khodorkovsky resigned as chief executive.

No one would deny that these events made Abramovich even richer: Putin's favourite oligarch had first proposed the creation of Yuksi – the marriage of Yukos and Sibneft – at the beginning of the year, committing himself to the point of promising to pay a $1 billion penalty should he withdraw for any reason. But the driving force behind the company to which he was entrusting his future was now in jail, and in Putin's Russia there are informal solutions to most issues. Abramovich had lost a close

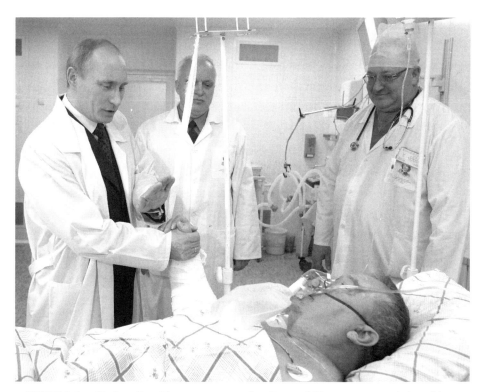

WHEN the Air Landing Troops commander General Shamonov was injured in a road accident he received a surprise visit from Putin at the Burdenko Hospital – named after Nikolay Burdenko, the man who pioneered Russian neurosurgery.

ally in the Kremlin when the President's Chief of Staff, Alexander Voloshin, resigned in protest over the handling of the Khodorkovsky affair, but the move brought Abramovich and Putin even closer together.

Yukos had already bought 20 per cent of Sibneft's shares for $3 billion in cash, valuing Abramovich's company at $15 billion and giving it a 26 per cent stake in the combined group in return for the remainder of the sum. This left Abramovich in the unfamiliar position of being the junior partner and, with Khodorkovsky indisposed, leadership of the merged entity had passed, not to Sibneft's CEO Eugene Shvidler, but to one of Khodorkovsky's associates, Simon Kukes. This rendered the entire operation vulnerable to a political attack which it would not have to face if he – as Putin's favoured oligarch – or Shvidler was in charge.

Just before the start of a meeting of shareholders on 28 November, Abramovich suspended the merger. Was he about to take advantage of the conglomerate's new weakness for personal gain? Or was he acting on the President's orders?

A core shareholder demanded that he should pay a penalty of five times the $1 billion agreed in the merger contract for unwinding it, return the $3 billion down payment with interest, and relinquish Sibneft's 26 per cent in Yukos.

The exiled oligarch Leonid Nevzlin – a rogue Yukos shareholder – and two others subsequently offered to give up their shareholdings in return for Khodorkovsky's freedom, but Khodorkovsky himself rejected the offer before anyone had a chance to consider it. Part of the reason was to emerge later when – incarcerated in a Siberian prison and serving an eight-year sentence – he made declarations on a website he was somehow able to maintain, proclaiming that he was Putin's enemy and not Russia's.

KHODORKOVSKY'S FINAL aim was – and probably still is – to achieve political power. He had made money, an unimaginable amount of money, building a business so huge that it was his country's fourth biggest commercial enterprise. In short, he'd been there, done it, and now had other things to prove. Such success seems to have made him contemptuous of those who wielded political power but had never made their mark in business.

The extent of Putin's control over Abramovich was made clear to me and writer Dominic Midgley when I put to the Kremlin an allegation Berezovsky had made to us in the course of research for our separate biography of Roman Abramovich.

At his heavily fortified office in Mayfair Berezovsky alleged to Midgley and me that Abramovich had made him sell his Sibneft shares for $1.3 billion when they were worth two or three times that amount (an allegation which has since become the subject of a High Court battle between the two men). Berezovsky further claimed that Abramovich turned up during his French exile and told him that unless he complied: 'Putin will destroy our company and we will both end up with nothing.'

Back home that night, I communicated Berezovsky's accusation to the Kremlin, making sure they knew that unless there was a swift response, the story – clearly detrimental to the President – would be published. The following morning I heard back from Moscow – not from the Kremlin but from the office of Abramovich, who had diligently refused to co-operate in any way with our biography of him. The oligarch was concerned that Midgley and I were getting 'too much negative information' and he was dispatching one of his most senior lieutenants forthwith to meet us in London. Abramovich was, it turned out, doing exactly what he had been told to do.

As Yukos ran deeper and deeper into trouble, Abramovich (or perhaps his Kremlin sponsors) saw a way to profit from the mess. Former Yukos manager Nevzlin's efforts to penalise his new partner and to free his imprisoned one both having failed (his powers were greatly curtailed by the fact that he was now in self-imposed exile), Abramovich was free to forge ahead with a plan to unbundle the merger and profit from its abortion. If he thought he was being greatly helped by Putin's dismissal of his Prime Minister Mikhail Kasyanov – whose crime had been to express his 'deep concern' over the way the Khodorkovsky business was handled – then Abramovich had not bargained for the appointment of his successor, Mikhail Fradkov, a former head of the Tax Police.

Abramovich could expect no kid-glove handling by the new man, who was as hardline as his boss when it came to dealing with the oligarchs who, he believed, had tricked the nation out of 60 per cent of its assets.

If ever Putin had wanted an opportunity to turn up the heat on Abramovich, then this was it. He declined to take it, however. Abramovich surged ahead, using every technique in the book to get his money – and more – out of Yukos. At one point during that London meeting engineered by the Kremlin, I asked his right-hand man why the businessman didn't simply repay Yukos the $3 billion he had received for the shares in Sibneft and call it a draw. 'But they want more,' he exclaimed.

The authorities were pounding Yukos for billions in taxes and penalties and the government had frozen its assets, making it unable to pay anyone.

By early September 2004 Abramovich's holding company had clawed back 57 per cent of the 92 per cent it had transferred to Yukos, after a court ruled that the issue of the new shares Yukos had used to finance that stake was illegal. At another court hearing there was more good news for Putin's man: the 14.5 per cent of his company he had transferred for 8.8 per cent of Yukos' treasury sales was also rescinded. He then took further steps to start recovering the rest, for which he had received $3 billion in cash.

Why was the fate of these two oligarchs and their companies so different? In an interview with the newspaper *Izvestia*, Paul Klebnikov, the American editor of the Russian version of *Forbes* magazine, said: 'I think one of them is simply a personal friend of the President. And the other is just an independent man. If the law is applied so strictly to one oligarch, why is it not applied in the same way to the other, who has offended public morals much more seriously?'

This point of view was widespread: if they condemned Khodorkovsky, why didn't they condemn them all? The explanation from the powers-that-be was that if someone proved that Potanin, Aleksperov, Abramovich, Yevtushenkov, or whoever else it might be, had stolen – by failing to pay due taxes – vast sums of money from the state, and taken Yukos' attitude of not wanting to return that money, then Putin could never forgive them. And why should he? Today, the steely-faced president is regarded as one of Russia's strongest leaders. He would also argue that his is a policy not based on unproven generalisations, but rather on the kind of real investigations that are conducted in any other civilised state. After Khodorkovsky's arrest, oil taxes collected rose instantly 15-fold, and although no one would claim it has stopped altogether, the misappropriation of Russia's oil money has fallen dramatically. There are still problems: a number of companies have been

PRESIDENT (Bill) Clinton reckoned Boris Yeltsin had picked his successor when he first met Putin in September 1999 at an APEC meeting in Auckland, where Putin was standing in for his president. 'Putin presented a stark contrast to Yeltsin,' Clinton wrote in his diary. ' Yeltsin was large, stocky and voluble. Putin was measured and precise... and extremely fit from years of martial arts pratice.'

extracting the cheaper oil from many of Russia's wells, in particular in Evenkia. Of the thousands of wells containing oil, at least half have been abandoned. Barbarous methods of extraction have resulted in up to 25,000,000 tonnes of oil being left in the ground each year – that's equivalent to the entire output of oil-rich Azerbaijan. Since his arrival in office, Putin has made it his business to challenge the companies responsible.

Just a few hours after he had given *Izvestia* his thought-provoking interview, Paul Klebnikov was murdered on a Moscow street as he walked home from the *Forbes* office on Ulitsa Dokukina. It was around 10 o'clock in the evening; four shots were fired at him from a passing car. It took five minutes for an ambulance to get to him and then, bleeding to death, he had to wait a further 20 minutes for the arrival of a surgeon at Municipal Hospital No. 20, a clinic with a good reputation. Putin had lost a useful media ally.

Klebnikov's most obvious enemy was the subject of his biographical book *Godfather to the Kremlin: Boris Berezovsky and the Looting of Russia*. Berezovsky had sued *Forbes* in 1996 over an article in which Klebnikov called him 'a mighty prince among bandits', accusing him of the assassination of the television presented Vladislav Listyev. Only a few hours after Klebnikov's death, Berezovsky said that he (Klebnikov) had been playing a dangerous game: 'Obviously someone didn't like the way he was behaving, and this someone decided to get rid of him... To publish a list of the richest people in the country [as Klebnikov had done in *Forbes*] was tantamount to giving their names to the Public Prosecutor. Standards are different...'

17

Trusted Friends

SO WHO DOES Putin turn to when the world turns on him? While his spokesmen were busy dealing with the response to the Klebnikov matter, Putin is understood to have paid a visit to the Sretensky Monastery.

Until the late 14th century the land on which the monastery was built had been known as Kuchkovo Field. In 1378, the last of the Velyaminov military leaders was executed there and shortly afterwards the ancient church named after the Blessed Mary of Egypt was built. The monastery was founded in 1395, by order of Great Prince Vasily Dmitrievich, son of Dmitri Donskoi, who also built the church of the Vladimir Mother of God in memory of the salvation of Moscow from Tamerlane's attack on the day when the miracle-working icon, the *Vladimir Mother of God* was brought from Vladimir to Moscow.

It is traditionally believed that the estates of the semi-legendary Lord Kuchka and Kuchkovo Field were both in the region of Lubyanka Street; in the 12th to 14th centuries the road from Kiev and Smolensk ran through here on its way to Vladimir on the Klyazma river, Great Rostov and other cities. By this road, in 1382, Dmitri Donskoi travelled to mobilise his forces against Tokhtamysh – the prominent Khan of the White Horde, forcing the Khan to withdraw from Moscow after destroying the city. During the Tamerlane invasion, which in 1395 reached the city of Yelets, this road was used to take the *Vladimir Mother of God* icon, from Vladimir to the Kremlin, where it was met by the Muscovites at the place where the Sretensky Gates now stand. At the place where the icon was met, a church was built, and then the Sretensky Monastery, the cathedral of which stands there to this day.

It was in the adjacent cellars of the Lubyanka, the home of the NKVD (later the KGB and FSB), that thousands of priests and laymen were executed. It is believed that Putin, while working as an agent in the famous Lubyanka offices, just next door, approached the head of the Monastery, Father Tikhon, and the unlikely pair soon became friends.

Archimandrite Tikhon – the honorary title that the revered clergyman would go on to inherit – started out in life as a scriptwriter. Born Georgii Aleksandrovich Shevkunov in 1958, he graduated from the screenwriting department of the All Russian Institute of Cinematography. Father Tikhon was the spiritual son of Father Ioann (Krestyankin), one of the most influential religious figures of the last 100 years – a man who attributed his survival of the brutal Soviet regime, during which time he had been imprisoned and persecuted, to his enduring faith. Father Tikhon had met his mentor – a man long-recognised as one of Russia's true prophets – when he joined the Pskovo-Pechersky monastery as a novice; little did either man know at that time the level of influence the young clergymen would go on to have. 'Putin's confessor' first rose to prominence in 1990 when, as an ideological activist of the conservative wing of the Russian Orthodox Church, he used his significant skills as a writer to compose the article *Church and State*, in which he openly expressed exceedingly controversial views on democracy. He wrote: 'A democratic state will inevitably attempt to weaken this country's most influential Church by bringing the ancient tactic of "divide and conquer" into play'. Not a view that many of Putin's fellow leaders would share or wish him to pay much attention to, alhough Tikhon is not entirely alone in his thoughts. Here in Britain, Father Stephen Platt, an Oxford-based Orthodox theologian, agrees: 'We live in a society, which, in spiritual terms, many would think has lost its way. Officially, Britain is still a Christian country. The bishops of the Church of England, for instance, still sit in the House of Lords. Although the Queen remains head of the

Church of England, it is debatable how much impact that has on the life of the average Briton. Muslims, who are not afraid to shout about their faith, consequently have the loudest voice in religious terms.'

In 2008 Father Tikhon went on to establish himself as one of Russia's most erudite figures with his controversial film *The Fall Of The Empire – The Lessons of Byzantium,* an ominous essay about the necessity of a huge country such as Russia avoiding a repeat internal dilution of power.

PUTIN IS UNDERSTOOD to have met, and became friends with, Father Tikhon after his wife's road accident in 1993, which caused him to rethink his life. Such was the monk's power of spiritual healing by that time – at least in the minds of his adoring public – that many believed Archimandrite Tikhon would succeed Alexei II as Patriarch of All Russia, although in fact this was not possible under the rules of the Russian Orthodox Church, since he is not even a bishop. However both men had made tremendous contributions to the cause of uniting the two Orthodox churches. Putin claims to have had no involvement in the choice of Alexei II's successor, Patriarch Kirill, but Kirill has expressed confidence in Father Tikhon by allocating him considerable responsibilities: he is head of the Sretensky Stavropignalny Monastery, Executive Secretary of the Patriarchal Cultural Council, Rector of the Sretensky Spiritual Seminar and co-Chairman of the Church Social Council for Protection from the Alcohol Threat.

Father Tikhon is not short of well-placed friends. Among his parishioners is Lieutenant-General Nikolay Leonov – who served in the KGB from 1958 to 1991 and during the 60s and 70s worked in the First Central Management Unit as its deputy head, at some point alongside Putin. Today Father Tikhon and Leonov are both members of the editorial board of the magazine *Russky Dom.* Leonov was also a political commentator on a television programme of the same name which used to be broadcast on the Moskoviya channel. Indeed, he was believed to be the guiding light behind both the magazine and the TV show.

The individual many consider to be Putin's spiritual adviser also has some interesting views on censorship: 'Censorship is a normal political tool in any normal society that should uproot all forms of extremism. Personally I am in favour of it both in the religious and the secular spheres. Sooner or later society will come to the sober realisation that state censorship is absolutely necessary. Let us recall how, in his youth, Pushkin railed against censorship and could hardly write "censor" without rhyming it with "fool", although later he supported censorship.' However, the religious leader's conclusion owes something to poetic licence: he based it on Pushkin's letter to Yazykov (November 1826), in which Pushkin described the Tsar being his 'censor' as of 'great benefit' (albeit Pushkin chafed against Tsar Nicholas' censorship, especially in his diaries and letters to his wife).

So it comes as no surprise to learn that the first to congratulate Putin on becoming President was none other than Father Tikhon, who rejoiced in his predecessor's exit and condemned the 'era of Yeltsinism'.

ALTHOUGH HE HAS never sought outrightly to exploit whatever relationship he has with Putin, Father Tikhon let his guard slip somewhat in an interview with *Profile* magazine when he declared: 'I have with much interest learned from quite a number of articles about my special closeness to the President, about my supposed influence on him, about my participation in solving of Church and even state problems. Based on these newspaper "facts", analysts in their turn make conceptions, global prognoses and so on and so forth. What can be said about that? First of all, in social and political circles there is an unshakeable conviction that somebody directs the President of Russia. Unfortunately it has been that way for the last 15 years. Parties of influence changed, but it wasn't particularly difficult to determine them. However, something different takes place today. Both those who for many years controlled the former presidents, and those who have served their interests (not forgetting their own) hectically look for and cannot find the source of influence on Putin. Who controls him? The oligarchs? No. His family? No. The military? The FSB? No. The West, the international circles, the media? It's a pity, but "no" too. It turns out to be Father

Tikhon, your humble servant. But in reality Putin is independent, and that quality is getting strengthened to the joy of many, and to the panic of a few. God willing, this President will be "managed" only by God, his conscience, his love for Russia and common sense.'

Father Tikhon went on to answer a question about whether or not the state was using the Church for its own purpose in pursuing the war in Chechnya. 'Orthodoxy implies non-resistance to evil,' Tikhon replied, 'the idea that the Church appeals for docility to evil is absolutely false. In reality there is nothing more alien to Orthodox Christianity than the assertion that one shouldn't oppose evil. As for Chechnya, Russia has forgone a lot. When it consented to sign the Agreement of Khasaviurt it was the same attempt to pay off as in the time of Dmitry Donskoi. The invasion of Dagestan by Chechen rebels in November 1999 forced Russia to unsheathe its sword again. Love your enemies, beat the enemies of your Fatherland, treat God's enemies with disdain.'

When Father Tikhon was asked if it was true that 'because you are the keeper of many state secrets you have [for example] an armoured executive class Audi-8 at your command,' he replied: 'Once we took humanitarian aid to Grozny and the rebels pursued us for several hours; and in spite of the fact that we had an entire military detachment with us, they would have caught us if it wasn't for God's help. In Moscow I have a seven-year-old Audi-6, which is consecrated and, therefore, spiritually armoured.'

Some might accuse Father Tikhon of being indiscreet for even discussing a spiritual ward, especially when that ward is the country's leader. It is known that when they are together he is required to discuss all matters (the monk probably knows more about what goes on in Putin's life than anybody save Igor Sechin). He says that work is part and parcel of his confessees' personality: 'Putin sets a very important example for all of us and for Russia in general by being the first true Christian head of state since the last tsar, Nicholas II'. Orthodox leaders regarded Boris Yeltsin as an atheist. He hardly ever set foot in the small private chapel next to the presidential office, whereas Putin prays there on a daily basis – no mean feat for a man who served so long in the KGB, a body dedicated to atheistic state ideology.

Never one to shy away from controversy, Father Tikhon spoke out in favour of Putin's decision to go to war against Islamic extremism in the northern Caucasus, suggesting that Western society was weak and decadent, especially in Europe, and not up to taking on the challenge presented by an 'aggressive' Islamic culture 'bent on world domination'.

'Russia,' he concluded, 'has no allies but its weakened army and weakened navy.'

LYUDMILA PUTINA'S near-death car crash in 1993 gave her too a newfound yearning for religious succour, which she rarely voices: 'I don't

WHEN PUTIN was presented with this 10-week-old tiger cub, he took it home to Novo-Ogaryovo but, knowing that soon it would grow up, he handed it over to visiting journalists, who presented it to Moscow Zoo.

like to talk about my faith in public,' she says. 'It is a very personal thing, but I do believe faith can unite people. I believe that to achieve the harmonious and bright future that we all dream of, humanity must unite under one faith. Or at least we must respect the existence of other faiths without war or spite. Russian Orthodoxy advocates first and foremost love and tolerance of your fellow man.'

PUTIN IS CLEARLY drawn to actors (his favourite was the late Austrian-born star, Romy Schneider), theatre (he likes the Sovremennik) and ballet, so it comes as no surprise to learn that another friend is Nikita Mikhalkov, who is also Russia's leading film director. Putin is fascinated by the stories Mikhalkov can tell him of the distinguished artistic family he was born into. His great-grandfather was the imperial governor of Yarolslavl; his father, Sergei Mikhalkov, is best known as a writer of children's literature – although he also wrote lyrics to both the Soviet and Russian national anthems. Nikita's mother, the poet Natalia Konchalovskaya, was the daughter of the avant-garde artist Pyotr Konchalovsky and grand-daughter of another outstanding painter, Vasily Surikov. Nikita's older brother is also a filmmaker, Andrei Konchalovsky, primarily known for his collaboration with Andrei Tarkovsky and his own Hollywood action movies including *Runaway Train.*

'Vladimir doesn't exactly sit at the feet of Mikhalkov, but he listens in silence when the director launches into stories about the adventures of his career,' says someone who has spent time in the company of both men. 'It's been quite an illustrious career too. Mikhalkov made that film *Dark Eyes* starring Marcello Mastroianni as an old man who tells the story of a romance he had when he was younger. He is also internationally known for *Close to Eden* and *Burnt by the Sun*. Mikhalkov himself appeared as Tsar Alexander III in his 1998 epic, *The Barber of Siberia*. Putin's seen all of his films; he loves movies, especially Westerns – he's a big cowboy fan.'

Mikhalkov, who also arranges private parties at his villa, where Putin is 'able to let his hair down', rarely speaks publicly about the President, although in 2005 he expressed his fear that Russia might be in for 'instability' if Putin failed to run for a third term in 2008. 'Playing heads-

or-tails with a country such as Russia every four years – who's going to get it? – means experiments that can end up in catastrophe for us,' he said.

ROMAN ABRAMOVICH certainly doesn't have it all his own way when it comes to bending the leader's ear. While he is regarded in Kremlin circles as a man Putin can do (commercial) business through, Abramovich is never quite at ease around him and, as far as one can judge, it is fellow oligarch Oleg Deripaska whose company Putin is least averse to.

Deripaska, 16 years Putin's junior, is the oligarch who knows best how to enjoy himself. A former student at Moscow State University, he built his fortune in aluminium after watching how others made their money during a spell as a broker on the Stock Exchange. He and Abramovich – once bitter rivals – cornered almost all of Russia's aluminium market in 2000, by which time Deripaska had seen something his partner had never witnessed – a tragic loss of life in the pursuit of personal fortunes: more than a hundred executives were murdered in the aluminium wars. He himself received a number of death threats and narrowly survived an assassination attempt when a grenade was launched at him.

Deripaska became a member of the Family by marrying Polina Yumasheva, the daughter of Boris Yeltsin's son-in-law and former Chief of Staff, Valentin Yumashev. He had no difficulty adhering to Putin's decree that the oligarchs should keep their noses out of politics – his only interest in whoever was occupying the Kremlin was in getting government approval for his various dealings. Putin also regards Deripaska as something of an international ambassador: he looks approvingly on how the oligarch has ingratiated himself in London society, forming a close friendship with Lord (Peter) Mandelson, regarded by many as Britain's Sechin, and another with financier Nat Rothschild (a member of the UK's leading banking family), who helped him to secure a visa to the US, where he had previously been banned for several years amid allegations that he had links with organised crime.

From the President's point of view, however, the oligarch serves another useful purpose. One Kremlin observer told me: 'Putin gets Deripaska to keep an eye on Abramovich, and Abramovich to watch over

Deripaska. Vladimir is very careful whom he trusts.'

However, Deripaska learned the hard way that Putin is no pushover when he attempted to lay off workers at a factory he owned in Pikalyovo, northern Russia, despite the fact that the government had given him substantial subsidies to safeguard their jobs. Putin was in St Petersburg, preparing for the arrival of world business leaders attending an economic summit in the city, when he heard that the workers had blocked a motorway to protest. They had not received their wages and their families were going hungry.

Ordering Deripaska to meet him at the factory, Putin set off in a people transporter for the 150-mile trip to Pikalyovo. Dressed in jeans, an open-neck sports shirt and a nylon anorak he stormed into the building, to which the media had also been hurriedly summoned. Facing the oligarch across a table in front of the assembled workers, he demanded to know why everyone had been running around 'like cockroaches' just before he arrived. 'Why was no one capable of making decisions?' he demanded before ordering Deripaska to explain to their audience why they had not been paid the money already provided by the state. Finally he threw a pen across the desk at his humiliated skiing partner and, before making an abrupt exit and returning to St Petersburg, ordered him to sign a contract which would resolve the dispute to the workers' satisfaction.

Says the businessman friend of Putin's who briefed me about Deripaska's activities: 'I wasn't there, I watched it on television. It was magic stuff. A lot of people thought the whole thing had been stage-managed for the benefit of the TV audience but I know when he's angry, and he was fuming. Deripaska deserved that dressing-down and he knew it.'

THE ONE MAN who can draw Putin out of his shell and get him to party is Italy's boastful, lady-loving former leader Silvio Berlusconi. He is not just the politician who is top of Putin's 'most popular' list. The pair travel thousands of miles to attend each other's birthday celebrations and Vladimir so much admires the Italian's lifestyle that he even has Silvio's tailor copy his suits for him. Even the whiff of scandal which

ALL'S WELL that ends well: Once Putin had reached agreement with Ukraine's
President Leonid Kuchma about Russian pipelines that run through his country, he
took him and visiting German Chancellor Gerhard Schroeder to dinner at
St Petersburg's most favoured restaurant, the Podvorye, to celebrate the deal.

blew east over Russia's leader from the hotspots of Italy failed to dent
their relationship.

Despite the scandals which abound about Berlusconi's estate, Putin
has visited Villa Certosa on the Mediterranean island of Sardinia, where
guests at parties usually include a bevy of attractive girls. In 2008 the Italian
leader said he had flown in a troupe of dancers from Rome to entertain
Putin, who is 16 years his junior. In October 2009 Berlusconi cancelled a
meeting with Jordan's King Abdullah in Rome, scheduled to discuss the
Middle East peace process, and instead turned up in St Petersburg 'bearing
fine wines' for Putin and a determination to join in the Russian leader's
birthday celebrations, despite rising speculation at home that he was
putting their special relationship ahead of his country's interests. The
official line delivered by Putin's spokesman Dmitri Peskov was that
Berlusconi's surprise trip was 'a private visit but with working content'
that would include talks on energy. Peskov denied that Berlusconi would
be attending a party at a villa on Lake Valdai, south of St. Petersburg.

Mindful, however, of the possibility that they might be photographed out and about together, Peskov added: 'I can't exclude that they will be celebrating his birthday. However, it's not the main reason for the visit.'

But it was the 'Putin's bed' story in July 2009 that caused the greatest amusement to readers of tabloid newspapers.

A party girl, Patrizia D'Addario, who took a tape recorder along when she – allegedly – enjoyed a night with Berlusconi at his residence in Rome, says she has a recording of the Italian Prime Minister calling to her from the shower to wait for him in Putin's bed, 'the one with the curtains'. The Russian Prime Minister's office was obliged to deny that Mr Putin had ever given Mr Berlusconi a bed.

It is not only Berlusconi's womanising behaviour which poses a threat to Putin's no-nonsense reuation. His attempts to speak for the Russian leader can be less than helpful. As the former European Commissioner Chris Patten reflects on one summit meeting: 'Prime Minister Berlusconi went a step further and acted, in his own words, as President Putin's defence attorney at a toe-curlingly embarrassing press conference, giving him extravagant cover on Chechnya, the Yukos affair and media freedom.'

What actually happened was that at a press conference in Rome a reporter from the French newspaper *Le Monde* had asked Putin about the rule of law in Russia – a hot topic at the time because of concern within the EU and elsewhere over the arrest of Khodorkovsky and the alleged abuses of human rights in Chechnya.

Before Putin could utter a word, Berlusconi grabbed the microphone and began a somewhat confusing rant: 'In Chechnya, there has been terrorist activity that has produced many attacks against Russian citizens and there has never been an equivalent response from the Russian Federation'. And as regards the arrested Russian tycoon, the Italian tycoon, who has himself faced numerous charges over his media business dealings, said he had direct knowledge of 'specific violations' of Russian law by the oil giant Yukos under Khodorkosvky and he knew personally 'that within the Russian Federation there's now a desire for transparency, correctness and the fight against corruption' .

Putin nodded affirmatively, but the look on his face said it all: he didn't need an impromptu attorney; he was perfectly capable of defending himself. When he finally got the microphone from Berlusconi's clutches he told the *Le Monde* reporter who had asked the question: 'It is my understanding that you are assigned that task and you have to fulfil that task'. In other words, the journalist was only doing his job.

Realising that Putin had provided an excellent answer to *Le Monde*, Berlusconi did his best to defuse the situation by saying he would request only one euro 'for acting as your attorney'.

When he was America's president, George W. Bush tried to use the Putin-Berlusconi alliance to his own advantage. In January 2003 he summoned the Italian leader to Washington and, in a meeting at the Oval office, asked him to use his influence on Putin to get his support for a United Nations Security Council resolution for the invasion of Iraq, which Bush and Blair had already decided would begin a few weeks later. Berlusconi flew to Moscow for a meeting with Putin on 3 February, but was told that partying was one thing, politics was another.

Putin wasn't going to be lectured by Bush on how to behave in the international arena. Rather than risk irritating his pal by pushing the matter, Berlusconi ditched the requests he had received in Washington and the two men went out to dine at the Italian restaurant both men favour, Trattoria, on Leninsky Prospect, where the management proudly displays a photograph of its most distinguished client.

Despite political differences, Putin and Berlusconi remain close friends. The former loves his Italian counterpart's sometimes macabre sense of humour. Says one of my Kremlin sources: 'Mr Berlusconi has a fund of jokes and can always make Mr Putin laugh when the going gets tough'.

BEFORE BERLUSCONI took his crown, Putin's favourite foreign politician was the lover of Kristal champagne and Cohiba Havana cigars Gerhard Schroeder. Putin was impressed by the German Chancellor's £5,000 Brioni suits, but that was before Berlusconi came along with his own sharp tastes. Not that Russian-Italian relations are confined to fashion: Russia is probably the only European country in which Gianni Rodari,

Federico Fellini, Sophia Loren, Toto Cutugno and Adriano Celentano (and for the greatest lovers of literature, include Dante Alighieri) are not some sort of 'exotic foreigners', known only by the well-informed, but are considered as much their own as many other Russian and European cultural figures.

Back then Putin was sufficiently close to the Schroeders for the two families to spend the Orthodox Christmas together in 2001, and after a night at the Bolshoi he took them on a sleigh ride through the streets of Moscow. He even arranged for them to adopt a child from an orphanage in St Petersburg. But Schroeder lost his shine when Angela Merkel seized the chancellorship and Putin offered him a highly paid job – as chairman of Nord Stream, a gas pipeline between their two countries.

The deal also cost Schroeder popularity in his homeland since as Chancellor he had long championed the cause of Putin-controlled Nord Stream and his government guaranteed to pay up to a billion Euros if Gazprom, the Russian gas supplier, defaulted on a loan connected to the deal. 'By taking this job, Schroeder has made himself a salesman for Putin's politics,' said Reinhard Bütikofer, a leader of Germany's Greens. Schroeder brushed off the criticism as 'a lot of nonsense'; reportedly suggesting he might sue one German tabloid for allegedly overstating the salary Putin secured for him.

Schroeder did not sue. And a good job too: Putin would not have approved of his name being dragged into a high-level court action involving his relationship with the ex-Chancellor. In any event Schroeder was by now an employee, and as Lord Browne says: 'If you can be hired then you most definitely will not be as respected as you were in your former role. Their attitude is "If we hire you, we own you".' But whatever the attitude, Russia has always been a favourite foreign employer for Germans – there have been 2,400,000 of them registered in Russia since 1913. Gerhard Schroeder reinstated the trend, following in the footsteps of many world-famous *Russlanddeutsche*, including Alexander Benkendorf, Heinrich Schliemann and Otto Schmidt.

But the man who is probably Putin's closest personal friend is Arkady Rotenberg, the man he met at the Trud athletic club and who became his favourite judo sparring partner when both were teenagers. Like Putin, Rotenberg and his brother Boris have come a long way since their impoverished days in Baskov Lane. Today the brothers have earned their places in the *Forbes* list of Russia's richest people, with an estimated worth of $700 million each, thanks largely to their deals with Gazprom. In addition to the SMP bank, they also own Stroygazmontazh, which is one of the largest suppliers of gas to the largely state-owned company and regularly produces 17% of all the gas extracted in the world. In 2009 alone Stroygazmontazh won 19 Gazprom tenders. It did not require tenders to secure contracts to build pipelines for Gazprom to supply gas to Sochi, site of the 2014 Winter Olympics, and another to Vladivostok, host of the 2012 Asia-Pacific Economic Cooperation summit.

Despite official denials, Arkady Rotenberg remains in close touch with Russia's leader, but declares that 'knowing high government officials has never hurt anyone in our country, but it has by no means helped everyone. For me it's unacceptable to use such connections.'

PUTIN and Patriarch Kirill light candles at the Holy Saviour's Icon in the Valaam Monastery.

18

The Fair Sex

PUTIN'S FONDNESS for the opposite sex is a major talking point among those who know him well – that is, when they feel safe from being quoted. When someone who claims to be close to the then-President was asked if he had a mistress, he replied: 'So what if he has? That would be no big deal in Russia, just as it isn't in France. It's only you people from Britain who make such a fuss about it. He is just very discreet; he doesn't want his family hurt by embarrassing publicity. Suffice it to say he's a good husband, a provider: he puts food on the table and he considers that is his main obligation as a husband and father.' Another insider, however, is sceptical, saying that 'Russia is definitely far more conservative than France, and while Putin indeed is a "red-blooded male", he is too busy for philandering. Putin already said he "loves all Russian women". So that gives him plenty of choice if he wants it.'

When she was asked if her husband admired other women, Lyudmila answered: 'I think beautiful women attract his attention... What men aren't attracted to beautiful women?'

However, there had not been the slightest whiff of scandal in Putin's private life until the year after he was elected President. That's when he had the misfortune to learn the hard way what it's like to be on the receiving end of tabloid journalism.

HE HAD GONE to a villa at Nikolina Gora on the outskirts of Moscow, the home of his friend, the film director Nikita Mikhalkov, to celebrate the opening of the Moscow International Film Festival. Among the glitterati present was the aspiring Australian actress and model Peta Wilson. According to more than one guest on the night (27 June 2001) Wilson made a beeline for the President and behaved in a provocative manner. But according to an extraordinary account of the event published in Rupert Murdoch's popular tabloid, *The Sun,* the statuesque blonde claimed it was the other way around – that Volodya flirted with her, despite the presence of her then-fiancé, the actor Damian Harris.

No one is denying (especially Wilson's publicist!) that Putin spoke to the actress and that he told her how much his wife enjoyed her performances in the television series *La Femme Nikita*. He even – jokingly, apparently – asked her if she would like a position in his administration – 'obviously as a bodyguard!'

But according to *The Sun's* bizarre version of events, one of Putin's bodyguards led Harris out of the room, explaining in broken English that it might make the President feel uncomfortable if her fiancé was close by while he chatted to her. Putin is then said to have presented the actress with a diamond necklace as a symbol of his admiration for her work before handing her vodka and canapés. Wilson claimed later to have been embarrassed and concerned about her missing boyfriend: 'My boyfriend had been beside me, but when I looked around, suddenly he wasn't there… It was a nightmare.'

Another guest that night, the actor Jack Nicholson (who received a white fox-fur boa as a souvenir of his first visit to Russia), said: 'I didn't see anything like that. He didn't strike me as the kind of man who would give diamonds to a girl on a chance meeting, he was circumspect and dignified.' None of the other guests noticed anything untoward about Putin's behaviour and his friend, the host Nikita Mikhalkov, says that Wilson had 'drunk too much' and it was definitely her who did the flirting, despite the presence of her boyfriend. 'When Peta Wilson blames the Russian President for pestering, she indulges in wishful thinking,' he added. And as for the trinket, Mikhalkov – who had organised the event as a private celebration of the Moscow International Film Festival, of

31 JULY 2009. Prime Minister Vladimir Putin visiting Chkalov Island in the Sea of Okhotsk while on a working trip to the Khabarovsk Territory.

which he was president – insisted the gift was not a diamond necklace but a souvenir pendant, which Putin had handed over on behalf of the Mercury Jewellery Company.

ALTHOUGH MRS PUTIN had every reason to be satisfied with that explanation, she is less likely to have been similarly placated over a *Pravda* story the following year headlined 'Vladimir Putin's girl has become Miss Universe 2002'. The subject of the story was Oksana Fyodorova, a voluptuous police lieutenant from St Petersburg, who won the Miss Universe title that year. And whose photo is said – dubiously perhaps – to hang on the wall of the President's office in the Kremlin.

The Kremlin had been accused of manipulating the result of the Miss Russia contest, which Ms Fyodorova won on her way up to the Miss Universe title, 'because she is a favourite of Vladimir Putin'.

When interviewed, Miss Fyodorova giggled and would only say that the man in her life was 'called Vladimir'. When this turned out to be one

Vladimir Golubev, a notorious St Petersburg villain, who had spent several years of his life in prison for serious crimes, the former detective was stripped of the Miss Universe title, the organisers citing her unwillingness to carry out the duties that went with the job.

As for Golubev, he moved to Moscow and befriended several oligarchs after being taken water-skiing without skis by gang leaders whom he had upset in the imperial city of his birth.

During his second term as President Putin was reported as saying that there were not enough beautiful women in his United Russia party. Everything had been decided by men since the days of Communism. That was quickly put right with a platform of stunning ladies, including four former athletes who had starred in topless photoshoots as well as Svetlana Zakharova, the elegant principal ballerina of the Bolshoi. They quickly became known as 'Putin's babes'. The top debutante among the new Duma intake was Svetlana Khorkina, a 28-year-old leggy blonde who was a seven-time Olympic medal-winning gymnast. She had caused a scandal by appearing nude in *Playboy* magazine.

Another was Svetlana Zhurova, a former Olympic speed-skating champion who had also stripped for a men's magazine and had elected to go into politics to promote sport and youth. Natalia Karpovich, a mother of seven, a boxer and bodyguard before she entered politics, had also appeared in a magazine wearing only her boxing gloves. Yet another of Putin's babes was the curvaceous 24-year-old gymnast Alina Kabayeva, who had also posed semi-nude, on a fur rug.

The whole thing almost rebounded on the Head of State when in April 2008 it was reported that Putin would divorce Lyudmila after he stood down as president two months later, and marry young Kabayeva. Nearly 30 years his junior, the former gymnast had joined the United Russia party as a Duma deputy the year before. The story broke just days after the party had elected Putin its leader.

Putin was dining with his friend Berlusconi at the Italian prime minister's villa in Sardinia when the story was published in the circulation-hungry newspaper *Moscow Korrespondent*. Berlusconi laughed, but Putin didn't say a word. His face hardened when he was questioned about the story at a joint press conference held the following day. He told journalists: 'You referred to an article in one of our tabloids. Other publications of that sort mention other successful beautiful young women and girls. I think it will hardly surprise you if I say that I like all of them. And indeed, all Russian women.' The President went on to say that it was wrong to interfere in private lives. However, he admitted: 'The public does, of course, have the right to know how people in public life live. But here too, of course, in Russia, certain boundaries exist.'

Then he added ominously: 'I have always taken a dim view of those who poke their noses into other people's lives with their erotic fantasies.'

While an air of humour prevailed in the room at that moment, back in Moscow the story was having serious repercussions. The owner of *Moscow Korrespondent,* Aleksandr Lebedev (yet another former KGB man), angrily accused his own staff of lying when they tried to explain how the report came about and after its offices received two 'nuisance' visits from the FSB, he closed the paper down. Following a raid on his National Reserve Bank by 200 armed police officers, he considerably stepped up his own security. Lebedev – a long-standing critic of Putin – believes the story of Putin's involvement with the young gymnast could have been planted to bring about the paper's downfall; he had powerful enemies on Russia's shadowy gambling scene after drafting (in his former capacity as a Duma deputy) a law to expel Moscow's casinos. He subsequently moved to London, where he bought the ailing *Evening Standard* and *The Independent* newspapers.

Increasing rumours spread about Putin's 'romance' with Kabayeva in December 2009. Widespread publicity was given – but only outside of Russia – to a report that Ms Kabayeva had given birth to a son, yet none of her friends – including sportswoman Elena Voropaeva, who saw her nearly every day – had noticed that she was pregnant. Kabayeva posted this notice on her blog: 'Dear friends. It's against my rules to comment on rumours, but I've decided to make an exception just this once because I can't ignore all your kind words. I promised to tell you about the most important events in my life on my site. So, when I become a mom (which has not happened yet), I will make sure to write about it. At any rate, thank you to everyone who congratulated me and was worrying about me. That's the only reason I make an exception to my rule – not to pay any attention to the rumours.'

'SO IS PUTIN attractive to women?' I asked the wife of a former Swiss ambassador to Moscow. 'To me he's not, I find him cold, he has no charisma. He is exactly what you would expect of a spy. But I know that Russian women fancy him, probably because of the power. To me he's very much the old Soviet-style kind of man. I had a long conversation with his wife once – our children went to the same school in Moscow – and she told me that she tried to support him in public at the beginning of his presidency, but he got criticised for it as Gorbachev did with the very outgoing Raisa constantly at his side.

'The Russian people don't want that and I don't think Putin wants it either. He has that old Soviet thing about the wife's place being in the

EIGHTEEN months into his presidency, it was Dmitry Medvedev's turn to take his Prime Minister to dinner to discuss progress.

home, looking after the family. He can't understand why Tony Blair seems to have taken Cherie everywhere with him. Lyudmila is a very charming lady but I don't think she is completely over the trauma of her motor accident, she doesn't enjoy being constantly under scrutiny.'

Contrary to what the Ambassador's wife said, however, the refrain from the popular Russian pop song by all-girl group Singing Together – *I want a guy like Putin* – would seem to sum up the view of a large number of his nation's women. But what do men think of him? One Western ambassador to Moscow told me: 'He has a remarkable ability to pick up on the mood of the person he is talking to. Psychologically he is quite astute, which probably owes something to his KGB training. You see it in the people – the men, at least – who have met him, they come away with a completely different impression than the one they went in with. So yes, I like him, he makes himself likeable, he wants to be liked. That's my first impression of him. My second is about his remarkable memory. He forgets nothing, no-one. The second time I met him was at a reception at the Kremlin for National Day. There were 3,000 people in the room and he came up to me knowing exactly who I was and remembered what we had previously talked about – and my country is no superpower. It was extraordinary. He is a most interesting personality, highly intelligent. Very impressive.'

Whatever his dalliances, there is one woman for whom he undoubtedly has a soft spot: the Governor of St Petersburg, Valentina Matviyenko. Under his patronage the 62-year-old chemistry graduate has become the most powerful woman in Russia. The striking blonde took over Putin's home city in 2003, when Vladimir Yakovlev resigned 'ahead of schedule'. This was the man Putin had called a Judas when he successfully stood against Vladimir's father figure Anatoly Sobchak in 1996 and, now that he was president, Vladimir wanted him out of the city, just as Yakovlev had hounded him out when he defeated their ex-boss in the election. Once Matviyenko was safely elected (greatly helped by the President's endorsement of her in a controversial televised meeting), Putin found a new job for Yakovlev – he was given the dubious honour of becoming the president's representative for the Northern

PUTIN accompanies Lyudmila Narusova, the widow of St Petersburg's first Mayor, Anatoly Sobchak, to lay flowers on the grave of his mentor in the city's Nikolskoye cemetery.

Caucasus: 'equivalent to being UK Minister for Northern Ireland during the Troubles,' as Peter Truscott observes in his 2004 biography *Putin's Progress*.

Now in her early sixties, Matviyenko rose up through the ranks after graduating from Leningrad's Chemistry and Pharmaceutics Institute in 1972. In 1998 she became Deputy Prime Minister of the Russian Federation with responsibility for social issues, education, sports and culture. Prior to that she was a diplomat and long-serving government official, serving as Russian Ambassador to Malta (1991-1995) and then to Greece from 1997 until taking up the post as Russia's first ever woman governor.

Matviyenko was feared, but she was fair. She spoke out in favour of pensioners and did everything Putin asked of her. Working in St Petersburg was difficult for her: Matviyenko's home was in Moscow, where her invalid husband lived – unable to leave because a change of climate would adversely affect his health. Putin had a difficult task to persuade her to stand in the election for governor against her main rival – also a woman – a police colonel who had served as Deputy Mayor under Yakovlev. But after Putin summoned her to the Kremlin to discuss this issue, Matviyenko ultimately agreed to go for it.

One of Russia's most fervent supporters of Putin, she is also a firm believer in the system he heads. When asked whether it wouldn't be better for the country to be a parliamentary republic headed by a Prime Minister with no President, she replied: 'No, this wouldn't suit us. We are not ready for such an experiment. The Russian mentality needs a Tsar, a President. In one word, a boss.' In the opinion of most of the inhabitants of St Petersburg, the city has today such a boss and a strict one at that: Valentina Matviyenko.

Putting her petticoat power to good use in 2009, she also persuaded Putin – a man not known for his love of art – to take time out from running the country to paint a picture for a children's charity auction she was staging in St Petersburg. The pictures were illustrations to the letters of the Russian alphabet based on motifs from Gogol's novel *The Night Before Christmas* – one for each letter of the Russian alphabet. Putin chose the letter U and the word *uzor*, or 'pattern', and painted a frosted window with a cruciform frame as his subject, although it is unclear how much of it he actually painted himself. (Later, against the background of the gas crisis in Ukraine, this sketch was, ironically, renamed *Freezing Ukraine*, as a punishment for the natural resources being 'stolen' in Ukraine.) To Matviyenko's obvious delight, his work fetched the highest price at auction, although that sum was beaten by half a million dollars the following year, when a black-and-white photograph of the Kremlin taken by his presidential successor, Dmitri Medvedev, raised $1.7million.

When I asked his businessman friend what quality Putin most admired in Mrs Matviyenko he said: 'Her assertiveness. She's a no-nonsense lady who delivers what she says she will. Oh, and by the way, she always gets what she wants.'

19

In Putin's Wake

In July 2003 the investigative journalist Yuri Shchekochikhin was found dead in his Moscow apartment. The hospital to which the 53-year-old's body was taken said his sudden death was due to an unspecified illness, but his family and friends insist he had been poisoned by radioactive materials. In the hospital the medical documents – including the death certificate detailing the reasons for his death – mysteriously disappeared. Shchekochikhin's friends expressed the opinion that he had been the victim of a political killing, though a subsequent report indicated that the campaigning journalist – who famously stood against the war in Chechnya – may have died as a result of drinking impure alcohol, and Shchekochikhin was known to like his drink.

Shchekochikhin was not just a dedicated investigative journalist; he was a conscientious Russian law-maker, having made the transition to new-style politician, less keen on grandstanding and hand-wringing than on the daily grind of persuasion and planning. He was elected from the Ukrainian town of Lugansk in 1989 to the Congress of People's Deputies, the first and only semi-free parliament the Soviet Union ever had. Its chaotic, freewheeling style gave him a taste for trying to turn campaigning into action. Although he went back to journalism as the Soviet Union fell apart at the end of 1991, he soon felt impelled to return to the political stage and in December 1995 he was elected to the Duma for the liberal Yabloko party. He was re-elected in December 1999

PUTIN ventured into the Moscow suburbs to train with the Russian national boxing team at Chekhov.

and at the time of his death was deputy chairman of the parliamentary security committee.

The reporter-cum-politician who made enemies in high places was writer and deputy editor for the opposition newspaper *Noyava Gazeta*, outlining the contentious results of his investigations into the Moscow apartment bombings, allegedly directed by the FSB. He also drew attention to a corporate scandal known as the Three Whales Scandal and another called The Grande involving contraband furniture on an unprecedented scale. These crimes were said to involve high-ranking FSB officers and were related to money laundered through the Bank of New York. One of his exposures resulted in the enforced retirement of the First Deputy Head of the FSB, Colonel-General Yuriy Zaostrovtsev, after his personal interests were linked to the Grande affair.

Shchekochikhin had also reported on corruption, not only in the Moscow municipal administration, the Defence Ministry, the Prosecutor-General's office and the Russian military forces in Chechnya; the year before his death – as part of his attempts to broker a peace deal in the region – Shchekochikhin travelled to Liechtenstein to meet Akhmed Zakayev, the aforementioned envoy to the Chechen rebel leader, the late Aslan Maskhadov. Zakayev (now living in the UK, where he has been granted political asylum) is regarded as a war criminal by the Kremlin, and Putin still frets about not being able to extradite him and imprison him on Russian soil.

More recently Shchekochikhin had been withering in his criticism of President Putin's leadership and what he regarded as the resurrection of Soviet methods. 'We are returning to where we have escaped from,' he complained. 'We are being driven ever more insistently back to the radiant past.'

Journalists reporting on his death insisted that Shchekochikhin's body be exhumed, but by the time this was done any traces of poison would have disappeared. Hence it was recorded that he died of an 'unspecified illness'.

There was initially the same diagnosis – unspecified illness – in the case of Alexander Litvinenko, the former security agent who died after eating out at a London sushi restaurant, but on the day after his death in a hospital in the capital, the doctors who conducted an autopsy were unanimous in their conclusion that Litvinenko's death was the result of acute radiation poisoning. He had, they stated, been poisoned with Polonium-210.

A former KGB officer, like Putin, Litvinenko took three weeks to die – plenty of time in which to rail against his killer or killers. Like Shchekochikhin – who made similar testimonies in two of his published books – the dying renegade security agent had accused the secret service of being behind the Moscow apartment bombings, which – publicly attributed to Islamic militants – had formed part of the Kremlin's basis for the war on Chechnya, together with a number of other terrorist acts in his country. British doctors, powerless to save him, declared: 'Litvinenko's murder represents an ominous landmark: the beginning of an era of nuclear terrorism'.

In the hours before he died, the spy who had risen to the rank of Lieutenant Colonel in the FSB and who had become Boris Berezovsky's colleague (some would even say his saviour) devoted his last ounces of strength to dictating a statement from his hospital bed in which he thanked the doctors, his wife and the British Government for protecting him since his defection six years earlier.

Then he turned his mind to the Kremlin and the Russian security services that regarded him as a traitor. 'As I lie here, I can distinctly hear the beating of the wings of the angel of death,' he said. 'I may be able to give him the slip, but I have to say my legs do not run as fast as I would like. I think, therefore, that this may be the time to say one or two things to the person responsible for my present condition.'

And then, in a direct reference to Vladimir Putin – whom he falsely claimed to know personally – he went on: 'You may succeed in silencing me, but that silence comes at a price. You have shown yourself to be as barbaric and ruthless as your most hostile critics have claimed. You have shown yourself to have no respect for life, liberty or any civilised value. You have shown yourself to be unworthy of your office, to be unworthy of the trust of civilised men and women.'

Subsequent investigations by British authorities into the circumstances of Litvinenko's death led to serious diplomatic difficulties between the British and Russian governments. Unofficially, British authorities asserted: '[We] are 100% sure who administered the poison, where and how'. However, they did not disclose their evidence in order, they said, to avoid prejudicing any future trial. The main suspect in the case – a former officer of the Russian Federal Bodyguard Service (FSO), Andrei Lugovoy – remains at liberty in Russia to this day. The British government did everything it could through diplomatic channels to extradite him, but without success. Lugovoy was made a member of the Duma, which means he now enjoys immunity from prosecution – a move then-Prime Minister Gordon Brown tried to counter by expelling four Russian envoys from the UK*.

On closer examination, the initial charge that Lugovoy sprinkled polonium into Litvinenko's coffee at the hotel bar is absurd. As any physicist could have explained to those making the claim, polonium is a detonator for an atomic bomb; a fuel with a tremendous destructive force. One gram of polonium is not just an explosive; one gram would be enough to wipe out a *division* of the enemy. The cost of one gram is 26,000,000 Euros. Even if former Federal Bodyguard Service officer Andrei Lugovoy had had just one milligram of polonium in his hands, he, and all those present in the bar of the Millennium Hotel, in the adjoining rooms and even on the street outside, would have died in 10 days at most. And if – as the investigation report suggests – Lugovoy *poured* polonium into the coffee, the cup of coffee would have immediately exploded into fragments; the table at which they were sitting with Lugovoy (and his wife and child, whom Lugovoy brought with him to the meeting) would at once have burned completely, as would the tables nearby.

Litvinenko's was not a death any world leader is likely to have

---

* Boris Kagarlitsky, a political dissident both of the Soviet Union and of post-Soviet Russia, said the Russian authorities were unlikely to have orchestrated Litvinenko's death: 'Personally, I don't think that a decision like this was made at a high level. For the Russian authorities, Litvinenko's killing causes more harm than good. This is so obvious that I don't think Russian authorities or even secret-services heads are as incompetent as to not understand this,' Kagarlitsky said. 'Because this is happening under the eyes of the whole of Europe and, to put it mildly, it doesn't improve the reputation of Russia and its current leaders.' He maintains that certain individuals were most likely to have poisoned Litvinenko with the aim of discrediting the Kremlin.

British novelist and historian Rupert Allason also said he would be most surprised if the FSB had tried to kill Mr Litvinenko because it would fly in the face of 65 years of confirmed practice, as 'neither the FSB nor the KGB has ever killed a defector on foreign soil and their predecessors, even under Stalin, did so only once, in the case of Walter Krivitsky in Washington in 1941'. Despite some reports that a recent Russian counter-terrorism law gives the President the right to order such actions, in fact the law in question refers only to 'terrorists and their bases' abroad.

PUTIN'S wife Lyudmila says he dislikes media presence when he goes to church,
but he was obliged to let a photographer record this moment, when he attended the
reunification ceremony of the Moscow Patriarchate and the Russian Orthodox
Church Outside Russia at the Cathedral of Christ the Saviour. He is flanked by
Metropolitan Laurus (left), head of ROCOR, and Patriarch Alexy II.

sanctioned. His diatribe against Putin was full of so many absurd
accusations that few took him seriously. Here is another example: two
years after his death it was disclosed that he had given an interview to
The Times in which he said that Putin had been vetted by Roman
Abramovich before President Yeltsin decided he was the man to succeed
him. The former FSB agent, with close links to both Boris Berezovsky
and the Russian Mafia, had also claimed that he was investigating the
death of his friend, the award-winning journalist Anna Politkovskaya.

Politkovskaya – who was included in the *New Statesman's* 2006 list
of 'fifty heroes of our time' – exposed Russian atrocities in Chechnya
during Putin's war and took the then-President to detailed task in her
book *Putin's Russia*: *Life in a Failing Democracy*. The winner of a number
of prestigious awards, Politkovskaya went to great lengths to point out

that she was not an investigating magistrate, but somebody who described the life of the citizens for those who could not see it for themselves 'because what is shown on television and written about in the overwhelming majority of newspapers is emasculated and doused with ideology'.

Her opponents insisted that she was more of a social activist than a journalist and, in going to Chechnya, she was pursuing political aims: Politkovskaya's anti-Russian reports were in great demand in the West and Chechnya became her political hobby-horse. Politkovskaya's book *Putin's Russia*, written, again, primarily for a Western audience, was to some extent her own confession that 'we ourselves are guilty of Putin's policy... We have allowed him to see our fear, which has only deepened his determination to treat us like cattle. The KGB respects only the strong. And eats up the weak... If you want to carry on working as a journalist, don't forget that they demand from you that you absolutely cringe before Putin. Otherwise, death may await you – from a bullet, poison or a court sentence – this is what our special services, Putin's guard dogs, think necessary.' Nevertheless, *Novaya Gazeta*, where Politkovskaya worked, exercises its right to attack Putin in virtually every edition. Its Chief Editor, Dmitri Muratov, regularly pays official visits to the Kremlin for meetings with Dmitri Medvedev. In much the same way *Moscow Echo* radio provides a voice for most discontented journalists – Kiselev, Shenderovich and Latynina among them – with no fear of being censored or closed down; it has to be said that no one thinks of taking the 'Echo' off the air and introducing censorship.

Politkovskaya was finally killed with two bullets to the head in the elevator of her Moscow apartment building on 7 October 2006. The date was Putin's birthday. Putin's opponents outside of Russia wasted no time in rushing into print with the suggestion that he and he alone was directly responsible for the writer's death. Some balance was restored by Mark Ames in an article he wrote for *The Exile* titled 'Where is America's Politkovskaya?' He described her murder as 'a juicy opportunity to demonise Putin and Russia and ridiculed the 'clues' so many had 'uncovered' to pin the blame on Putin. 'Why don't we have someone as courageous as [Politkovskaya] was to tell the story of how we razed Fallujah to the ground, Grozny-style,' he demanded, adding: 'Why isn't there a single American willing to risk almost certain death the way Politkovskaya did in the pursuit of truth and humanity?' For good measure, he added: 'And what about all the journalists murdered during Yeltsin's tenure?'

Immediately after Politkovskaya's murder, Reuters published an article titled 'A bitter enemy of Putin has been shot in Moscow', demonstrating to Russians at least that her death was the latest ace in the hands of the political technologists. The article insinuated that Putin had ordered her assassination. A number of major reports continued the theme, going so far as to suggest that Politkovskaya's death on Putin's birthday was actually his present to himself. It was not only his birthday; it was the eve of his visit to Germany to sign a major energy contract. It is a ludicrous thought that he would have ordered an assassination and timed it for his own birthday just as he was about to meet Angela Merkel at an all-important energy summit.

Fred Hiatt, commenting in the *Washington Post,* pulled no punches in an article which virtually accused Putin of murder. He wrote: 'No investigation is necessary to name the chief guilty party in these deaths. It is the atmosphere of cruelty which has reigned and flourished for the time of Putin's rule.' This was as good an attempt as any to accuse Putin of Politkovskaya's death. It has to be said that, like most Russophobes, the authors of such articles have chosen to ignore obvious contradictions.

Politkovskaya was the 13th journalist to die in suspicious circumstances since the year 2000. At *Novaya Gazeta*, one of the newspapers for which she wrote her provocative articles as a 21-year-old reporter, Elena Kostyuchenko – who idolised Politkovskaya – raised her eyes to the ceiling and said: 'You come to work, see your colleagues and think "Who's next?"' The answer to her question was on its way. It was to be one of her *Novaya Gazeta* colleagues, Anastasia Baburova.

Twenty-seven months after Politkovskaya's assassination, one of the lawyers who had represented her case was murdered in broad daylight as he left a press conference in Moscow, less than half a mile from the

VISITING Cape Point, the extreme south-western point of the African continent, on the Cape of Good Hope.

Kremlin's shimmering gold towers. Stanislav Markelov was not only a human rights lawyer, he too was a journalist who wrote investigative articles on Chechnya. Baburova, a politically active journalist working for Russia's main liberal newspaper, tried to go to his assistance, but she too was shot dead by the masked gunman, who used a pistol fitted with a silencer in what was clearly a well-planned operation. President of the Russian Federation Dmitri Medvedev sent his condolences to her family and ordered an official investigation into the killings, which resulted in two members of a neo-nazi nationalistic group, Nikolay Tikhonov and Yevgenia Khasis, being charged. They were convicted after one of the pair was reported to have confessed.

It subsequently emerged that just a few days before he died, Markelov had phoned one Visa Kungayev to tell him he had been threatened with death if he refused to drop an international court appeal against the early release of Russian army colonel Yuri Budanov. Budanov had been sentenced to 10 years in prison after being convicted of the 2003 murder of a Chechen woman: Kungayev's own daughter Elsa.

Ivan Safronov did not die immediately, despite falling four floors from a window in his Moscow apartment block. Witnesses say he tried to get to his feet after hitting the ground, but then collapsed for the final time.

The police say the death of the well-respected journalist, who worked for *Kommersant*, had all the hallmarks of suicide – though they were willing to consider the possibility that he was 'driven' to kill himself. But his friends insist he was not the sort to take his own life. He was happily married with children, loved his work and was awash with job offers. On his way home that fateful day he had bought a bag of tangerines, which lay scattered in the stairwell from which he is supposed to have thrown himself.

In 2007 Safronov became the 20th Russian journalist to die in suspicious circumstances since 2000. The majority of them shot, stabbed or poisoned, the journalists have two things in common: apart from the murders of Markelov and Baburova, no one has ever been convicted of any of their killings – or in most cases even arrested – and all of them had criticised someone with serious assets, people who tend to show little restraint in dealing with their enemies.

'In Russia,' said Oleg Panfilov, president of the Moscow-based Centre for Journalism in Extreme Situations (CJES), 'whenever you are investigating something that could destroy someone else's business, it always generates a reaction – often it is murder.'

A specialist in military matters, Safronov had revealed embarrassing failings in the Russian defence programme. Shortly before his death, he was reported to be working on an exposé of Moscow's secret arms deals with Iran and Syria; something that, if true, would have caused further scandal. 'He covered themes that could provoke a reaction,' said Mr Panfilov.

According to Panfilov there was a direct link between such intimidation and the presidency: 'The problem is with Putin himself. He showed his true colours with Politkovskaya's death.' In the eyes of many, he appeared dismissive and slow to react. 'Putin takes pleasure in launching verbal attacks on journalists,' Panfilov went on. 'It is he who defines the atmosphere in which we work.'

And so the list of those media critics who died for their profession goes on. But how do those close to him believe that Putin reacts when yet another one falls and the blame is laid so close to his door?

'You have got to understand he is human,' said one of his confidants, relaxing in the Polo Bar of the Westbury Hotel in Mayfair on a visit to London. 'He does believe in the sanctity of life, but the lives he protects are those of the people he both leads and serves. Those who go over to the 'other side' become, in his eyes, the enemy and yes, that includes journalists who try to turn people's hearts and minds against their nation's government.

'Take the case of Litvinenko. Of course Putin didn't have him poisoned, but I know he didn't shed a tear when that man died. He saw him as a Russian who had betrayed his country. People like him and some of the others you mentioned cost loyal Russian lives. When we send our soldiers into places like Chechnya and Georgia, we are sending many of them to their deaths. For reporters to go there and try to demoralise them by sending home hurtful dispatches is – and I know Putin shares this view – tantamount to high treason.

'How would you have felt if some of your journalistic colleagues had gone to Northern Ireland to stir up feeling against British soldiers during the 'troubles'? Volodya does feel there is a need to ensure that journalism is not allowed to become the enemy of the state, but he's not a murderer, he wouldn't stoop to that.

'I must also remind you that many of the killings referred to were Russian Mafia jobs, which other journalists used as an excuse to turn their dead colleagues into heroes and laud themselves in the process. Journalists rattle a lot of cages, not just the Kremlin's.'

Putin's attitude to political assassinations when he is not on a public platform can be almost casual. An instance is his reply to a question from the journalist Elena Tregubova about an allegation by Boris Berezovsky

PUTIN aboard the Russian Air Force One, as the presidential plane is known. The wide-bodied aircraft is as luxoriously fitted out as its American equivalent and is a Nuclear Command Post when the President is on board, in case a crisis should develop while he is airborne.

that the FSB planned to murder him. Tregubova alleges he replied: 'Personally I do not rule out for myself that these people did intimidate Boris Abramovich Berezovsky. After all, there was an attempt on his life and it was easy and simple for him to believe that yet another attempt was being planned. But I personally consider that with the help of the [Litvinenko] scandal, the officers were merely ensuring themselves a labour market for the future. After all, some of them are now even working in his own security detail. That's precisely why I liquidated this unit.'

Afforded an opportunity by *Time* to discuss the unsolved murders of journalists, however, Putin delivered a very different response: 'To give you an absolutely frank answer without any politics involved at all, I am also very worried about this situation. I will not speak out about what happens in other countries where many journalists have also lost their lives, including Iraq, where the number is probably even higher. This is not the point and I do not want to point the finger of blame somewhere else. Let us talk about the situation in Russia.

'There are several aspects to this problem. First of all, the media community is all part of Russian society, which is made up of people who want to live better and enjoy all the benefits of civilisation. At a time when capital is in its initial stages of being built up, many people, journalists included, are tempted to earn some extra money on the side. This has led people to enter into relations with business, sometimes criminal business, to be drawn into this environment, begin defending the interests of one group against another and end up becoming part of the struggle for economic gains and wealth, This struggle always leads to victims. That is one category. The second category of journalists who have become victims are those who are sincerely fighting corruption.

'These are especially severe losses, of course. This is the area to which the state should pay the greatest attention. I do not exclude that such losses have also taken place here, but I see this as personal losses because such people are without doubt working in the interests of Russia, working to make Russia stronger from within, and we will do everything we can to protect such people and guarantee their security and the possibility of carrying out their professional activity.

'As you know an investigation [into the murder of Anna Politkovskaya] has brought results, but there are problems with the evidence. It is also no secret to you if you are involved in Russian affairs that Miss Politkovskaya did not play any significant role in Russian political life. Insinuations that she was a danger for the authorities and so on are therefore nonsense. She was no danger at all. I think that her murder was simply a provocation against the authorities. No one ever talked about her. Only a limited number of people – you could count them on your fingers – knew about her activities and now all the country and the whole world is talking about her. I think this is just a deliberate provocation – a sacrificial victim was chosen and a woman was killed, that is all.'

Some may consider that his response avoided the point. Putin's friend, the businessman to whom I spoke at the London hotel, was more succinct in his reply when I put *Time's* question to him: 'Look, the fact

of the matter is that Volodya has tried not to allow his important work –
he sees it as his mission – to suffer from getting emotionally involved in
these killings. As in other countries many, many murders happen in
Moscow but we cannot ignore the fact that in the case of most of those
you refer to there is a common denominator – Vladimir Vladimirovich
Putin. None of us who know the man, as opposed to the politician,
believe that he is capable of organising cold-blooded murders as some
have accused him of doing.

'However, it would be a naive and foolish fellow who did not see that
many of the victims were in fact irritants to Russia's leader – a man who
has devoted his life to improving his country's lot, rescuing the economy
and ensuring that Russia stands tall in the world – and that these are not
random killings, but the work of an individual or group of individuals.
Knowing him as I do, I cannot believe that in his heart of hearts Volodya
does not regret killings which would appear to have been carried out in
his name. No sane man could sleep comfortably in his bed at night
knowing that there is a trail of blood leading to his door. But Putin cannot
afford to show emotional weakness – this is a man who has to send troops
into battle knowing full well that there will be innocent casualties.

'People die so that others might live, that is a sad truth about
civilisation and has been through the ages, but take it from me: Vladimir
Putin is no more a murderer than, say, Winston Churchill was.'

Whatever accusations are levelled against Putin by journalists who
have encountered the sharp edge of his tongue, he cannot be accused of
harassing every reporter who crosses his path. A notable exception is
Andrei Kolesnikov, a lean and hungry journalist who has written two
books about Anatoly Chubais and, in his capacity as a senior *Kommersant*
journalist, is a member of the Kremlin pool. Kolesnikov's articles often
border on the satirical and he is known to poke fun at Putin – an offence
which would merit automatic expulsion for any other member of the
pool, but not for one of three ghosts who compiled *First Person*, Putin's
'autobiography'. It may seem a mere journalistic trifle, but when Putin
met his French counterpart Jacques Chirac, Kolesnikov wrote the
following:

'When the journalists were leaving the negotiating room, Vladimir Putin reached for his handkerchief, used it and then could not restrain himself and… offered it to Chirac. Chirac politely declined and showed that he had a handkerchief [of his own].' Such temerity would have earned a scolding at least from Dmitri Peskov, but I am reliably informed that when Kolesnikov reports such detail it is greeted with a smile in the Kremlin.

Kolesnikov – who has been writing for the paper since 2000, when it was owned by Boris Berezovsky – once went so far as to inform Putin that he had lost the feeling of living in a free country, although he tempered the remark by adding that he did not have the fear one would expect when living under a dictatorship. Putin picked his reply carefully: 'You don't think that maybe this is what I am aiming to achieve – that one feeling would disappear and the other would not yet be born?'

So why has this widely-read man not suffered the same fate as his *Kommersant* predecessor Elena Tregubova and had to flee the country? Kolesnikov's editor Andrei Vasiliev states quite simply: 'Putin really likes [Kolesnikov's writing].'

Kolesnikov says of his prey: 'He [Putin] is a very secretive person in all aspects. Closed in a way he was taught in the KGB, and closed in a way a person is closed, based on his natural instincts. I cannot say I know this person. Once I heard a remark from one documentary movie-maker, making a film on Putin. He said, "When I see Putin I think I know what he is really thinking about; moreover I think he is thinking about what I am really thinking of all this". This is a man, a director, who seriously lives with such an idea. It lightens up his entire life. He switches on a television and a drama unfolds in front of him: Putin is saying something and in his mind seeks advice from him. And that is it, you can easily set up an appointment with a psychiatrist after that. All that I know of Putin, I tell. I have nothing to hide because I don't really know that much. Once a trendy magazine asked me about Putin, and then, after I told them everything, they were afraid to publish it. I was very surprised. I write about people I see every day and am not worried there will be any problems. If I was worried, I would probably not have written a single article.'

20

The Money Trail

'ON THE VERY DAY when he put it on for the first time, he pulled the sleeve of the shirt down over his wrist so that no one could see it, because he felt… well, a little embarrassed. Now he doesn't give a damn,' says Vladimir Putin's friend, referring to his leader's $60,000 Patek Phillipe Perpetual Calendar gold wristwatch. In August 2009 he gave this watch to the son of a shepherd during a one-day visit to Tuva.

In its place he acquired a Blancpain watch, which costs around $8,000, but was obliged to part with that too during a visit to a weapons factory in Tula. Viktor Zagaevsky, one of the factory workers, who had just asked a question about an economy problem, suddenly called out, in a fit of boldness: 'Vladimir Vladimirovich, give me something to remember you by!' Putin took off the Blancpain and handed it to him.

SUCH GESTURES OF generosity put Putin in danger of becoming the political equivalent of Elvis Presley, who would buy expensive cars and jewellery for some poor person he saw looking longingly into a showroom window. When Russia's chief rabbi, Berel Lazar, went to his Novo-Ogaryovo residence to tell Putin he was setting up a fund to build a Jewish museum of tolerance, the man who once told Jewish jokes surprised him by saying without hesitation: 'Good idea, I will donate one month of my salary to the fund'. A generous gesture; one month's salary was equivalent to more than £8,000.

ALWAYS ONE to surprise, Putin declined his chauffeur driven Zil limousine and drove himself in his beloved 1956 GAZ-21 Volga when he attended the opening of the Adler tunnel near Krasnaya Polyana.

When I heard about the two vanishing watches I went back to mine and Putin's mutual friend and asked him: How does Putin see fit to buy such expensive timepieces when George Bush always sported a $50 Timex? 'Because one is Vladimir Putin and the other is George Bush. It's as simple as that.' When Lord Browne was asked if he believed that Putin was now a very rich man his reply was diplomatic but interesting: 'Who isn't? I'm sure his family is. But you never know, I don't suppose anyone knows how much money he's got. Who knows that...?'

SO HOW RICH is Putin and where has it all come from? One man has devoted much of his recent life to finding the answer to those questions: Stanislav Belkovsky.

Mr Belkovsky is a Russian political expert with contacts deep within the Kremlin and the White House, and he believes the Russian leader is now one of the richest men in the world, with a fortune close to $40 billion. It has to be said that not many in Russia pay attention to Belkovsky's assertions and his frequent appearances on tabloid-type sensational television programmes do little to enhance his personal reputation.

When he was asked at a press conference on 14 February 2008 whether he was the richest person in Europe, as some newspapers claimed, and if so, to state the source of his wealth, Putin said, 'This is true. I am the richest person not only in Europe, but also in the world. I collect emotions. And I am rich in the respect that the people of Russia have twice entrusted me with the leadership of such a great country as Russia. I consider this to be my biggest fortune. As for the rumours concerning my financial wealth, I have seen some pieces of paper regarding this. This is idle chatter, not worthy of discussion, plain bosh. They have picked all this from their noses and smeared it across their pieces of paper. This is how I view this.'

BELKOVSKY, IN HIS book (which collects dust on the shelves of all major bookstores in Moscow – contrary to assertions about all such writings being suppressed) alleges that Putin effectively controls 37 per cent of the shares in Surgutneftegaz, an oil exploration company which is also Russia's third biggest oil producer. That shareholding alone would be worth $20 billion, but that's not all: Belkovsky's sources claim Putin also owns 4.5 per cent of Gazprom and at least 50% of Gunvor, a mysterious Swiss-based oil trader founded by his friend Gennady Timchenko, through which the state company Rosneft sells 30-40% of its oil.

'He may also own or have some interests in other business that I don't know about yet,' says the reckless political expert. 'Putin's name doesn't appear on any shareholders' register, of course. There is a non-transparent scheme of successive ownership of offshore companies and funds. The final point is supposedly Zug.'

The liberal group struck back, granting *Kommersant* an interview with Oleg Shvartsman, a previously obscure businessman, who claimed that he secretly managed the finances of a group of FSB officers. The Secret Servicemen had, he said, $1.6 billion banked in various offshore accounts – not bad for men whose average pay is less than $50,000 a year. Shvartsman declared the officers were involved in 'velvet reprivatisations' – the forcible acquisition of private companies at below-market value with the intention of turning them into state-owned firms.

The First Deputy Chairman and CEO of Alfa Bank, Oleg Sysuev, described Shvartsman's *Kommersant* interview as 'very serious, truthful and scary'. Quoting Vladimir Putin, he said that 'there are lots of idiots who want to rub shoulders with United Russia – and in this case – to do good turns to those in power'.

Senator Farkhad Akhmedov, co-owner of Nortgaz, on the other hand, said that 'people like Shvartsman must be turfed out of the business community'. Akhmedov promised to ask the Prosecutor's Office to 'probe into the circumstances of the case' because if 'businessmen are stuck in their holes, there will be as many Shvartsmans as snow in the Arctic'.

The head of the Federal Politician Council of the Civil Force Party, Alexander Ryavkin, sacked Oleg Shvartsman from the party's supreme council following a request by party leader Mikhail Barshchevsky. Barshchevsky said in an interview with *Kommersant* that they had no knowledge of Mr. Shvartsman's 'dubious dealings'.

Our 'mutual friend' would not be drawn on the subject. When I put the political writer Belkovsky's assertions to him, his response was brief and uncharacteristically muted: 'I know nothing [of this], if you want to print it, print it. I would not confirm this information to you'.

It is no secret that the rich and powerful men close to Putin include Gennady Timchenko, owner of the oil company Gunvor, and Yury Kovalchuk, who heads the Russia Bank and is its largest shareholder. *Forbes* lists him as the 53rd richest person in Russia and estimates his fortune at $1.9 billion. Kovalchuk and Putin are long-standing acquaintances, but Kovalchuk, who is regarded as an exceptionally astute operator, made his first millions long before Putin arrived in Moscow. In May 2008 Kovalchuk won the right to buy a controlling packet of shares in the newspaper *Izvestia* from Gazprom. The newspaper is among the most widely-read publications in Russia and is regarded as being Russia's 'voice'.

To his credit, Kovalchuk does not interfere in the paper's editorial policy, so his media empire does not lose 'journalists with conscience', as happened frequently in the case of newspapers belonging to Berezovsky and Gusinsky.

IN GENEVA, WHERE he lives with his wife Elena and their three children, Gennady Timchenko refused to see me and share his views about Vladimir Putin. But in a penthouse office high above the City of London, his UK spokesman Stuart Leasor told me later: 'They [Putin and Timchenko] know each other, they met in the early 90s and they see one another on certain occasions, but I wouldn't say they were friends. Mr Timchenko financed a judo club* in St. Petersburg with which Mr Putin also has a connection, but that doesn't make him Putin's bagman. It does no harm to Gunvor and [Timchenko's other company] Volga Investments to let people believe they are friends if they want to, but that's stretching things.

'As for Mr Putin having anything to do with Mr Timchenko's business, there was a great conspiracy theory about who the mystery third party shareholder in Gunvor was and people put two and two together and made five – i.e. was it Putin? Gunvor made a big mistake in refusing to talk to the press – oil traders historically only give out information on a need-to-know basis – but I can tell you the third party was a Swedish businessman who was not an oligarch – in Russia you're a pauper unless you're a billionaire. He had 10 per cent of the company. It wasn't Putin.

'Gunvor has been accused by the Yukos camp of screwing the Russian company because their company's main assets were taken over by Rosneft and, like Gunvor, Rosneft has a trading arm in Geneva, for healthy tax reasons. The trading arm of an oil company is most important. It's one thing to go to a producer and buy 100,000 tonnes of oil but how do you get it from the wellhead to where you want it to be?

* The Yavara-Neva Judo Club in St Petersburg, which Timchenko finances is run by Putin's close friend Arkady Rotenberg. Putin is the club's honorary president.

Gunvor has excellent facilities and a good relationship with Russian Railways. Mr Timchenko knows how to play the Russian game.'

WHEN I ASKED Leasor about the worrying image of his boss conveyed to me by my diplomat friend, he replied: 'Mr Timchenko lives a pretty ordinary life. He is not like those steely-eyed, no-neck oligarchs [and here he names three prominent oligarchs] who had people killed off. He doesn't have a gang of bodyguards following him everywhere; when he goes on holiday with his wife and children he stays in a relatively modest villa, not in a seaside palace or on an ocean-going yacht, and he wears Pringle diamond-pattern pullovers.

Putin rebuts the charge that while Russia's poor get poorer, those men close to him are getting richer. '[If] you know who and how, write to us, to the Foreign Ministry, if you are so confident,' he said in an interview with *Time* magazine, adding, 'I presume you know the names, you know the system and the tools. I can assure you and everyone who would listen to us, watch us and read us, that the reaction would be swift, immediate and within the prevailing law.'

Although the names to which he refers are known to most of his citizens, there is no record of anyone having written in response to his statement. In any event, Putin is immune from prosecution under article 91 of the Russian Constitution, which states that 'A president of the Russian Federation who has ceased to exercise his authority has immunity. He cannot be called to account under criminal or administrative liability for deeds he has committed during the period of exercising the powers of President of the Russian Federation, or be detained, arrested, searched, interrogated or placed under personal surveillance, if the said deeds were committed in the course of dealing with matters connected with his exercise of the powers of President of the Russian Federation. The immunity of a President of the Russian Federation who has ceased to exercise his powers extends to the domestic and service premises he occupies, the transport vehicles he uses, means of communication, documents and baggage belonging to him, and his correspondence.'

PUTIN visits the St Panteleimon Russian Orthodox Monastery on
Holy Mount Athos.

ONE LEADING RUSSIAN academic says of the 'billionaire President'
theory, 'If he were in possession of a fantasy fortune he would have a
hard time spending it. Can you really imagine Putin, Russia's Robin
Hood, joining the ranks of the oligarchs in a spotlight he's destined to
live in for the rest of his life? He would face the total contempt of the
Russian people, and he knew that very well before putting his Robin
Hood hat on. If he were an oligarch at heart, he would have opted out of
the Russian presidency a long time ago – he would make much more
money out of public life. Putin drives Ladas, not Bentleys, he likes fishing
in Siberia, not swimmimg on the Côte d'Azur; and skiing in Sochi, not
Courchevel. He's a patriot and an action hero, the discreet charm of the
bourgeoisie in parochial Zug or Lichtenstein is not his destiny. His
mission is Russia, Russia and once again Russia.'

In any event, no one can question the fact that Russia has prospered under his leadership. While George Bush and Tony Blair concerned themselves with Iraq, Putin rarely gave time to what he regarded as irrelevancies, and instead concentrated on building Russia's energy power. As a result, by 2007 net inflows of foreign investment had grown to $10 billion from $1.62 million in 2004. In that period America had doubled its import of Russian oil to 400,000 barrels a day, and Europe had increased its requirement of the commodity from 12 per cent to almost 30 per cent.

But it was Russia's gas that Europe needed even more: Europe bought close to 150 billion cubic meters – about 40 per cent of its entire need. And furthermore, a number of leading analysts have noted that Russia's control over gas, which is Europe's 'life blood', is on the increase. Germany alone took 40 billion cubic meters; no wonder Chancellor Merkel was reluctant to castigate Putin for Russia's military action in Georgia. Meanwhile China and, to a lesser extent, India, were buying everything Russia had to sell – not only oil and gas but nickel, copper and coal. And as for coal, the Ukraine is almost entirely dependent on Russia for fossil fuels – a reliance that the NATO countries could never hope to cater for should the country incur Putin's wrath by responding to its overtures. More than one leading analyst pointed out that Russia was consolidating its grip on Europe's very lifeblood. Its economic confidence was growing by the day and the West was on notice that it would pay a high price for intruding on its buffer zones.

Putin had the brilliant Alexei Kudrin – educated at the University of Leningrad and another 'graduate' of Mayor Sobchak's office – to thank for masterminding the upswing in Russia's fortunes, and as a result he was the only remaining liberal reformer to survive the Cabinet reshuffle in 2007, which even cost German 'the thinker' Gref his job.

However, even Kudrin was incapable of improving Russia's fortunes when it came to producing goods other than its natural commodities to sell on the world market. Tourists shopping in Moscow and St Petersburg for Russian-made products would soon discover that most of what they took home was made in China.*

Kudrin left the Russian government after a spat with Dmitri Medvedev in September 2011 but many believe he will be restored to high office once Putin is President again.

IN DECEMBER 2009 one of Khodorkovsky's lawyers, Robert Amsterdam, joined the chorus of those anxious to find out what was happening to Russia's assets. He riled Putin when he demanded, 'What happened to the country's largest, most transparent and most successful oil company, and who pocketed billions from [its] illegal expropriation?'

The previous month Putin had likened Khodorkovsky to the Chicago gangster and killer Al Capone, who was accused of many crimes but ultimately charged and jailed for tax evasion. And in an emotional outburst when he was asked in a subsequent televised call-in programme when Khordokovsky could expect to be released from prison, Putin went off-message and declared: 'Unfortunately, no one recalls that [any] of the Yukos security chiefs is in jail too. Do you think he acted on his own initiative and at his own risk? He had no actual interest. He was not the company's main shareholder. It's obvious that he acted in the interests and under the directives of his bosses. How he acted is a separate matter.' And then he added a damning sentence: 'At least five murders have been proven**.' Amsterdam's response was swift: 'Leaving aside for just a

* Kudrin, Gref, and Mikhail Zurabov, ministers of Health, Economics and Trade respectively, had all come under fire for economic reforms they tried to implement. Many of the reforms had to do with replacing free benefits, such as medical care and transportation, with cash benefits. This replacement angered many of the elderly because transportation costs are increasing. Protests took place across Russia. The President reprimanded Kudrin on national television, and a few members of the Duma went on a hunger strike for a short period of time. A no-confidence vote against Mikhail Fradkov's department was called by the Duma in early February, but it failed. Some analysts saw the whole affair as an attempt to either discredit or perhaps get rid of one of the three men by other members of the cabinet. However, this was never proven and at that time Kudrin, Gref, and Zurabov all retained their jobs.

** Putin seems to have been referring to the killing of the Mayor of Nefteyugansk [a region in which one of Yukos's main oil fields was located] and four other men. Alas, moment the fact that Khodorkovsky is not a murderer, and has never been charged [with] involvement in any such violence, the logic and timing of this argument is ridiculous.'

BY NO MEANS EVERYONE has shared the advocate's accusatory view. His client is described thus by the highly charged Moscow-based American banker Eric Kraus: 'Khodorkovsky – and his lieutenants, the vicious Nevzlin and Lebedev – were notorious for callous brutality. The privatisation of Apatit alone filled up a medium-sized graveyard in the Urals. Russia may be a sometimes brutal place, but people like him made it far more so. Despite the best efforts of the Russian state, Yukos/Menatep retains control of its stolen billions parked abroad (it is for this reason that the Russian administration rightly fears Khodorkovsky – clever, vicious, infused with a sense of mission, with unlimited access to Western corridors of power and controlling a multi-billion dollar war chest – back on the street he could be infinitely more pernicious than Berezovsky). This money is channelled through a dense network of political fixers, right-wing think tanks, Washington political operatives, PR and government relations firms (notably APCO, run, disconcertingly, by one Margery Kraus… no relation!), law firms such as

---

if the KGB man-turned-President knows that, then he is unable to prove it. The only 'evidence' of Khodorkovsky's connection with the gunning-down of Mayor Vladimir Petukhov, on Khodorkovsky's birthday in June 1998, is the testimony of one Sergey Mavrodi, who claimed that Yukos Vice President Leonid Nevzlin instructed the company's head of security, Alexey Pichugin, to arrange for two of his 'old buddies' to carry out the murder, and gave him '$200,000' for the undertaking – money which was paid to him by Khodorkovsky's father, Boris.

Mavrodi says he gained his information from Pichugin's own lips when they shared a prison cell – Mavrodi was incarcerated for his part in running a pyramid scheme which defrauded Russians out of $1.5 billion. Pichugin was in prison after confessing to the murder of Valentina Korneeva, a former Yukos high-flyer, who was allegedly eliminated to prevent her from revealing information about the company to the government, for which she went to work after leaving Khodorkovsky's service. Pilchugin says the same killers were assigned to dispatch Evgeny Rybin, to whom Yukos owed $100 million for the purchase of an oil field.

Nevzlin fled to Israel in 2003 to avoid prosecution. He was convicted of murder in absentia and faces a life sentence if he ever returns to his homeland.

Robert Amsterdam (essentially a very effective political huckster posing as an attorney), with scores of Western public figures on the payroll.'

Shortly before Khodorkovsky's arrest in October 2003 Putin had one of his quite frequent meetings with Lord Browne of BP. He knew Browne had seen Khodorkovsky about investing in Yukos, but without success. Khodorkovsky had unnerved Browne with his talk about getting people elected to the Duma, about how he could make sure oil companies did not pay much tax, and about the powerful people he controlled. Putin's comment was illuminating: 'I have eaten more dirt than I need to from that man,' he said.

Dirt? Browne, ever the English gentleman, was not offended, though he says he believed that the interpreter had cleaned even that up in his translation.

21

Putin's Pride

'VLADIMIR IS THE SAME person as he was as a child,' says someone who has known him for more than 20 years, when invited to share his views on the Russian leader's psychological make-up. 'He can be a Machiavellian so-and-so. He has never trusted America, particularly Bush, and he didn't believe a word Kissinger said. Clinton? Well, Vlad liked him, but Clinton wasn't on his level. He believes, he knows, the United States was out to plunder the Russia he is so proud of, using the oligarchs, and that Alan Greenspan had carefully worked out a plan to that end. As for Barak Obama, well, the jury's still out.

'You must understand that Putin is a man who acts responsibly. He doesn't attack first, he is a peace-loving man. But if someone encroaches on the interests of his country – whether it is little Georgia or mighty America – there will be a commensurate response.'

PUTIN'S PSYCHOLOGICAL make-up was also studied in some detail by one former diplomat who worked with him and says: 'He is very clever in that he doesn't make enemies – apart from the obvious ones like Khodorkovsky, where he obviously had no choice. Where he has replaced people who were in power under the old regime, he hasn't cast them out into the desert. They always got new appointments, maybe a little less important ones, but probably more financially rewarding by way of compensation. He is a person who cannot abide having enemies, because he knows you can't control them and he has to watch his back all the time'.

Evidence that he cannot abide *confrontation* is shown in the treatment of his cabinet. He avoids going to meetings, knowing full well that they will probably end in full-blown battles. Afterwards he will see members individually, listen to their arguments and give the impression that he agrees with each and every one of them. Then he goes away and proceeds on the course he always intended to.

The senior British diplomat who briefed me on his return to London added this: 'You know the situation in the Kremlin when he was President was that things hadn't actually changed under Putin as much as people thought they had. It's still a very Byzantine system and you don't know who exactly has the power. I have a feeling that if you went to see the boss in any department – including Dmitri Medvedev's now – you would open the door and there would be Putin. He has a very big job in balancing the different centres of power and in that respect he is extremely clever. He pulls it off every time, but he knows that nobody – I repeat nobody – devotes as much thought and attention to the detail of running the country as he does and that puts him on a higher plane than anyone who serves him.'

One of Putin's oldest friends, Sergei Roldugin, sums him up in more human terms: 'He was always a very emotional person, but he just couldn't express those emotions. I often told him how terrible he was at making conversation and that's one of the reasons he has no friends other than the people who work with him.'

Nevertheless, Roldugin adds: 'Volodya has a very strong character. Let's say [when we were young men] that I was a better soccer player. I would lose to him anyway, simply because he's as tenacious as a bulldog. He would just wear me down. I would take the ball away from him three times and he would tear it away from me three times. He has a terribly intense nature, which manifests itself in literally everything.'

Roldugin is equally interesting on Putin's hunger for learning: 'Sometimes Vovka and I would go to the Philharmonic after work. He would ask me about the proper way to listen to a symphony. I tried to

MEETING with representatives of the democratic youth antifascist movement
NASHI (Ours) in the Sochi presidential residence, Bocharov Ruchei.

explain to him about Shostakovich's Fifth Symphony; he can tell you a lot,
because he loved it terribly when he first heard it and I explained it to him.
And then Katya and Masha took up music. I'm the one to blame for that.

    'I'm absolutely convinced that our lecturers, with their highfalutin
talk about music, are wildly wrong. The propaganda for classical music
is really missing the mark. I explained to Volodya what a normal person
should see and hear. I would say, "Listen, the music has started. That's
the peaceful life – they're building communism. You hear that chord ta-
ti, pa-pa? And now the fantastic theme is coming in. Look, there it goes
– those brass instruments are playing. That theme will grow. And there's
the peaceful theme, from the beginning. The two will clash now, here
and there, here and there." He just loved this terribly.'

    Putin's passion for music – although he says that Lyudmila is
responsible for 'dragging me to the opera' – is not the only side of the
friend Roldugin remembers so clearly: 'Once, at Easter time, Volodya

called me to go to see a religious procession. He was standing at the rope, maintaining order, and he asked me if I wanted to go up to the altar to take a look. Of course, I agreed. There was such boyishness in this gesture – "nobody can go there, but we can" [he said]. We watched the procession and then headed home. We were waiting at a bus stop and some people came up to us. Not thugs, but students who had been drinking. "Can I bum a cigarette off you?" one of them asked. I kept silent but Vovka answered: "No you can't." "What are you answering that way for?" said the guy. "No reason," said Volodya. I couldn't believe what happened next. I think one of them shoved or punched Volodya. Suddenly somebody's socks flashed before my eyes and the kid flew off somewhere. Volodya turned to me calmly and said "Let's get out of here." And we left. I loved how he tossed that guy! One move and the guy's legs were up in the air.'

Roldugin's anecdote illustrates how Putin's prowess in the martial arts allowed him to overcome his diminutive stature when – literally – push came to shove. When his friend Silvio Berlusconi suffered a broken nose, cuts and two broken teeth after being hit with a souvenir model of Milan's gothic cathedral following a 2009 rally in the city, Putin telephoned him to praise his 'macho behaviour' in the wake of the attack. Dmitri Peskov said Putin had told the Italian leader that he 'had behaved in a manly way in an extreme situation'.

ONE TRAIT WHICH bothers those who come into regular contact with him is his inconsistency, something which is hard to spot from his cool, calm and calculated public demeanour. 'Vladimir can be charming one day and vile the next, there's no accounting for his mood swings,' says a prominent Russian businessman who has had many encounters with him. 'You rarely get to know what causes him to change so drastically in such a short space of time.'

On the other hand, someone who has spent a considerable time in Putin's company admits: 'If you do what he tells you to, you're safe; if you don't, you are liable to get the rough end of his tongue or even see him weep.'

For a man who has been seen to weep in public just once – at Anatoly Sobchak's burial – that seems an extraordinary admission. But according to Lyudmila he burst into tears that flowed for hours on the afternoon of Black Friday – Friday, 3 September 2004 – after being told that dozens of children were among the hostages shot or burned to death in a siege at a school in Beslan, North Ossetia.

Two days earlier Putin had been on holiday at the presidential residence, Bocharov Ruchei, in the hills above Sochi – his home away from home. It was a hot day and the president was making the most of the sub-tropical climate he enjoys so much on his frequent vacations there. He had already found time to swim in the Black Sea, within view of the naval ship which is always on duty there while the city's most exalted resident is in town.

And then came the horrifying news. An armed group, mostly Chechen and Ingush terrorists, had broken into School No. 1 on Comintern Street in the town of Beslan. They had taken about a thousand people hostage, forcing them into the school sports hall, which they immediately mined. There was a particularly large number of people in the school that day as it was the beginning of the school year, and many of the children had arrived with their parents. The bloodbath began at exactly 9.30 a.m.; seven people were killed in the first attack.

Twenty minutes after the siege began Putin returned to Moscow. This was the second time in the last eight days that he had had to interrupt his holiday: 10 days earlier he had returned to the capital after terrorists blew up two passenger aircraft with a loss of 90 lives. It was clear that the terrorists had launched an all-out war.

SOON AFTER HIS plane landed Putin proved he meant business by conducting a meeting with Rashid Nurgaliev, the head of the Russian Ministry of Internal Affairs, Vladimir Ustinov, the Prosecutor General, Nikolai Patrushev, director of the FSB, and General Vladimir Pronichev, commander of the Russian border guards. Nurgaliev was to say later that Putin was very angry: 'I have never seen the man in such a temper. He was in a vile temper'. This is disputed by the man himself, who told the

American interviewer Mike Wallace on the *60 Minutes* programme in May 2005: 'I don't remember one time in my five years as President of the Russian Federation that I lost my temper. I think that this [would be] absolutely unacceptable.'

Putin's first action was to place a call to North Ossetia's President, Alexander Dzasokhov, ordering him to hand over command of the counter-terrorist operation to the FSB. That allowed him to send in the *Spetsnaz*, his Russian commandos under the command of General Tikhonov. He went on to order the closure of North Ossetia's borders and barred all flights in and out of the capital, Vladikavkaz. Then he disappeared from public view for the ensuing events, apart from a brief television appearance the following morning to declare that his main concern was for the lives of the hostages. For the following two days Putin never left his Kremlin office other than to pray in the adjoining chapel. He grabbed a few hours' sleep on a makeshift bed, but admits that he sorely missed his daily exercise routine, which he could rely on to keep him focused.

Just as they had done at the outset of the terrorist act in Dubrovka, the bandits demanded that their mobiles should not be switched off. When an explosive device was set off in the sports hall, the children and teachers tried to flee, but a number were shot from behind. At this point special forces troops of the Alfa group rushed in to save the children. One of the soldiers was the fourth to be carried out. He had died with a child in his arms, trying to shield the youngster with his own body.

The total number killed was 334, of whom 186 were children – children younger than Putin's own daughters.

SHAMIL BASAYEV was to say later that Beslan had been chosen by the Chechens because its airfield was used by Russian fighter planes during the bombing of Grozny, although he admitted later that he would have preferred to target a Moscow school, but such an operation was beyond his financial limitations.

At 4 a.m. that morning, Putin boarded the plane kept on standby to take him to Beslan. Once there, he visited hospitals treating the injured in the dead of night, though few of the town's 35,000 inhabitants were asleep. This was one of the toughest days of his presidential life: 700 of his countrymen had been saved but hundreds had perished.

Putin made a brief television statement in which he admitted the weakness of the existing security system. 'The weak get hit,' he declared. His whole appearance showed that he was extremely tired and emotional. 'It's hard to speak. A terrible tragedy has taken place in our country. Throughout the last few days, each one of us has suffered deeply and felt in his heart everything that has gone on in the Russian town of Beslan…'

AFTER A LONG ENQUIRY Deputy Prosecutor General of Russia Nikolai Shepel was later to find no fault with the security forces' handling of the hostage crisis: 'According to the conclusions of the investigation, the expert commission did not find any violations that could be responsible for the harmful consequences'. To address doubts, Putin launched a Duma parliamentary investigation led by Alexander Torshin, resulting in a report, which identified 'a whole number of blunders and shortcomings' by the local authorities.

IN THE DAYS following the attack Putin took steps to consolidate both his own power and that of the Kremlin. He signed a law which replaced the direct election of regional governors with a system whereby they are now proposed by the President of Russia and approved or disapproved by the elected legislative of the federal subjects. The election system for the Duma was also amended, eliminating the election of Duma members by single mandate district. The Kremlin went on to tighten its control over the Russian media, so it came as no surprise to Putin when his critics charged that his circle of *siloviki* had supposedly used the Beslan tragedy as an excuse to increase their own power and return to the country's authoritarian past. America's Secretary of State Colin Powell said that Russia was pulling back on some of its democratic reforms, while George Bush expressed concern that Putin's further moves to centralise power in Russia 'could undermine democracy there' – a comment Putin treated with contempt.

VISITING the *Orlyonok* (Little Eagle) All-Russian Children's Centre on the
Black Sea coast near Tuapse.

Dismissing foreign criticism as Cold War mentality, Putin resisted the opportunity to remind Bush of how power in the US was centralised in Washington, leaving it to his Foreign Minister Sergei Lavrov to remind the Americans that Russia had its own affairs under control..

Putin's undoubted pride in Russia is matched only by his love of his native city, the city he still often refers to as Leningrad. Known as the Venice of the North because of its 300 bridges, St Petersburg is rated worldwide for its culture. Pushkin, Nabokov and Tolstoy all wrote there and Dostoevsky set his Crime and Punishment in the city. Millions of tourists from all over the world flock to Russia's second biggest city – and Putin's home town – annually, many to inspect the incredible collection of three million pieces of artwork from the Stone Age to modern times in the Hermitage Museum, part of the Winter Palace. On some days the visitors almost fill St Isaac's Square, their cameras pointed upwards towards the towers of St Isaac's cathedral, the fourth highest domed cathedral in the world.

If his rise to ultimate power brought about radical changes at the expense of some freedom of expression and democracy as other nations know it, Putin can be appreciated for having instilled national pride, the kind of pride he harbours personally for the city of his birth. Just days before he hosted the G8 summit in St Petersburg in July 2006 he received the 'happy news' that Shamil Basayev, the butcher of Beslan, had been executed by the FSB in the Ingush village of Ekhazhevi. This was a moment in Russian history equalled only in subsequent years by the Americans' capture and killing of Osama Bin Laden.

The happy news did much to boost Putin's mood for the great show-off event of his presidency. He had easily outspent the sums lavished by his guests on previous summits. He had restored the Konstantinovsky Palace, founded by Peter the Great, to its former magnificence and even ensured that rain would not fall on his parade by ordering Russian fighter planes into the air to 'burst' clouds before they could reach the skies over the city.

Just in case anyone thought that he was genuflecting in the face of George W. Bush and Tony Blair, Putin referred to America in his pre-summit State of the Union address as 'Comrade Wolf' and warned the British Prime Minister to stay clear of making corruption charges by telling him he knew all about Scotland Yard's investigation into the dealings of his chief fundraiser, Lord Levy.

It was evident to one and all that Putin's psyche was in good shape, but what of his physical condition?

Both during his past presidency and his turn as Prime Minister, Putin has pursued a punishing keep-fit programme in order to maintain his exceptionally high energy levels. His long morning runs and marathon swims would defeat many a man half his age. He has no alarm clock – he wakes when he is ready – eats modestly only when he is hungry and these days, as has been said, rarely drinks anything stronger than tea, although he will often clutch a glass of wine to make drinking guests feel comfortable. He scarcely ever leaves for Moscow before noon, regularly works in his office past midnight, and never gets into his bed before 2 a.m.

A former European ambassador to Moscow tells me: 'He called me one night to suggest we went out "right away" to ski. I said "Vladimir, it's past midnight". "Exactly," he replied. "The slopes will be empty".' The ambassador went, although he resisted Putin's persistent efforts to get him on skis.

IT CAN BE SEEN that right from boyhood Putin has never been an easy man with whom to make friends and his friendship can easily be lost. On a political level that friendship with Tony Blair was severely strained over the British Prime Ministers' pro-American stance during the Iraq war. But really it was on a personal level that Putin decided he wanted nothing more to do with Blair. No one was more acutely aware than Putin that the British Prime Minister had insulted Russia by sending his bumbling deputy John Prescott to represent him at a most significant event in Russian history. The 2005 celebrations in Moscow were to pay tribute to the Russian fallen on the 60th anniversary of the Allied victory over Nazi Germany – the most important day in the nation's commemorative calendar. Presidents Bush and Chirac and Chancellor

Schroeder all turned up in person.

What Blair had thrown away, France's new president, Nicolas Sarkozy, picked up when he and Putin met for the first time following the G8 summit in June 2007. However, it seemed to many observers that the felicitations had gone a little too far when Sarkozy turned up late for a press conference – and seemingly a little the worse for wear – explaining that he had been with Mr Putin. His explanation for slurring his speech and nervous laughter as he invited a stunned audience of reporters to question him was that since he was running late he had taken the stairs four at a time: 'I do not touch a drop of alcohol,' he said.

A French journalist's account of a meeting with him some time later in Moscow is worth recounting: 'Sarkozy does not touch a drop of alcohol, so something else explained why his spirits were so high when he regaled us late last night on his dinner with Vladimir Putin. Sarko was unstoppable as he held forth in a little room in the National, the old Soviet hostelry, now transformed into a luxury hotel, which is opposite the Kremlin and Red Square. In three hours at Putin's dacha, two minds had met as they surveyed the world and Russia's resurgence as a power, Sarko said: "It was a long, very long discussion. Enthralling, very intimate. I felt a real desire to exchange ideas and to understand".

'Something seems to happen to Sarko when he meets Putin. It was after their first meeting, at the G8 summit in Germany last June, that he acted like such an excited schoolboy that the video of "Drunk Sarko" became a YouTube hit. The French President arrived in Moscow talking of Putin's "brutality" with Russian natural gas and warning how tough he would be with the uncooperative Kremlin. The cosy old Franco-Russian days were over and we would see what we would see, as the French say. Yet there he was overflowing with admiration for the soon-to-resign Tsar — and claiming that he had won a big concession from him over policy on Iran's nuclear programme.

'It seemed once again that Sarko was incredulous that he was playing world statesman, accepted as one of the big-boys, *dans la cour des grands*. Putin, he said, had confided in him his possible plans for staying on in power by becoming Prime Minister once he stands down as President next year. He had sounded Sarkozy out on his own ideas for putting a two-term limit on France's five-year presidency. Putin is weighing the pros and cons of continuing power and he is extraordinarily lucid on the matter, said Sarkozy.

It is always fascinating to see Sarkozy up close like this. He was even joking that he had something in common with Putin because he had been chief of the French secret service for four years – as Interior Minister under Jacques Chirac. "What makes you think I'm an ordinary President?" he quipped to the group of reporters who had come from Paris to sit at his feet. Chirac would never have made a crack like that. Nor would he have chatted so openly after a session with his good friend Vladimir. Sarko is really different.'

'REALLY DIFFERENT' might also describe how Putin comes across to others, and – if they ever meet to compare notes – Blair and Sarkozy might certainly testify to that. He behaves in a way that will command the utmost attention from whomever he is with. As Vladimir Pribylovsky, the director of the political think tank Panorama, puts it: 'In the West he tries to be Gorby. For the East he tries Stalin's image. For pensioners he looks like the father of the nation. For young people he is a sportsman. For those who are Orthodox he is in church with a candle.'

Although he usually makes his point with a frankness that verges on rudeness, at times Putin can be deliberately indistinct and the court he has surrounded himself with tends to operate according to the old Russian village principle of *'Ne vynosit' sor iz izby'*– which literary translates as 'Do not carry rubbish out of the hut', i.e. 'Do not tell tales out of school'.

In recent years Putin has made obvious moves to improve his tough-guy image outside of politics. In November 2010, wearing a patriotic helmet emblazoned with the Russian flag and Russia's national symbol, a double-headed eagle, he drove a Renault Formula One car on a deserted stretch of road outside St Petersburg at speeds of up to 150mph. Photographers were on hand to record the stunt, as they were when he harpooned whales in the Arctic, dived in a miniature submarine almost a mile beneath the earth's surface to the depths of Lake Baikal, piloted a jet fighter, rode a Harley Davidson with biker gangs, and took a long road trip across Russia's far east at the wheel of a Lada.

He had previously posed for cameramen stripped to the waist, riding a horse through rugged terrain on one of his ventures into the Siberian region of Tuva. Wearing only green fatigue trousers and a hat similar to the one worn by Indiana Jones, his eyes hidden behind reflective sunglasses, he looked every inch the Hollywood player.

IN REALITY PUTIN seems to have no interest in image-building and does not give a second thought to the pop star following that has grown up around him. His supporters say 'he is above all of that. He just gets on with his job'. They suggest that he is a superstar in the political firmament, but he does not bother paying attention to such things.

22

Putin's Legacy

AND SO IT CAME to pass. On 24 September 2011 – exactly as the businessman with close personal ties to Vladimir Putin privately predicted in a London square six years earlier – Putin had accepted a nomination from his successor to be Russia's President once again.

'I think it would be correct for the congress to support the candidacy of the party chairman, Vladimir Putin, to the post of president of the country,' said the sitting President, Dmitry Medvedev, at the ruling United Russia party's annual congress. 'For me this is a great honour,' Putin responded.

There was something in it for Medvedev too, of course. He was to swap places with Putin and become Prime Minister after the presidential vote in March 2012.

As predicted yet again, a change in the constitution would mean that Putin's first term back in the Kremlin would be for six years instead of four and he could serve a further six-year term, meaning he could stay in place until 2024. It would not be all be plain sailing – he warned of unpopular measures to cope with the global financial turmoil: 'The task of the government is not only to pour honey into a cup, but sometimes to give bitter medicine'. But there would be good times, too: he was to be the man in charge of Russia for the 2014 Winter Olympics in Sochi as well as the 2018 World Cup.

But can he really hang on until he is 72? Some outside Russia see this as a daunting prospect, but at home Vladimir Putin has established such respect within the grassroots that no alternative seems to be even on the most distant horizon, or indeed desired by the Russian people. In a 2007 interview with newspaper journalists from G8 countries Putin had spoken in favour of longer presidential terms in Russia, saying: 'A term of five, six or even seven years in office would be entirely acceptable.'

For his part, Dmitry Medvedev was never keen to see his position as that of a temporary caretaker. But as a realist, he knew from the day he first became President that he could never outshine Vladimir Putin, however much he wished to make his own strong mark in Russian history with his proposals for radical reforms.

IF IT HAPPENS, 20 years as President would see Putin coming second only to Stalin, who served 31 years as Russia's leader. But does he see himself carrying on where Stalin left off? Although he would most certainly wish to distance himself from Stalin's worst excesses, there can be no doubt that Vladimir Vladimirovich Putin has studied the life and times of the man who, as General Secretary of the Communist Party, ruled his country for so long. 'But don't compare him with Stalin,' said our businessman at a London restaurant during one of his frequent visits on matters Russian. 'Stalin is the man who saved the Soviet Union, but although he and Putin had similar goals they had very different ways of achieving them.'

In June 2007 Putin organised a conference for history teachers to promote a high school teachers' manual, *A Modern History of Russia: 1945-2006,* which portrays Stalin as a cruel but successful leader. Putin said at the conference that the manual would 'help instil in young people a sense of pride in Russia' and he pressed home the point that the human suffering caused by Stalin's purges paled in comparison to the United States' atomic bombings of Hiroshima and Nagasaki. At a memorial for Stalin's victims, Putin said that while Russians should 'keep alive the memory of tragedies of the past, we should focus on all that is best in the country'.

Putin's understanding of Stalin's modus operandi was rumored to cause a rift between him and Dmitri Medvedev in November 2010. Medvedev was insistent that his government should acknowledge that Stalin personally ordered the wartime massacre of 22,000 Poles by NKVD in the Katyn forest. Prime Minister Putin was rumoured to be against the admission, but Medvedev won and the government officially expressed 'deep sympathy for the victims of this unjustified repression' in 1940.

Putin sent a chill down many Western spines in the summer of 2007 by announcing the resumption on a permanent basis of long-distance patrol flights by Russia's strategic bombers, which had been suspended since 1992. America's official response to the threat of a new Cold War was almost mocking: 'If Russia feels as though they want to take some of these old aircraft out of mothballs and get them flying again, that's their decision,' said US State Department spokesman Sean McCormack. In Moscow, McCormack's statement was greeted with derision by the Air Force Chief General Zelenin, who said that in reality America shivered when the patrols were resumed; the Russian aircraft had in fact been considerably upgraded.

Putin's announcement had been made during the SCO (the Shanghai Cooperation Organisation) summit in the shadow of Russian-Chinese military exercises – the first ever held on Russian territory – and the general consensus was that he was inclined to set up an anti-NATO block or the Asian version of OPEC. But when he was presented with the suggestion that Western observers were likening the SCO to a military organisation which would stand in opposition to NATO, Putin brushed it off with a bland lawyerly statement: 'This kind of comparison is inappropriate in both form and substance'. He left it to his Chief of the General Staff, Yuri Baluyevsky, to expand on the comment. 'There should be no talk of creating a military or political alliance or union of any kind [because] this would contradict the founding principles of the SCO,' he said.

Putin continued on his course of subtle sabre-rattling by making the first visit by a Soviet or Russian leader to Iran since Stalin went there for the Tehran Conference in 1943. After a meeting with the country's president, Mahmoud Ahmadinejad, he held a press conference to declare that 'all our [Caspian] states have a right to develop peaceful nuclear programmes without any restrictions'. It emerged only later that he had agreed with Ahmadinejad and the leaders of Azerbaijan, Kazakhstan and Turkmenistan that none of them, under any circumstances, would let any third-party state use their territory as a base for aggression or military action against any other participant.

He stepped up the pressure on NATO by ordering Defence Minister Anatoly Serdyukov to send 11 ships, including the aircraft carrier *Kuznetsov*, into the Mediterranean for the first major sortie there since Soviet times. The ships were backed up by 47 aircraft, including strategic bombers, in what Serdyukov made clear was an effort to resume regular Russian navy patrols on the world's oceans.

With the energy tool firmly in his grasp, Putin certainly does not need bombs or guns to wage war, but he had clearly set out to demonstrate that Russia still had military muscle in the unlikely event that it be required. Protest marches were organised by a civil front group called Other Russia, led by the former world chess champion Garry Kasparov and national-Bolshevist leader Eduard Limonov. In the subsequent demonstrations more than 150 people who attempted to break through police lines were arrested.

However, the marches received little support among the general public, according to popular polls. Indeed, the march in Samara held in May 2007 during the Russia-EU summit attracted more journalists providing coverage of the event than participants. When he was asked in what way the marches bothered him, Putin answered simply that such demonstrations '[should] not prevent other citizens from living a normal life'.

During the march in his home city of St Petersburg the protesters blocked traffic on Nevsky Prospect, much to the annoyance of local drivers. Putin telephoned his close friend, Governor Valentina Matviyenko, urging her to follow the softly-softly approach he had adopted in Moscow. Sure enough, her subsequent statement was a mild one: 'It is important to give everyone the opportunity to criticise the authorities,' she said, 'but this should be done in a civilised fashion'.

Eventually Kasparov went too far and he was arrested on charges of public order offences as he led a march towards Pushkin Square. The arrest infuriated many and the President was obliged to deny that he was trampling on democracy; instead he accused the opposition – in this case Kasparov's Other Russia – of trying to destabilise the country. But he kept a close enough eye on the proceedings to be able to point out that during his arrest the chess-playing dissenter was speaking English rather than Russian, suggesting that this clearly indicated Kasparov was targeting a Western audience rather than his own people. It lent weight to his assertion that some of his domestic critics were being funded and supported by foreign enemies who would prefer to see a weak Russia.

In his charge against Kasparov, Putin strayed off-message when he chose the moment to take a side-swipe at George Bush: 'I do not want to offend anyone,' he began, recalling the debacle of the 2000 US presidential election, 'but let us recall that the election of the [then] President of the United States were associated with certain difficulties. The fate of the President was resolved in a court of justice rather than by direct plebiscite. In Russia the head of Russia is elected by secret ballot and in the US by an electoral college. As far as I remember, in the first case the college voted for a President who has less than half of the popular vote. Is this not a systematic problem in American electoral legislation?'

The events on Moscow's streets inspired Boris Berezovsky to announce from his exile in the UK that he was plotting a revolution to overthrow Putin. In an interview with *The Guardian* Berezovsky said that Russia's leadership could only be removed by force. After Putin's spokesman Dmitri Peskov declared that Berezovsky's remarks were being treated as a crime that would cause the British authorities to question the status of his asylum, the oligarch subsequently softened his words saying that he backed 'bloodless change' and did not support violence.

In a speech at a United Russia meeting in Luzhniki – widely interpreted as evidence that he advocated a one-party system – Putin declared: 'Those who oppose us don't want us to realise our plan... They need a weak, sickly state! They need a disorganised and disoriented society, a divided society, so that they can do their deeds behind its back and eat cake on our tab.' The speech did nothing to assuage the critics, but then, it wasn't intended to.

IN AN INTERVIEW with *Interfax* on 28 January 2008 Mikhail Gorbachev sharply criticised the state of Russia's electoral system and called for 'extensive reforms to a system that has secured power for President Vladimir V. Putin and the Kremlin's inner circle'. It should have come as no surprise to Gorbachev that following his attack on the President, Putin ceased all contact with him. Gorbachev's interview did not score him any points at home, but it did win him some dubious praise in the United States: the *Washington Post* observed in a leading article: 'No wonder that Mikhail Gorbachev, the Soviet Union's last leader, felt moved to speak out. "Something wrong is going on with our elections", he told the *Interfax* agency. But it's not only elections: in fact, the system that Mr. Gorbachev took apart is being meticulously reconstructed.'

Such criticism had little effect on the reigning President. Even when 10,000 people took part in an anti-Putin rally in Lyudmila's home town, Kaliningrad, with protesters characterising him and his government as 'corruptioners [*sic*] and liars', and demanding resignations, including his own, the protests did nothing to sway the man himself off course. In reality, Putin pays little, if any, attention to the actions of dissidents. When he was asked about their marches, he simply shrugged his shoulders and said: 'They don't bother me'.

The leading man celebrated his birthday that autumn with long-term friends at the Chekhov restaurant in St Petersburg, a tourist haunt where the menu now includes 'the President's meal' in memory of the occasion.

ONE OF HIS staunchest supporters assured me: 'Despite enjoying the growing challenges of the job, I suspect he is growing tired of certain aspects of it, fed up with it even. He's no Margaret Thatcher. Vladimir likes to enjoy himself, and that's where guys like Abramovich, Berlusconi and Deripaska come in, because they go out and have fun. They have yachts and private planes. I think he pays private visits to a certain villa in Spain, but then he's entitled to his time-off and he would never tolerate the kind of publicity that always seemed to surround Tony Blair on his holidays.'

Lyudmila Putina is obliged to tolerate Silvio Berlusconi's often vulgar behaviour, but regards it as a small price to pay in return for the privacy his villa on the Mediterranean island of Sardinia affords Russia's first family when they holiday there. But even Berlusconi knows that when his friend's wife and daughters are in situ he has to keep his behaviour in check; Lyudmila has invested much of her life into raising two superb daughters, although she insists on sharing the credit with her husband: 'Volodya said in his autobiography that he grew up in a loving atmosphere,' she says. 'I would add that he was raised with a strong work ethic and we try and instil this in our daughters. A child must be fully occupied in his or her spare time. For example, our daughters have been taught the violin since they were tiny. I also worried about the girls' health and made sure that all the hard work didn't take its toll on them. We never demanded that they got high marks at school. I consider that the main thing is knowledge.'

As if in a desperate bid to convince the world, Lyudmila went on to say how much her husband loved his daughters and always went to say goodnight to them even when he came home late.

On another occasion, however, Lyudmila lamented the fact that her husband had never been able to take as active a part in raising the girls as she would have liked. But she understood that he was busy doing the best for the development of democracy in the country, spending almost all his time and energy to unite Russia.

Nevertheless, Lyudmila – who says that she and Vladimir go to church together about once a month – added, 'To me the President of Russia is first and foremost a husband'.

PUTIN WAS IN Beijing for the Olympic Games when, on the evening of 7 August 2008, he was informed that Georgia's president, Mikhail

FOR THE Russian leader no holiday is complete without a photo opportunity. He
sent this snap home from a vacation in Tuva.

Saakashvili, had embarked on an invasion of South Ossetia – one of his country's two breakaway enclaves – going on to capture the southern half of the country, up to and including the suburbs of its capital Tskhinvali. Putin had warned the Russian people two years earlier that he suspected Georgian leaders of planning to settle their country's territorial disputes by force, and as a mark of protest he had deported a number of known Georgian criminals in what provoked a bitter diplomatic row. But he had also carefully laid the plans for battle if his warning proved to be right.

Russia waited 36 hours before unleashing its full military might on the Georgian invaders. Even as Putin sat in the VIP box for the opening ceremony of the Olympic Games in Beijing, Russian tanks, soldiers and warplanes were surging south to engage with Saakashvili's forces. At that point, according to the then Australian Prime Minister, Kevin Rudd, seated two rows behind him in the Birds Nest Stadium, Putin found himself being castigated by the man in the seat next to him: George W. Bush, the very man, as it turned out, that Putin would blame for starting the war – albeit a brief one – that was to ensue.

Putin kept his cool. Even as the athletes paraded before him and Bush railed against him in the heart of the Chinese capital, Russian planes were already bombing a military base outside the Georgian capital of Tblisi.

Instead of returning to Moscow from Beijing, Putin flew to Vladikavkaz, the capital city of North Ossetia, Imperial Russia's traditional staging post for campaigns in the Caucasus, and which neighbours South Ossetia, where the armed conflict was taking place. There he declared: 'Georgia's actions are criminal, whereas Russia's actions are absolutely legitimate. The actions of the Georgian authorities in South Ossetia are obviously a crime. It is a crime against its own people, first and foremost.' And while his soldiers fought just across the border, Putin added: 'A deadly blow has been struck against the territorial integrity of Georgia itself, which implies huge damage to its state structure. The aggression has resulted in numerous victims, including among civilians, and has virtually led to a humanitarian catastrophe, but time will pass and the people of Georgia will give their objective judgments on the actions of the incumbent administration.'

Putin was to claim that, since he was in China at the time the order was given, it was President Medvedev who had taken the decision to attack.

Finally he went home to Moscow for a pow-wow with Medvedev, who had never left the Kremlin throughout the crisis. In all, 10,000 Russian soldiers and their tanks crossed the border into Georgia, bombers and fighter jets flew regular sorties and ships of the Russian navy were deployed menacingly off the Georgian Black Sea Coast; this was not the work of the newer Kremlin occupant. As his mentor Anatoly Sobchak had once said of Putin: 'He is as tough as nails and sees his decisions through to the end'. In any event, the Russian forces stopped short of reaching Tbilisi; their presence in the country was enough and it was all over in two days.

Back in the White House, Bush summoned reporters to the Rose Garden and called on Putin – the man whose eyes he had once looked into and 'seen his soul' – to announce an immediate ceasefire, recalling his troops from the conflict zone: 'Russia has invaded a sovereign neighbouring state and threatens a democratic government elected by its people. Such an action is unacceptable in the 21st century,' he said.

Meanwhile, in Moscow, Putin's men were displaying evidence to support Putin's theory that America had orchestrated Georgia's invasion of the tiny independent republic. The Russian Deputy Chief of Staff, Colonel General Anatoly Nogovitsyn, showed off a colour copy of what he said was a US passport for a Texan named Michael Lee White, which had been found in the basement of a house in a South Ossetian village among items that belonged to the Georgian attackers.

Putin hardly needed any evidence. He was sufficiently sure of himself to press on and, in response to Bush's harsh criticism, he racked up the tension by saying that Russia had hoped the US would restrain Georgia – a country with which it had such special ties that even the main road to Tbilisi airport was known as George Bush Boulevard. 'The American side in fact armed and trained the Georgian army,' he said.

'Why hold years of difficult talks and seek complex compromise solutions in interethnic conflicts? It's easier to arm one side and push it into the murder of the other side, and it's over.' Later he added: 'We have serious grounds to think that there were US citizens right in the combat zone. And if that's so, if that is confirmed, it's very bad. It's very dangerous.'

Ignoring a ceasefire pledge by the Georgian president Mikhail Saakashvili, Putin had ordered tanks and armoured vehicles to keep going. After days of fighting the Russian soldiers had seized a military base and four cities, while Saakashvili was still calling for an emergency meeting of the UN Security Council.

After mediation by the French presidency of the European Union, the parties reached a preliminary ceasefire agreement on 12 August, signed by Georgia three days later and by Russia on 16 August; but fighting did not stop immediately and, after signing the agreement, Russia pulled most of its troops out of Georgia, but left others to establish buffer zones and create checkpoints within Georgia's interior which were to remain until the following October. On 26 August Russia recognised the independence of South Ossetia, but America still grumbled that Georgia had lost some of its territories.

Three weeks later, as Medvedev did his best to look masterful addressing Russia's Security Council about the Georgian crisis, Putin returned to the area, suitably adorned for the jungle setting in combat boots and camouflage fatigues, and accompanied by a TV camera crew. In the bizarre event, the President saved the crew by firing a tranquilliser dart at a tiger which was charging towards them. Showing how happy he was that the crew had been saved, and that the tiger would live, the normally serious Putin rewarded them with a rare triumphant smile.

'At least,' a man in the Kremlin Press Office said to me two days later, 'it wasn't like [Leonid] Brezhnev. He liked hunting bears and wild boar, but he got so sick towards the end, they had to drug the animals and tie them to trees so he couldn't miss'.

The good humour Putin displayed on his jungle mission did not last. One month after the conflict, during a three-hour lunch for some of the world's leading Russia-watchers under the restored dome of a former sanatorium in Sochi, he turned the air blue with his defence of his country's much-criticised actions: 'Russia had no choice. They [the Georgians] attacked South Ossetia with missiles, tanks, heavy artillery and ground troops. What were we to do?' If his country had not invaded, he said, it would have been like Russia 'getting a bloody nose and hanging its head down'.

Then he went for his media audience. 'What did you expect us to do? Respond with a catapult? We punched the aggressor in the face as all the military text books prescribe.'

While his guests chewed their smoked duck and sipped nervously on their wine, Putin prodded a finger and chastised them for staying silent when the Georgian invasion began. And he was not finished: he accused George Bush of acting like 'a Roman emperor' and warned Poland and the Czech Republic against hosting US missiles.

Warming to his theme, he went on: 'If my guesses are confirmed, then that raises the suspicion that somebody in the United States purposefully created this conflict with the aim of aggravating the situation and creating an advantage for one of the candidates in the [forthcoming] battle for the post of US president,' he said. Later still, he became more specific, suggesting that Bush's verbal attack on him had been 'cooked up in Washington to create a neo-Cold War climate that would strengthen Republican candidate John McCain's bid for the White House'.

The chief diplomatic adviser to Nicolas Sarkozy, Jean-David Levitte, revealed later that when the Russian tanks were just 30 miles from Tblisi, on 12 August, Putin told the French President (who was in Moscow trying to broker a ceasefire) 'I am going to hang Saakashvili by the balls'.

Sarkozy thought he had misheard. 'Hang him?' he asked. 'Why not?' Putin replied. 'The Americans hanged Saddam Hussein.' Sarkozy tried to reason with him: 'Yes, but do you want to end up like Bush?' Putin who, for once, was briefly lost for words, responded: 'Ah, you have scored a point there'.

The whole tone of Putin's outburst served to further underline the belief that he was calling the shots in Moscow and not Medvedev, who was

PUTIN and Archimandrite Tikhon Shevkunov, head of the Sretensky Monastery, laying flowers at the tombs of the anti-Bolshevik White Guard commanders Denikin and Kappel, and the emigré philosopher Ilyin at the Donskoy Monastery.

Sarkozy's official host at the Kremlin meeting. The language was in keeping with his fondness for coarse imagery: in 1999 he had vowed to chase down Chechen terrorists wherever they were — 'if we get them in a toilet – pardon me – we'll rub them out, even in the outhouse,' he declared.

THE GEORGIAN EPISODE severely strained relations between the Russian government and Her Majesty's Ambassador to Moscow. Never one to mince his words, Sir Anthony Brenton said in September 2008: 'I think we're in quite a dangerous moment now, because we have seen an upsurge of anti-Russianism in the West and an upsurge of anti-Western feelings here in Russia. There is a real danger of political confrontations of one sort or another. I think it is really important that we get those sort of events under control... We have serious disagreements – not least about Georgia – but we need to be able to resolve these in an atmosphere which recognises the very important shared interests we have.'

Cambridge-educated Sir Anthony, who had taken up his post in 2005, had been caught up in flash mob acts orchestrated by the youth group *Nashi* – nicknamed the Young Putinists – who gathered outside his official residence and chased him around Moscow even when he was out shopping: 'I think it was a deplorable manifestation even by *Nashi* [standards], an insult not only to me but to the United Kingdom. It was unpleasant for my family. We had [the Young Putinists] outside the house from early in the morning.'

But it wasn't only the *Nashi* who persecuted the Ambassador and his family. An embassy source who had bravely agreed to meet me for coffee at the closely-observed Sovietsky Hotel admitted: 'Things have got pretty bad, what with the row over them refusing to extradite Andrei Lugovoy, the forced closure of British Council offices, the row over BP-TNK and now the standoff over Georgia, it's made life pretty unpleasant here for us Brits; they seem to think we're all spies again. They've definitely stepped up the bugging, the eavesdropping.

'It's explosive. I don't know how Sir Anthony has been able to stand it. Did you know they chased his Range Rover through the streets of Moscow at high speed one night? We've been getting signals for some time now that their Foreign Ministry wanted him out of the country and if they can do that to Bob Dudley [the chief executive of BP-TNK] who's to say they didn't cause Sir Anthony's departure? He's going any day.

'I think the British Government's stand over Georgia was the last straw for Putin. That really rattled his cage.'

IT WOULD BE wrong to conclude from such an episode that there is widespread anglophobia in Russia; on the contrary, there is considerable empathy towards Britain and its culture. Following the 7 July terrorist bombings in London in 2005, the Russian public offered condolences to the UK. People carried flowers to the British Embassy in Moscow and the general mood was clearly on the side of the victims. Putin himself condemned the attacks, declaring: 'All civilised countries should unite in the fight against international terrorism'.

BY THE END OF 2008 Putin's intolerance of those who procrastinate had become even more apparent when Russia found itself involved in yet another international dispute, this time with Ukraine over the latter's gas debts. The previous March (2008) he had ordered Gazprom to reduce supplies to Ukraine because it was not paying its bills. This affected 18 European countries, who reported major falls or cutoffs of supplies of Russian gas transported through Ukraine.

Some 80 per cent of Russian gas headed for the EU passed through pipelines in Ukraine territory, a service for which Ukraine received 17 billion cubic meters of the product in payment for the corridor facility it provided. That still left Ukraine with a bill for six to eight billion cubic meters to meet its domestic needs, and it was not paying up. Putin accused the Ukrainians of stealing Russia's gas by siphoning off large quantities from the pipelines, and he demanded the country hand over the complete infrastructure in payment for its debts.

Europe's urgent cry for the two countries to resolve their differences endorses the statement made to me by his businessman friend the previous year that Putin's huge control over natural resources could bring much of the world to its knees 'without firing a shell or a bullet'. This has nothing to do with diplomacy, he simply knows the strength of his country and therefore his own strength, and is not afraid to employ both. But Ukraine had a strong bargaining card: since so much of Russia's mighty Gazprom revenues came from gas pumped across its territory Putin might be able to exert pressure when Europe shivered but a total shutdown would cost his economy dearly and that he simply could not afford. So in November 2009 he flew to the Crimean resort city of Yalta to forge a new agreement with Ukraine's Prime Minister Yulia Tymoshenko. Russia would lift penalties it had intended to impose on its neighbour; transit fees paid by Gazprom would be increased by 60 percent, and the price of gas supplied to Ms Tymoshenko's country would be pegged to market rates for the first time.

The Ukrainians had bowed their heads in submission. Europe breathed a sigh of relief. Putin had demonstrated once again that actions speak louder than images.

In the midst of the Ukraine gas crisis, Putin had to deal with questions about whether or not he had paid £20,000 for a private performance by a London-based band which impersonates the Swedish superstar group, Abba. Bjorn Again's manager, Rod Stephen, said that the band had been flown to Moscow then driven 200 miles north by bus to a remote location near Lake Valdai, where they were accommodated at a military barracks. It was only as they prepared to perform in a tiny nearby theatre the following night that they apparently learned who they were supposed to be entertaining. Aileen McLaughlin, who impersonates Abba's famed blonde Agnetha Faltskog, claimed that Putin and a woman companion were sitting on a sofa veiled by a lace curtain and that they and six others clapped along as they sang their versions of *Waterloo, Gimme Gimme Gimme* and *Dancing Queen.* They said they were not invited to meet their smallest ever audience, but were driven straight back to the barracks after giving the performance.

Although this was probably no more than a publicity stunt by the band, the Prime Minister's spokesman was obliged to distract himself from the Ukraine crisis in order to deny that Putin had been anywhere near a group of Abba impersonators. It would certainly not have done much for the Prime Minister's street cred: perhaps unwisely, Dmitri Medvedev had been at pains to let it be known that he favoured the heavy metal band Deep Purple.

Although Putin himself may have been seen to be gliding across the waters with relatively little effort, a PR machine was all along operating below the surface at desperate speed, attempting to change the Russian people's view of their leader. Those managing it, however, were as inexperienced in their task as Putin had been in his when great office was thrust upon him. Relatively early in his presidency a pop record was sent to Russian radio stations by an anonymous source. Supposedly by an all-girl group Singing Together, the song was called *Takogo kak Putin* (Someone like Putin), and the general idea of the incredibly crass lyrics was that the girls' regular boyfriends 'get stoned, have too many fights and don't look after us properly':

I want a man like Putin who's full of strength
I want a man like Putin who won't be drunk
I want a man like Putin who won't hurt me
I want a man like Putin who won't run away

The record was well – indeed expensively – produced and with so much airplay the tune caught on with its young target audience, but no one was able to buy it, since it never appeared in the shops. Other politicians envied Putin the popularity it reflected, but the Kremlin disowned it.

Similarly, a Vladimir Putin fan club, posting its address as The Kremlin, Red Square, Moscow, declared that it stood for 'A strong Russia; centralised government (because Russia cannot survive as a decentralised state), the reunification of traditional Slavic and Orthodox lands such as Ukraine and Belorussia that were stolen by clandestine groups and Western powers' and 'the imprisonment of all oligarchs who robbed Russia'. On the day he stepped down from the presidency, his 'fan club' posted a notice hailing him as 'the man who made Russia enter the century as a superpower once more'.

The notice concluded: 'Our group will not change its name nor will it change its principle. We will always be loyal to the path that Putin has chosen, a path that, instead of being dictated by liberalism, socialism or any other -ism, is chosen only in the best interest, irrespective of what -ism it has to be against or follow. For that we thank Vladimir Putin for eight amazing years. We wish him good health and a long life.'

Though he may never even have been aware of the fan club, Putin`s relatively young and virile image was especially welcome after the sickly Yeltsin years. Remember, he had dived to the bottom of the world's deepest lake, Lake Baikal, in a mini-submarine, attached a tracking device to a white whale (warning it not to be 'naughty' as he went) at a research centre and, during President Obama's visit to Moscow, he stole the limelight by joining a group of Hell's Angels-style bikers called the Night Wolves. Dressed all in black and wearing shades, he even boasted that he had performed a wheelie.

IN OCTOBER 2010 Putin's PR spinners were back at work. They persuaded him – and I'm told he took a lot of persuading – that since his family-man image had taken a battering from whispering campaigns about his fondness for beautiful young women in general, and claims that he was going to marry the gymnast Alina Kabaeva in particular, he should take part in an 'at home' video with his wife and daughters. The result was a ham-fisted 11-minute film which was posted on the Government's website. He appeared awkward and rarely met Lyudmila's gaze but concentrated his attention on the couple's black Labrador, Connie. For her part Lyudmila looked nervous and drawn according to *The Times.* Furthermore, she was not wearing her wedding ring. Russian women switch their wedding ring to their left hand if they are divorced or widowed and Mrs Putin had previously been seen wearing a gold ring on her left hand, although it has never been established whether or not it was her wedding ring.

The obliging Mr Peskov stated that it was 'not obligatory' for her to wear a wedding ring. 'It is not because they are not married,' he concluded to the surprise of everyone, including the Putins.

Quite how much the couple love each other is impossible to establish but there can be no doubt about the unprecedented affection the Russian people have for their leader. Indeed, having been such a popular president, Vladimir Putin was always going to be a hard act to follow. Throughout his term in the office, Dmitri Medvedev was taunted by claims on some occasions that he was Putin's puppet and on others that he and his Prime Minister were constantly at loggerheads. One of those who would have liked to divide and rule the two men was Moscow's mayor, Yury Luzhkov. He made it clear that when it came time to nominate the next President he would back Putin, but his disrespect for the sitting president cost him dear – precisely, his job. Luzhkov had written an article in the official government newspaper *Rossiiskaya Gazeta* challenging Medvedev's decision to suspend construction of a motorway from Moscow to St Petersburg – a project Putin had been known to favour.

But if the mayor – who controlled a budget of more than $30 billion and a city that was responsible for almost 29% of Russia's gross domestic product – sought to drive a wedge between Putin and the man he put into the Kremlin, then he failed miserably. Early on the morning of Tuesday 28 September 2010, an emissary arrived at Luzhkov's office to inform him that he had been fired. And if he expected Putin – whom he had constantly derided during his term as President – to rush to his assistance, then he was to be sorely disappointed. After conferring faint praise on him – 'to a certain degree [he has been] a symbolic figure of modern Russia' – Putin went on: 'It is evident that relations between the Moscow Mayor and the President soured. The Mayor is the President's subordinate and not vice versa, so [Luzhkov] should have taken the steps required to normalise the situation.'

They may have disagreed over Stalin's position in history, but no one in Moscow doubts that Putin and Medvedev were wholly in accord when it came to removing the city's most powerful man, the mayor whose wife rose to become one of Russia's three richest women.

MY FIRST VISIT to Dmitri Peskov's Kremlin office proved to be more dramatic than I could ever have imagined. It was bitterly cold on the night of 1 November 2006 and older Muscovites, swathed in huge overcoats, their heads wrapped in fake fur hats, were hurrying in all directions to get home; in stark contrast, brightly clad youngsters were heading for a multi-storey underground shopping mall offering franchises of Benetton, Diesel and Top Shop, electrical stores selling wide-screen television sets and washing machines, cappuccino bars and mobile phone shops, a McDonald's, an Irish pub and a travel agency offering holidays in Spain, Turkey and Egypt, where menus nowadays are available in Russian. It all constituted an outward and visible sign of Putin's economic success, for by this time the average wage was up by 13 per cent year-on-year to $415 – still low, but four times what it was when he became President – and consumer credit had mushroomed from zero to $40 billion. Even some of the oil, gas and metal oligarchs had been obliged to spread their entrepreneurial wings and diversify into the consumer market.

The mall behind me stood as a symbol of Westernisation just a stone's throw from the imposing set of buildings ahead of me, which housed the presidential headquarters.

Wearing a trilby hat lent to me by Putin's businessman friend (I had underestimated the need for headgear in this inhospitable climate), I reached the base of the enormously wide and high steps that lead to Red Square 10 minutes ahead of the meeting scheduled by the President's spin doctor, only to find that armed soldiers standing shoulder-to-shoulder were totally blocking access to Moscow's oldest and most famous square. I attempted to ask one to let me through, explaining that I had an appointment to keep. But I couldn't speak his language and he couldn't understand mine. He pushed me back with the arm that was wrapped around his Kalashnikov.

In desperation I phoned a Russian friend and explained the situation. He told me to hand my cell phone to the soldier so that he could apprise him of the 'importance' of my mission. Reluctantly the solider took my phone and whatever it was my friend said to him worked, for after a brief conversation the soldier stood aside for just a few seconds and with a contemptuous twitch of his head nodded me through.

Shivering from the cold, I climbed the steps, only to find when I reached the top and peered through the Resurrection Gate that the whole square ahead of me, which would normally be filled with tourists even at this hour, was in pitch darkness. In the distance I could make out the silhouette of the onion-shaped domes of St Basil's Cathedral, built in the 16th century by Ivan the Terrible. But that was about all. Picking my way carefully, I knew that to my right was the mausoleum housing the embalmed body of Lenin and to my left should be the GUM department store, normally brightly lit and bustling with its nouveau riche contingent of well-heeled shoppers. But tonight it was bathed in silence and an eerie darkness, its elegant steel framework and glass roof that blend surprisingly well with the medieval ecclesiastical architecture of its earlier construction, well hidden.

Then, suddenly, everything changed. Red Square was lit with a dazzling display of spotlights and silence was punctured by the deafening sound of military band music. It was then I realised that I was far from alone. In fact I was surrounded by hundreds of grey-coated soldiers who began to march in that menacing way those Russian soldiers do so well.

Now here was a problem: their four-abreast line stretched unbroken around the square. I had to get through that line to reach the Kremlin's 'business' entrance in the far right corner. It was a tricky manoeuvre but, seizing my opportunity when I spotted a small gap in the marching line, I managed it. Alas, that was not the end of the ordeal. Once through the entrance I encountered the strictest of security checks and found myself being searched, patted down and deprived of anything metal including my buckled belt and, alas, my precious tape recorder: thank God they did not take my note book. Even my overcoat was held in a cloakroom where, ominously, I spotted no others. Then a silent guard escorted me to an elevator and took me to an upper floor, where the doors opened onto a totally different sight: a wide, splendidly decorated arched corridor that was brightly lit and overheated. I fell into step beside the silent guard, who virtually marched me to an open door.

'Mr 'Utchins' he announced to Mila, the attractive secretary seated behind the desk. She stood up and welcomed me with a smile and an introduction in perfect English. Politely she explained that her boss had been delayed in a previous meeting, but as much as I tried to edge her towards the subject of Vladimir Putin, she steered the conversation round to Roman Abramovich, whose biography I had just written with Dominic Midgley. 'What's he like?' she persisted. 'I'm so interested in what he is doing in the UK.' Then the telephone rang and she spoke in her native tongue to someone I assumed was to be my host for the next hour.

Moments later a side door opened and there stood the tall, slim, beaming figure of Dmitri Peskov, Deputy Press Secretary to the President of the Russian Federation. With his reddish hair somewhat wild and sporting a thick moustache, he looked more like a fun-loving university graduate – despite the fact that he was 42 at the time – than the man who is the buffer between the international media and one of the most powerful men in the world.

Cordially he invited me to 'step inside', indicating the large room

WHEN he was asked about his friendship with Vladimir Putin, Archimandrite Tikhon (above) asked 'What are you trying to make out of me, some sort of Cardinal Richelieu?'

that is his office, crammed with the paraphernalia of a man with a restless mind. At one end books were piled high on a table, which was also used to display framed photographs; at the other a cosy fireplace with an armchair on either side. I was directed to one of the chairs and he took the other. Would I like coffee or Georgian tea? Like my host, I chose the latter and while we waited for its delivery I told him about my dilemma in the square outside. He laughed: 'Oh, that'll be the rehearsals for tomorrow's parade,' he explained. 'I should have warned you.'

And then the tea arrived, served in porcelain cups and with biscuits. So this was how the media could be charmed in Putin's Russia, I pondered. It could not have been like it in the days of Nikita Khrushchev and Leonid Brezhnev. Or could it?

As we ate cake and drank our tea by the fireside, I asked Peskov how would Vladimir Putin – the man raised in a cramped room with a peeling ceiling, who had been welcomed to London on a state visit, who had seduced an American president with his stunning blue eyes, a British Prime Minister with his good manners, the leader of Italy with his frequent fun-filled visits to the Riviera, and the French President with the Grand Cross of the Légion d'Honneur – like to be remembered?

Peskov shrugged his shoulders and replied: 'It doesn't matter to him. He lives in the now. What happens after he is gone is of no concern to him. As long as he gets home, whatever the hour, has his bowl of *kasha* [a kind of porridge] and perhaps a cup of tea to wash it down, he's happy.' I put to him what the businessman had said to me: 'He gets angry, you can always see it when he's angry on TV'. Peskov's comment was: 'Yes, he can get angry, but I've never seen him driven into a rage, he has impeccable self-control. Little things can trip him up, though. He likes going to church, but he hates it when there are photographers there taking his picture. That's understandable. Certain situations deserve privacy, respect.'

NEVERTHELESS, WHAT Peskov had to say – and in particular his guidance on matters of political importance dealt with elsewhere in this book – all seemed highly believable, with one exception. As I trudged back through the snow to my hotel that bitterly cold night, one thing he'd said puzzled me: did he mean that Putin really had no desire to leave anything to be remembered by, that he lives in the day? Surely no man with such greatness thrust upon him could possibly operate without a keen eye on the future? Putin's supporters insist that he thinks foremost of Russia's future, a true believer in the sentiment that you cannot live for the day. 'He believes that Russia's tomorrow always begins today', they insist.

Or did he perhaps mean Putin was not interested in personal glory? After all, I had by now been made aware of a town positioned more than a thousand miles east of Moscow. Deep inside Siberia, Khanty-Mansiysk is Putin's secret legacy. It is his equivalent of Poundbury, the model town in the English county of Dorset created by Prince Charles as *his* ideal for the future.

Khanty-Mansiysk is located in the heart of Yugra, Russia's richest region, providing 58 per cent of the country's oil. Putin installed his close friend Alexander Filipenko as the region's governor* and found a way to allow Yugra to keep a substantial amount of the oil revenue in order to provide comfort and facilities for its citizens which were to be the envy of the rest of the population – or would be if many of them knew about it. Those who lived away from Russia's main cities in the 'donor regions' always had to pay more in taxes than they received in the annual budgets to maintain the social sphere in their communities, and there's no denying this had increased under Putin – except, that is, in Ugra.

I journeyed across western Siberia to interview Filipenko for this book and to see Putin's dream for myself. The region was once one to which the Soviet Union dispatched its dissidents and most hardened criminals – usually to die from the bitter cold in winter, sweltering heat in summer or the total lack of medical facilities. Today that has all changed thanks to the oil riches, which provide heating and air-conditioning in abundance and an ultra-modern hospital. It is no coincidence that most of the splendid homes in Khanty-Mansiysk (where the crime rate is virtually zero and Russia's chronic incidence of alcoholism is hardly noticeable) are no older than Putin's period in power. Even the Russian film festival is staged there in the most amazing theatre east of the capital. One of Putin's last acts as President was to switch the 2008 Russia-EU summit from Moscow (to the dismay of the capital's mayor Yuri Luzhkov) to Khanty-Mansiysk, so that he could show off his dream town to other world leaders.

Perhaps he sees it as a 'soft' ideal, but Putin's Siberian project is not one that welcomes publicity. After I left I learned that Governor Filipenko had received a call from Moscow: The Interior Minister wanted to know why he had received me there, what I had asked and what I had been told. In the eyes of the Kremlin, both the Governor and I had apparently broken the rules. This view was endorsed a few days later when I received an uncharacteristically angry call from the friend Putin and I have in

---

* In February 2010 Putin, a keen believer in young blood and more women in high office, raised no objections as President Medvedev replaced Filipenko as Governor of Ugra with Ms Natalia Komarova.

LYUDMILA Putina in Canada, December 2000
© Alexander Korobko

common, wanting to know what I had been doing in Khanty-Mansiysk in the first place.

IN WRITING THIS biography of Vladimir Putin I was presented with numerous negative opinions, many of which seemed well-founded on first hearing. But, having spent years studying every aspect of his public and personal life, it seems impossible to reach any other conclusion than that Putin has been Russia's saviour. When he was suddenly catapulted into high office in 2000 the country was not just in bad shape, it was

falling apart. The signing of the Khasavyurt agreement could have meant
the beginning of the break-up of Russia, for within the agreement there
was a point about the possibility of Chechnya leaving the Russia
Federation, which would inevitably have led to a domino effect. Crime
levels were frighteningly high: this was brought home to me when I
encountered a young Moscow woman who, in a short space of time
before Putin came to power, had seen another like her shot in the head
in the courtyard of the apartment block they both called home. Not far
away she had witnessed a man blown up in his car as he left a smart
restaurant. The first victim was an estate agent who had got caught
between two antagonists in a relatively small property deal; no one knew
what offence the second had caused. My informant did not live in a run-
down suburb, but a smart residential area just 10 minutes' walk from the
Kremlin. Of course there are still murders on Russian streets, as there
are in towns and cities throughout the world, but journalists and authors
are not singled out any more than estate agents or restaurant customers.

Make no mistake, the world's biggest country was in chaos as the
Soviet system lived out its dying days. Boris Yeltsin gave the country
freedom when he tore up his Communist Party membership card and
became the first President of the Russian Federation in 1991, but under
his inept leadership the chaos only worsened. Experts thought it would
take three decades to get things right, but Putin did it in less than one.
Yes, there has been a price to pay. Russians have fewer political rights
today, but most seem to consider that a fair price to pay for the restoration
of law and order. Almost one in three heads of cities and small towns is
now serving a sentence in cases not far removed from corruption and
other breaches of the law, while the collection rate of taxes in the oil
industry has increased 15-fold.

The war in Chechnya has been halted and the activities of terrorists
have been considerably reduced, to a fraction of what they were when
the second President of the Russian Federation first came to power.

DESPITE HIS OWN dismissal of a grand epitaph, Putin will perhaps
be best remembered for restoring Russia's national pride and – in his

later period as Prime Minister – the establishment of open government. He has enjoyed rather less success to date in the war he has waged against corruption, which has for generations permeated its stench through public life, but he's working on it: when recently a man complained about the harm such corruption was doing to the country's military services, Putin personally ordered a thorough investigation of his complaint. 'If he is simply being mischievous then punish him,' was the message conveyed to the person he ordered to carry out the investigation. 'If not, then put right what he tells us is wrong.'

Russia has undoubtedly changed under Putin, but has he changed? 'Certainly,' says someone who has observed him in close quarters since the very early 90s. 'He was always self-confident but these days he lets it show. He has fun, he enjoys his popularity, in fact he enjoys life and I don't think you could have said that about him in times gone by. Nevertheless I believe it was always in his DNA. He is a most remarkable man and if DNA had been discovered when he was a boy I believe they could have told us all what an interesting man he was going to be, what an amazing life he was going to lead.'

Perhaps too much has been made of comparing him with Josef Stalin. As pointed out earlier in this chapter, Putin studied in great detail the man who once held his job, but the leader he really draws inspiration from is Pyotr Stolypin, born 150 years ago. Like Putin, Stolypin became Prime Minister at a truly dramatic period in Russian history, a time of great political and social turmoil. Constantly repeating his mantra, 'You want great upheavals, but we want a Great Russia', Stolypin fought hard and successfully to achieve peaceful reform when all around him were advocating revolution. Whereas Stalin wanted to shut the West out, Putin clearly wants Russia to be up there on the world stage, just as Stolypin did. Having dug deep into his own pockets to make a substantial contribution towards a Moscow monument to Stolypin, Putin subsequently solicited similar personal subscriptions from members of his government. He may well hope that one day his successors will do the same for him. Certainly, his re-election as President of the Russian Federation will mean he has plenty of time in which to continue wooing his countrymen, though if he is to finish the great task that Stolypin started there isn't a moment to lose. For it is not just at home that Putin has to prove himself. Republican Presidential candidate Mitt Romney asserts that America is 'an exceptional country with a unique destiny and role in the world'. As Russia is also one of the five permanent members in the UN Security Council, it has enough kudos to make similar statements and Putin may now be rethinking some of his earlier isolationist views, such as the one he expressed in 2007 when he said: 'I do not think that we should take some kind of missionary role upon ourselves... I therefore have no wish to see our people, and even less our leadership, seized by missionary ideas.'

We should remember the words of Dostoevsky, who put the challenge succinctly when he said: 'the destiny of a Russian is pan-European and universal... To become a true Russian, to become a Russian fully, means only to become the brother of all men, to become, if you will, a universal man'. If Putin's destiny is to become such a man, then we'll see the emergence of a new Russia, one with the moral right to call itself truly pan-European and universal.

Postscript

THIS BOOK WAS being completed right at the time of Russia's own version of the 'Occupy' – primarily directed against economic and social inequality – movement, the recent rallies in Moscow and other Russian cities in the aftermath of the alleged ballot-rigging in parliamentary elections. The protests began as numerous official reports of election irregularities came to light across the country, including allegations of vote fraud, obstruction of observers and illegal campaigning. Members of the Just Russia, Yabloko and Communist parties reported that voters were shuttled between multiple polling stations to cast several ballots. The Yabloko party reported that video footage was withheld from observers, and that they were not given access to ballot boxes, not allowed to monitor the sealing of boxes and were 'groundlessly removed from polling stations'. LDPR, the Liberal Democratic Party of Russia, also complained of many attempts to 'hamper the work of observers'. Even the ruling United Russia Party alleged that their main rival, "CPRF" (the Communist party,) had engaged in illegal campaigning by distributing leaflets and newspapers at polling stations and that at some polling stations the voters had been supposedly 'pushed' to vote for Communists...

'In a perfect world, even a single violation would be one too many', writes Anatoly Karlin, a blogger who's finishing a degree in Political Economy at UC Berkeley. 'And by all accounts there were many, many violations in this election: ballot stuffing, forced voting, roving "carousels", the works. But the world isn't perfect and elections are never entirely flawless, even in advanced democracies such as the US. For instance, the 2004 US presidential elections featured "caging" scandals, dodgy voting machines in Ohio, and a turnout exceeding 100 per cent in several Alaskan districts. But few would go on to argue that Bush's win was fundamentally illegitimate, because ultimately the official results reflected the will of the electorate. And why should standards be any stricter for the Russians?' The reality is that at the federal level, the results are fairly accurate – they perfectly correlate to pre-election opinion polls...

This suggests that the aggregate level of falsifications is probably at around 5 per cent, and almost certainly less than 10 per cent... Either way, "United Russia" won, and it won resoundingly; the will of the Russian people was not fundamentally subverted. When Hilary Clinton says that the Russian elections were 'neither free nor fair', she contradicts the opinion even of the OSCE observers, who were highly critical – as they have been with every Russian election after Boris Yeltsin left power – but acknowledged that, despite numerous technical flaws, 'the voters took advantage of their right to express their choice'.

And what prevented the opposition from handing in their mandates, an act which would have automatically annulled the recently held elections and triggered a rerun? Not doing so was perceived by many as confirmation that the opposition's claims to power are not serious.

ON 15 DECEMBER 15 2011 Putin gave a nationally televised press conference in which he dismissed the protests for trying to provoke 'coloured revolutions', and said that the white ribbons worn by the protesters looked to him like condoms (from an anti-AIDS campaign). Many were shocked by the comparison, but perhaps the revelation that the web site promoting the White Ribbons was created 2 months before the disputed elections, fomented Putin's sarcasm towards this new 'symbol' and fitted the theory that the protests were 'engineered'.

Engineered or a spontaneous ensign, the white ribbon didn't catch on as the Russian people, even the protesters themselves, largely reject the idea of any 'revolution'. 'As far as I understand,' BBC-quoted Twitter-user Arina said, 'the white ribbon is a symbol of revolution, whether it's white, snow-white or anything else. And this is not something that Russia needs.'

However, one unexpected thing that the protests demonstrated was that the notion of a notorious 'Russian riot, pointless and merciless' is clearly outdated and serves as a perfect example of 'literaturecy' and cliched thinking. Even if the protesters' criticism was supercharged and 'used' by some opposition leaders, the protests so far have been measured, intelligent and civilised – compared to London's riots (with burning cars and burgled shops, etc.) or with what's going on in other European countries. In a way, Moscow is further away from the 'Arab Spring' than London, not only because of Russia's leadership, but first and foremost because of Russian people, their education and their intelligentsia. Yes, a change is in the air, but this change (not just for Russia, but perhaps for the world) is coming not at bayonet-point, but with the pen. One of these pens may be – Putin's, if he will subscribe to a certain reform (be it the creation of a much-needed public TV – Russia's own BBC – or the return of elections for local governors).

So Putin will have to prove himself at home as much as on the world stage. For his people in many ways are much more demanding than those who elected Obama on the promise of a change and have it not-yet-delivered.

IN THIS SENSE, to paraphrase Pushkin's ironic maxim that 'what's fit for London' is not 'too early for Moscow', because 'intelligentsia' is, after all, a Russian word, and like *Veche* (a popular people's assembly in ancient Russia) is ingrained in Russia's soul. So, the Russian 'protests' are a lesson and an example not just for Russian authorities, but also for the world – both politicians and ordinary people. A lesson in civilised assembly. Without the values of education, without intelligentsia, democracy – in any country – can become ochlocracy (mob rule).

AS MUCH AS PUTIN needs to embrace the intelligentsia, the latter also needs to understand that it is far easier to criticise than it is to govern. Other than 'New elections!' what was the protesters' positive programme? That has not yet been made clear.

Yet it is clear that during Putin's reign an estimated 25% of the population has become part of what might roughly be called the new middle class: well-dressed, wired, connected to the Internet, able to travel abroad freely, and to splurge on consumer goods and appliances. Especially in Moscow and other major cities, shops and consumer malls bloomed. Construction cranes and scaffolding for reconstruction seemed to sprout everywhere. Food shortages disappeared, while private property ownership — and the number of Russians owning cars— soared. Indeed, in a sign of progress, Moscow, St Petersburg, Yekaterinburg, Nizhniy Novgorod, Vladivostok and other major Russian towns began to be plagued by nightmarish traffic jams – unimaginable in previous times.

New service industries were born, advertising became as ubiquitous as propaganda had been in the Soviet era and, for the first time in memory, world-beating Russian hi-tech companies appeared, such as Kaspersky Lab, the fourth largest computer security firm in the world, ABBYY, the optical text recognition firm, or Aquaphor, the world leader in water filtration and purification technologies. And the list goes on. This new growing class of technocrats is also Russia's quiet electorate, who are electing Putin by choosing his Russia as their base and entrusting it with their dreams.

'Bring it on, Bandar-logs', Putin said (with the audience breaking into applause) during his televised press conference, addressing those of his opponents who he suggested are pointless or impossible to deal with. 'I've loved Kipling since childhood.' One can say Putin's reference to Kipling's monkeys was quite offensive (yet one might find it a positive sign of a peaceful literary inclination). One way or another, but – deep inside – how many of us haven't ever imagined themselves in Kipling's universe, in the times when history was alive, to paraphrase Francis Fukuyama's *The End of History*? How many of us haven't ever dreamed about the brave and lively Jungle, which was an allegory of the politics and the society of the time, and, perhaps, a metaphor for Life? The Russian 'Jungle' is a paradox. The streets of Moscow are safer than London's, yet indeed there are Akela, Kaa, Bagheera, Baloo and Bandar-log out there as well, all mixed in the amazing circle of life which is Russia.

Another book comes to mind: *Time and Again* by Jack Finney. A modern New-Yorker, a participant in a secret government project, goes back to 19th century New York and decides to stay. New York in 1882 is far from perfect, corruption is a big problem. But back then in New York 'the streets could still fill with sleighs on a moonlit night of new snow, of strangers calling to each other, of singing and laughing. Life still had meaning and purpose in people's minds; the great emptiness hadn't begun.'

YOU CAN TRAVEL IN time or ... you can go to Russia. French banker and financial strategist Eric Kraus, the author of the well-respected Russia strategy monthly *Truth and Beauty (and Russian Finance)* did that 15 years ago when he fled his native Paris for Moscow, just in time to survive the 1998 financial crisis. He writes:

> '.......The challenge for Russia may be not the lack of democracy, but rather, its excess. In the 1990s, no Russian asked anything more of the State than to be left alone; this has changed, as a newly empowered middle class takes root, and the fearful turbulence of decades past fades from memories, the government has become mindful of its popularity ratings and exquisitely sensitive to the popular mood. A welfare state is rapidly taking shape, and though Russia is famously unpredictable, a European destiny seems most likely; at a time when the European social model seems threatened with imminent implosion, this may seem a counter-intuitive choice.
>
> All of this is still for the future, and as of this writing, Moscow is the only European city in which one can still feel free. Thus, in closing, a word to my many Russian friends who constantly threaten to decamp to that Europe which I fled in despair – at the bureaucracy and immobility, suicidal political correctness and crushing fiscal inquisition – 15 years ago: the

West has a great future – behind it. Go ahead, give it your best shot and good luck to you – but here's betting that you'll be coming back a lot sooner than you had imagined..."

And this new Russia, which even a cosmopolite would miss and want to come back to, has Putin's DNA embedded in its recent history, and, perhaps, the future, regardless of his own political fortunes... Does this mean that Putin has already survived his toughest test: the test of time?